The New Woman and the Old Academe: Sexism and Higher Education

The New Woman and the Old Academe: Sexism and Higher Education

by
Jonah R. Churgin

In memory of my beloved father, teacher and best friend, Professor Gershon A. Churgin, Emeritus: A lover of ideas, students and nature.

Library of Congress Catalog No. 77-91470

Copyright © 1978 by Jonah R. Churgin

Libra Publishers, Inc.
391 Willets Road
Roslyn Heights, New York 11577

Manufactured in the United States of America

Acknowledgments

Where I have quoted frequently or beyond what might be considered Fair Use, I have requested and graciously received permission from the following publishing houses, foundations and institutions.

Jonah R. Churgin

Abramson, Joan. *The Invisible Woman: Discrimination in the Academic Profession*. San Francisco: Jossey-Bass, 1975.
Astin, Helen S. *The Woman Doctorate in America*. New York: Russell Sage Foundation, 1969.
Bailyn, Lotte. "Notes on the Role of Choice in the Psychology of Professional Women." *Daedalus* 93 (Spring 1964): 701-707. Reprinted by permission of *Daedalus*, the Journal of the American Academy of Arts and Sciences, Boston.
Barzun, Jacques. *Teacher in America*. Boston: Little, Brown and Company in association with the Atlantic Monthly Press, 1945.
Bird, Caroline. "Women's Colleges and Women's Lib." *Change* 4 (April 1972): 60-65.
The Carnegie Commission on Higher Education. *Opportunities for Women in Higher Education: Their Current Participation, Prospects for the Future, and Recommendations for Action*. New York: McGraw-Hill Book Company, 1973. Copyright by the Carnegie Foundation for the Advancement of Teaching. Used with the permission of the McGraw-Hill Book Company.
Cole, Charles C., Jr. "A Case for the Women's College." *College Board Rev.'ew*, no. 83 (Spring 1972): 17-21. The College Entrance Examination Board is the grantor of permission and the holder of the copyright.
Edmiston, Susan. "Portial Faces Life: The Trials of Law School." *Ms.* 1 (April 1974): 74, 76, 78, 93. Copyright by *Ms.* Magazine Corporation. Reprinted with permission.
Feldman, Saul D. *Escape from the Doll's House—Women in Graduate and Professional Education*. New York: McGraw-Hill Book Company, 1974. Copyright by the

Carnegie Foundation for the Advancement of Teaching. Used with the permission of the McGraw-Hill Book Company.

Friedan, Betty. *The Feminine Mystique.* New York: W.W. Norton and Company. Copyright (c) 1974, 1963 by Betty Friedan.

Furniss, Todd, and Graham, Patricia Albjerg, eds. *Women in Higher Education.* Washington, D.C.: American Council on Education. Copyright 1974 by the American Council on Education.

Gardner, John W. *Excellence—Can We Be Equal and Excellent Too?* New York: Perennial Library, Harper and Row, Publishers, 1971.

Graduate Education for Women: The Radcliffe Ph.D. A Report by a Faculty-Trustee Committee. Cambridge: Harvard University Press, 1956.

Howe, Florence, ed. *Women and the Power to Change.* New York: McGraw-Hill Book Company, 1975. Copyright by the Carnegie Foundation for the Advancement of Teaching. Used with the permission of the McGraw-Hill Book Company.

Komarovsky, Mirra. "Cultural Contradictions and Sex Roles: The Masculine Case." *American Journal of Sociology* 78 (January 1973): 873-881. Permission granted by the University of Chicago Press.

Langdon, George, and Griffin, Clyde. *Report on Men's Education.* Poughkeepsie, New York, 1968.

Margolis, Diane R. "A Fair Return? Back to College at Middle Age?" *Change* 6 (October 1974): 34-37.

Mead, Margaret. "The Life Cycle and Its Variations: The Division of Roles." *Daedalus* 96 (Summer 1967): 872-874. Reprinted by permission of *Daedalus*, the Journal of the American Academy of Arts and Sciences, Boston.

Richter, Melissa Lewis, and Whipple, Hane Banks. *A Revolution in the Education of Women—Ten Years of Continuing Education at Sarah Lawrence College.* Bronxville, N.Y.: Sarah Lawrence College, Center for Continuing Education and Community Studies, 1972.

Rossi, Alice S. and Calderwood, Ann, eds. *Academic Women on the Move*. New York: Russell Sage Foundation, 1973.

Rossi, Alice S. "Equality Between the Sexes: An Immodest Proposal." *Daedalus* 93 (Spring 1964): 610-632. Reprinted by permission of *Daedalus*, the Journal of the American Academy of Arts and Sciences, Boston.

Sanford, Nevitt, ed. *The American College: A Psychological and Social Interpretation of the Higher Learning*. New York: John Wiley and Sons, 1962.

Simpson, Alan. "Coeducation." *College Board Review*, no. 82 (Winter 1971-1972): 17-23. The College Entrance Examination Board is the grantor of permission and the holder of the copyright.

"Smith College and the Question of Coeducation—A Report with Recommendations Submitted to the Faculty and the Board of Trustees by the Augmented College Planning Committee." Northampton, Mass, April 1971.

Weisstein, Naomi. "Woman as Nigger." *Psychology Today* 3 (October 1969): 20, 22, 58. Reprinted from *Psychology Today* Magazine. Copyright (c) 1969 by the Ziff-Davis Publishing Company.

White, Lynn, Jr. *Educating Our Daughters*. New York: Harper and Row, Publishers, 1950.

TABLE OF CONTENTS

Preface

It has been said that a preface is written last, read least and placed first. While this may be true in most cases, in this instance it was inscribed in my mind well before the completion of the book. For this work could not have been anticipated or pursued to completion without the continuous encouragement of four individuals.

Many people touch the lives of others, few have a lasting effect, and fewer still have an endearing impact. Either because the English language is deficient, or I am deficient in its use, I do not believe that I can express the depth of my gratitude to Dr. Donna Shalala, former treasurer of New York's Municipal Assistance Corporation; Professor Harriet Fields of the College of Mount St. Vincent; Dr. Jerry Haar, currently of HEW; and Dr. Catharine Stimpson of Barnard College.

Also, I would like to express the warmest thanks to my many Maryland colleagues. Specifically, I would like to acknowledge my former teacher, Dr. Francis Rourke of The Johns Hopkins University; Maryland State Senator Clarence Blount; former Deans Jeffrey Moss and Maceo Williams; the former Interim President of Morgan State University, Dr. Thomas Fraser; and Ms. J. Elizabeth Garraway, Executive Director of the Maryland Independent College and University Association.

Finally, I would like to thank my many friends at Washington College, particularly President Joseph McLain; Dean Robert Roy, Chairperson of the Washington College Board and Dean Emeritus of The Johns Hopkins University School of Engineering; former Dean Nathan Smith, my great mentor; and Dean Maureen Kelley. During my stay there, I looked upon them as scholars and considered them my dear friends.

Baltimore, Maryland   Jonah R. Churgin

INTRODUCTORY REMARKS

Discrimination against women is mankind's oldest prejudice. This is a story of that prejudice as it relates to one of America's foremost institutions, the educational academy. Mirroring the society of which it is an intrinsic part, we will see how academe affects and reflects societal attitudes and prejudices.

Viewed in the broader context, we will concern ourselves with the role that one institution played and how it was, in turn, affected by the society it served. With this in mind, we will begin our discussion with the rise of the women's movement, always mindful of the inevitability of the monumental changes the cloistered academy must soon embrace if it is to carry out its newly assigned functions successfully. In one sense, this is a case study of a movement impinging upon the traditional prerogatives of an institution; in another sense, it is a probe into what happens when the whole of society is at variance with one of its constituent institutions and of the reconciliation that must follow. While we propose recommendations for academe so that it might better accommodate the new societal expectations of women, the thrust of this presentation will concentrate on why revolutionary change is imminent. Such change will come about whether we can anticipate it or not. We are not saying what will be, but why "what is" is no more. We are disposing of a system, not proposing an alternative one. Certainly, that we cannot visualize society's reconstructed form with precision does not make the inevitability of change any less apparent. For in reviewing the course of human history, if we changed only at the tempo that we were ready, or were willing to accept, or anticipate, or at a pace amenable to our own temperament, then we might still be carrying out our dialogue in the cave.

PART ONE

WOMEN—A SOCIETAL PROBLEM COMES TO CAMPUS

Chapter I

ANATOMY OF THE WOMEN'S MOVEMENT

PHILOSOPHY OF THE MOVEMENT:
BETTY FRIEDAN'S CALL TO ARMS

The first kernels of reform that were destined to rack the very foundations of academe had innocent and largely unnoticed beginnings. Initially the women's movement, through which feminist ideas were given expression, was largely regarded as an external if not faddish phenomenon of no real import to the academy.

Various writings began to emerge in the 1960s, the most notable being Betty Friedan's *The Feminine Mystique*.[1] This pioneering work, published in 1963, was a flash success rekindling old embers that have grown brighter with each passing year. To Friedan, "The Feminine Mystique" defined the lot of the American woman as happily fulfilled in "occupation housewife." This happy image, supported by the mass media and reinforced by our educational institutions, had little basis in fact. These women were, to Friedan, quite despondent. Yet, as a characteristic shared by all of them, each believed her own unhappiness unique to herself rather than a condition caused by a social life-style shared by a generation of women.

Friedan's work could easily be described as signalling the start of the "Second Women's Movement." The two women's drives arose out of the general reform fever of their times. Women as integral members of society reflected the lethargy and energy of the time. Referring to the demise of the earlier movement, historians have erroneously concluded that it was a "single issue" affair and once the objective of suffrage was achieved, the movement naturally dissipated.[2] Yet a careful reading of the statements of those earlier women reveals that this thesis, while attractively simple, is grievously fallacious; for they too were concerned with a

1

galaxy of women's issues. Another theory for its demise is that they could not possibly maintain the momentum of reform in the war-weary lethargic society of post-World War I America, and that the women of those years simply did not have the power to singularly sustain their momentum given the prevailing climate of opinion. No matter how true this idea may be, times have changed: in the earlier days women formed merely one of many movements finding sustenance in the general reform atmosphere of the period and receiving their driving force from the few middle-class women in a largely lower-class society. Today, while the movement is still largely middle-class, we are in a middle-class society and women are no longer one among many, but first and all-encompassing. They can, to a considerable extent, dictate society's climate and direction.

A few years ago after the publication of her landmark work, Friedan described the motivation that compelled her to put her thought to paper. She was disturbed, she says, by women's lack of identity as individuals, about the lives they were forced to lead and about the frustration they were privately compelled to endure. What was it, Friedan observed, that deprived women of their natural destiny? To be defined not as individuals but in terms of their relationships to others? To her, the term that appropriately defined the condition that subjugated America's women was "The Feminine Mystique."[3] The only remedy for this social malady could come about through a total restructuring of "childbearing, education, and marriage. . . ."[4]

To Friedan, one of the ingredients contributing to the subjugation of the modern American woman was attributable to the ever lowering marriage age. The new vogue, pounded into the minds of impressionable young girls, was to look forward to being a suburban housewife who received daily ecstasy and intimate gratification from cleaning the kitchen floor or waiting for hubby to return from work.[5] Women were fast becoming impoverished mentally while simultaneously being placated by an ever higher standard of living. This was part of the problem. Since happiness is

2

largely defined by financial wealth, an unhappy woman who is also wealthy is, almost by definition, someone abnormal.

Under the guidelines of the "Mystique," the prevailing creed was to procreate:

> If the secret of feminine fulfillment is having children, never have so many women, with the freedom to choose, had so many children, in so few years, so willingly.[6]

This criterion, while it was regarded as inordinately natural, had not always held sway. Friedan describes how in the 1930s the mass media and other societal institutions, including the educational establishment, were more sympathetic to the notion of the career woman.

The transformation to the new ethos emerged in the late 1940s with articles in the mass media on "How to Snare a Male . . . Cooking to Me Is Poetry . . . The Business of Running a Home. . ." as the vanguard of a new offensive preparing women for a noncareer orientation.[7] Friedan depicts the vivid contrast with the articles of the 1930s which catered to and assumed a class of professional women. Articles by Walter Lippman, General Stilwell, Carl Sandburg and Margaret Sanger abounded. If people seek to evaluate themselves based upon the expectations of others, one may well imagine the educational impact that a sophisticated mass media must have had on the impressionable minds of young women. As time elapsed, women capitulated to the new realities and abrogated any contemplation of a meaningful professional career, preferring the promised eternal bliss awaiting them in matrimony.[8] Yet the happiness so often alluded to in the media was elusive in life. In college, women were educated to be men but socialized to act "like" women. The contradiction was all too apparent—in hindsight.

The relationship between the media and the educational world was intimate and reinforcing. Educators get their ideas from the information they absorb. Nowhere is this blending of the two worlds more harmoniously depicted than in the words of the great intellectual politician, Adlai

Stevenson. Speaking to the students of Smith College in the early 1950s, he enjoined them on the importance of domesticity. "Women," he said, "especially educated women, have a unique opportunity to influence us, men and boy."[9] The extent of this indoctrination is seen not only in the fact that a person of Stevenson's intellectual stature and prowess could utter such thoughts but that he could do so, unhesitatingly, at a prestigious women's college which was supposedly founded in the cause of women's ultimate emancipation. Moreover if the Stevenson creed was correct, what was the rationale for the continued operation of Smith College? What was the purpose of proving that women were men's equal in thought, so convincingly established at Smith, if they were to remain unequal in action? Looked at in this context, the expensive Smith experiment was a "successful failure."

As women were to live vicariously and complementarily through their men, it was only natural that the academic order should remain masculine. Society, through its media, socialized the young woman to accept her fate well before she entered the ivied columns. A college junior, asked about her ambitions, responded:

> I don't want to be interested in a career I'll have to give up.
> My mother wanted to be a newspaper reporter from the time she was twelve, and I've seen her frustration for twenty years. I don't want to be interested in world affairs. I don't want to be interested in anything beside my home and being a wonderful wife and mother. Maybe education is a liability. Even the brightest boys at home want just a sweet, pretty girl.[10]

The woman who comes to college is already sociologically maimed. At the college she is provided with the rationale for her supposedly different position and perspective in life. If a young girl had any remaining glimmer of hope about pursuing a career, the educational process through its various practitioners would show her the futility of her ambitions. The college and university curriculum, to the extent that it was concerned about women, stressed adjustment, not exploration. For example, the Freudians of the

4

post-World War II era held sway on campus and in society.[11] They claimed, among other things, that motherhood was a full-time occupation necessary both for the fulfillment of the mother and the well-being of the child and that, in order for the child to mature into a healthy human being, the constant adulation of the mother was absolutely indispensable. This imprisoned the woman as well as her children.

Why has American society been so reluctant to accord women new rights? Is it only the male ego that prevents the woman from assuming a career role? The Russians seem to have circumvented this hurdle by allowing women to enter many professions but then lowering the status of the professions they occupy. This gives the women a career but preserves the pretense of masculine domination. At first glance it seems odd that American men cannot grant their women as much. A possible answer lies in the difference in the economic system—"the business of America is business." All of America's institutions, including education, revolves around the business philosophy. The illustrations are many: the taxpayer helps to subsidize a science student with a fellowship to acquire a doctorate. This fellowship money helps to defray student expenses. The student graduates and takes her/his skills, acquired at public expense, to the private sector. These skills are then utilized to realize a profit from the public. This scenario is repeated in many different ways and is meant to demonstrate the intricate interdependency of institutions and the overriding business philosophy. What, then, would be the impact on institutions if women were accorded equality with men? The answer, of course, almost takes us into the "twilight world" of educated speculation. Certainly whole industries presently established might be instantly displaced. Women would no longer feel fulfilled by being acquainted with the different brands of detergents or live in dread of the woman visitor with the white glove who uncovers dust particles on her furniture. Her furniture might be a little less bright, but her brain would be dramatically less dull. Television programming in the daytime would be altered. Friedan illuminatingly provides us with an illustration why various industries would be eliminated:

5

> One of the ways that the housewife raises her own prestige as a cleaner of her home is through the use of specialized products for specialized tasks. . . .When she uses one product for washing clothes, a second for dishes, a third for walls. . .she feels less like an unskilled laborer, more like an engineer, an expert.[12]

Without question, a woman is crippled from birth by the "Feminine Mystique." Her ambitions are arrested because she is told that in marriage there is "happiness ever after." Strangely, very few books describe what happens "after." A youthful mind can innocently fantasize, but grim reality must take its toll. Similar to the ancient Chinese civilization which sought to retard the growth of the girl's feet, we attempt to limit the biological potential of the girl's mind.[13] To Friedan, the "Feminine Mystique" presents women with a contradictory choice: either be a human being and allow yourself to develop to the full extent of your abilities or be a woman.[14] She emphasizes that if the family system is to be saved, its structure must be revised, and notes that professional career women are happier in marriage than those who devote themselves exclusively to being full-time housewives.[15] Specifically: Friedan stresses that if women are to have fulfilling lives it is vital that the early marriage age be reversed, that women be encouraged to defer consummation of their marital plans.[16] Indeed, only if the marriage is contemplated as a genuinely equal partnership should women ever consider the union. To Friedan as well as others, the statistical correlation between earlier marriages and the subsequent forfeiture of career pretensions is nearly absolute.[17] In addition, various other assumptions must be laid bare. For example, it has frequently been held that if a woman truly desires a career she can assume one once her family child-rearing obligations are fulfilled. The assumption rests on the questionable premise that a woman can start or continue a career after a long absence from the work force. However, the premise that women alone must endure the burden of child rearing, with its concomitant sacrifice, should not go unchallenged. Also, under the cloak of the "Feminine Mystique," the college woman is too busy seeking an appropriate mate and contemplating imminent marital

6

bliss, and this is hardly conducive to laying the groundwork for a future career.[18]

Friedan suggests that, given the severe disadvantages women have had to endure, and recognizing the tremendous contribution they have made to the nation in terms of self-lessly maintaining the family, a massive GI-type bill should be implemented to allow women to reconstruct their lives. The consequences of such a proposal on women, men, education, and the general societal structure are too difficult to comprehend but nevertheless tempting to ponder. Society's institutions as they currently exist were predicated on values that have long since disappeared. But, the old vestigial structures and attitudes remain:

> Should a gifted child grow up to be a house-wife?... the gift of high intelligence is bestowed upon only one out of every 50 children... one question is in-evitably asked: "Will this rare gift be wasted if she be-comes a housewife?"... the majority find the job of being a housewife challenging.... In her daily role as nurse, educator, economist... she is constantly seeking ways to improve her family's life.... Millions of women... shop-ping for half the families in America do so by saving X stamps.[19]

Certainly X stamps has an interest in maintaining the present structure!

PHILOSOPHY OF THE WOMEN'S MOVEMENT

Like the Orwellian prophet in *Animal Farm,* "Old Major," the movement which was to develop from Friedan's call to arms did not always heed her program or take hold of her prescription for change.[20] The "Feminine Mystique" provides the rationale nevertheless. To Friedan, unlike many of the other prophets before her, goes the unfortunate distinc-tion of living to see her dream reach fruition. Had she died, she might have been instantly elevated as a lasting symbol for all, but by living she could be a leader only for some.

Notwithstanding these qualifications, the new feminist movement has many Friedanian overtones. Central to the feminists' belief is the notion that all political-economic systems have been biased against women. After all, there is overbearing sexual discrimination in the Soviet Union as there is in the United States and the class struggle is in essence a male competition for power from which women are patently excluded. While they may be the recipients of some of the emoluments of status, especially if they are married to influential men, they can rarely hold status in their own right. Consequently, the feminists maintain that all women are united in the same plight: they are all victims of a common socialization process that robs them of their identity and self-worth.

While women are generally united in their grievances, they are at odds over the appropriate solutions. Some women, especially those who identify with the earlier movement, hold the masculine model as the ideal for all and spurn any thought of wholesale deviation. Others claim that they should pursue their own destinies and renounce the idea that the masculine mold must be the standard for comparison. To them, different is not to be equated with unequal.[21] A third viewpoint, the one espoused here, maintains an "asexual" outlook: men and women are human beings first and foremost and any apparent societal differences based on sex are contrived, not innate.

Whatever else women may debate among themselves, they appear united in their condemnation of the contemporary family structure; for regardless of the profession they wish to enter or the life they desire to lead, their activities remain adversely curtailed as long as they remain the primary moving force in the marital arrangement.[22] In the past, if a woman of middle-class origins worked outside the home, it was generally viewed as temporary and incidental to her fundamental family obligation.[23] The woman's commitment in marriage was total; the man's partial.[24] Yet, the staggering divorce rate, seemingly incidental to women's drive for equality, is both a cause and effect of the new burgeoning consciousness. For the presumed conditions upon which the woman receives compensation in the form of lifelong companionship and security in exchange for her familial involvement no longer exist: she is required to commit herself to a husband who statistically may not be with her for a substantial portion of her adult life; equally, the only suitable profession for which she has generally been trained, and in which millions of women in the past were able to secure employment, teaching, is a rapidly diminishing option. Clearly, with divorce at epidemic proportions and in the absence of any emotional or financial security, women run the risk of becoming financially insolvent and emotionally destitute by clinging to old ways. In conjunction with this state of affairs, the question emerges: should society educate a girl to the realities of marriage? Can a devoted parent dare not to? However, to educate her to the new imponderables is to reorient her to be self-reliant.

Still another "problem" concerns the very real physical superiority of women.[25] As women live longer they face the prospect of spending even more time in a mental vacuum. What, after all, is a woman to do after her children are raised? Can she revert to the attentions of her husband who, however devoted he may be, has grown accustomed to his office life during the years of her maternal obligations? Undoubtedly, the evolution of the nuclear family is not an innovation that treats the middle-aged woman kindly, and even the most ardent traditionalists may be hard put to provide the rationale for the necessity "for women to confine their life expectations to marriage and parenthood."[26]

Today, regardless of their personal situation, women in middle age appear relegated to voluntary "make work" activities. Because such activities are nonpecuniary in an otherwise materialistic society, they are accorded a low status. Since status is intricately related to financial prowess, an individual who has to "give away" her or his services is in fact engaged in socially demeaning activities.[27]

Quite conspicuously, the changing life-style will decree a different role structure. The argument that biology is destiny is irrelevant and has been so for quite a few years. Mankind has allowed technology to alter his destiny; therefore why is womankind immune from the novelties of twentieth-century innovation?[28] Margaret Mead too emphasizes that differences

9

between the sexes may be needlessly exaggerated. After all, when a man is myopic we give him glasses and thereby eliminate the physical disparity between him and his keener visioned peers. So too, if a woman is a little slower at a particular occupation, is there a way to compensate for this discrepancy rather than exaggerate it?[29]

The inconsistencies in American society are blatant. While many millions of privileged women remain unemployed out of respect for the psychological theories of proper upbringing, this taboo seems peculiarly absent for working-class mothers who have been employed in unprecedented numbers for quite a few years.[30]

That societal standards are arbitrary and capricious can be seen in the politics of child-care centers.[31] For years women of the middle class were denied use of such services on the pretext that it would cause irreparable harm to future generations. However, society seems to be immune to the supposedly deleterious effects of child-care centers with respect to lower-class toddlers. Could it be that the establishment looks with favor on poorer females working for petty wages, thereby producing added goods and services under conditions that men would not tolerate? Alternatively, when it comes to the middle-class woman who would directly infringe on the job market of establishment males, a different rationale is imposed. Under the exigencies of World War II, with so many men out of the labor market, the government was less hesitant.[32]

If the argument about child care is strictly to secure the best interests of the child, then a vast network of child-care centers should be constructed.[33] Is not such an institution, which can provide professional help, preferable to the part-time domestic baby-sitters? Is it not better for the child to come from a household where the mother is not frustrated? And finally, does not the child benefit from the added income that the working mother can produce?[34]

Because of societal abuse inflicted upon women, they cannot help but question the fundamental rules by which they are governed. Must they, to be equal, compete in the degrading and dehumanizing masculine-contrived amoral world?[35] Is it good that people have been conditioned to

10

simulate a mechanical character in their daily existence?[36] Viewing the women's movements in this perspective, could we suggest that a golden opportunity might be lost if in reconsidering women's role we do not also question the very integrity of the society that perpetuated such discriminatory behavior in the first place? Alice Rossi suggests:

> The idea has been lost that many problems, even in the personal family sphere, cannot be solved on an individual basis, but require solution on a societal level by changing the institutional contexts within which we live.[37]

THE ELITIST-COLLECTIVIST DEBATE

With respect to changing society, one of the continuing controversies revolves around the structure of the various women's groups and focuses on whether they should be organized on the so-called "star system" in preference to the "collectivist" approach. To many women the star system, being inherently elitist, signifies the perpetuation of the old order that they are trying to replace. For the star system of society presupposes that the best would automatically rise to the fore, clearly implying that those who are left behind failed on "their own merits." Yet societal rules have been so designed as to guarantee that women, despite their own best efforts, could not easily succeed. Incontrovertibly, the meritocratic system that supposedly assures equal competition for all has, through the establishment of certain guidelines, assured virtual success for some. Granting the validity of these assertions should not negate the fact that there are differences among people. To Catharine Stimpson:

> "Stars" are often smart, hard working, courageous and skillful. . . . Trying to abolish the star system must avoid the risk of leveling pioneers, prophets, and the odd spirits who find joy in lonely work. Trying to demonstrate hierarchies must avoid the risk of inhibiting skill.[38]

The collectivist ethos has its origins in the egalitarian

11

ideal. It assumes that everyone is equal and is made unequal only through the arbitrarily imposed rules of society. The entire problem of ensuring equality becomes one of structure, not ability. In accordance with this philosophy, many aspects of the women's movement, especially in its earlier years, lent credibility to this notion by adopting a communal basis for leadership.[39] However, governing soon became difficult. Since everyone has to be immersed in the affairs of the "sisterhood," no one could speak as an individual, and since only individuals can speak, the defects were obvious: those with greater abilities were automatically accused of power aggrandizement. In order to maintain the semblance of equality, rules had to be promulgated that protected mediocrity by preventing talent from rising. Under the collectivist spirit, everyone had to succeed together. As we will see later in the work of John Gardner, the less talented, whoever they may be, derive tangible psychological benefits under a restrictive system, for if discrimination is societally based, failure is not personal. Under the new procedures, where success and failure lie in the province of the individual, the lack of such achievement must exact a grim psychic toll. Moreover, since women in the past were kept from competing, many may not have the requisite confidence in their own native ability to perform in a truly open system. Women, being untried, are uncertain.

Regardless of the validity of the collectivist-star debate, certainly at its inception the tactical use of the egalitarian clarion call was necessary if the movement was to unify. It is not surprising, then, that we saw feminists proclaiming:

> Elitism makes us look down on students, secretaries, factory workers, housewives, and all women who, for good reasons of their own or of the climate in which they live, do not share our professional status. Competition and jealousy make us niggardly in sharing ideas and support with our female colleagues.[40]

The necessity for a unifying principle was essential. Male mores have not only subjugated women but also served to instill among them suspicion that had to be dispelled if the

12

movement were to go forward. Women were told, in effect, that while they should defer to men, they should compete with other women. This socialization process has been so imbedded that perhaps the only effective procedure to combat it was to renounce competition altogether in favor of cooperation: "We have learned that women are not as important and interesting as men and that another woman is to be regarded with cautious dislike."[41]

Even if a woman had not been socialized as a youth to compete with other women, she might out of necessity adopt such a posture, no matter how unwillingly, as an adult. This is because career women were historically forced to compete for the few token positions allocated to their sex. Viewed in this perspective, it is understandable that they were reluctant to respond to anything but collective leadership.[42] Only when the system begins to modify, when everyone is equally subjected to the rules of competition, may women reevaluate this "tactical" decision. However, once they become a powerful and established voice, it does not necessarily follow that they should become competitive. At that juncture they are at the crossroads: should they seek to change society or merely join it? The cooperative stance within some feminist groups may be a means to gain access to competitive society rather than a microcosm of how they believe society should be formulated.

THE GENERAL REFORM MOVEMENT AND WOMEN STUDENTS

Naturally, it is essential to understand the philosophy and direction of the women's movement if we are to anticipate its impact on the campuses of America. Today's feminist revolution is especially intriguing for educators because in large measure it emanated from "activist" women students who were originally concerned with the issues of war and race.[43] As these students left the sheltered confines of academe they began to realize that the rights they were seeking for others were denied to themselves—both in society and on the campus.

13

These college women were fertile ground for the new ideology. Jessie Bernard observes that it is the "younger women. . . and the more educated women. . . who are more for women's rights."[44] These are the women who have the ability to see societal injustices, and themselves as victims.[45] Indeed, their very education prepares them for a life which they will not be "allowed" to lead, obliging them instead to acquiesce and accept positions for which they are obviously overqualified. Thus Jo Freeman observes that "twenty percent of all college-educated working women are secretaries."[46] Interestingly, "lower-class" women are not susceptible to this frustration. They are not affected by the contradiction in the media advertisements of secretarial schools enticing women college graduates to take their postgraduate training in an eight-week secretarial course while their male counterparts proceed to graduate and professional schools. A woman who had only a high school education is more fit for and consequently less resentful of the prospect of such employment.

Certainly the American middle-class woman, who has so much to offer by way of her education, is the person who is most patently ignored by society.[47] The lower-class woman has a vital role to play as an essential contributor to the family income, whereas the educated woman, marrying an affluent mate, is deprived of the right to feel needed. In a sense, we can say that women as a group should not be united because they do not suffer equally, and since the middle class has the most to gain, it is truly a sexual class movement. Yet even if we tentatively grant this assumption, the conclusion does not follow, for America is fast evolving into a predominatly middle-class society in which it is not uncommon for people to pass from poverty to wealth within the same generation. This is the American reality and birthright that cannot be denied. Therefore the problems of middle-class women today will be the problems of all women tomorrow. Over half of the nation's population cannot be expected to have the American dream of affluence be equated with uselessness. The survival of society, not only the happiness of its women, is in question.

In the past, whether the woman was a career professional or a housewife, she was a very poor change agent. As a career professional she was easily co-opted and as a housewife she was made subordinate. In either case she was afraid and isolated. However, today women students are truly the catalysts for change.[48] Not tied to a husband or the obligations of a family, still possessing the idealism of youth, and united in a college setting, the female student is in a pivotal position for determining the fate of the movement.

Indeed, to an impressive extent, women students were the embodiment of the women's movement—inculcated with its ideals and mobilized for action. A *New York Times* correspondent writes typically of 1975 Barnard graduates:

> The graduates tended to have several things in common: A burning desire for a career or an advanced degree. A feeling that they want to change what they consider, for the most part, is a lousy world. A wish for marriage and the family—but with the provisions that they will still be able to work.[49]

If the college women who participated in the general reform movement were in turn affected by it, so too were their older sisters who graduated only a few years earlier under the banner of the "Feminine Mystique." For example, in 1971 at the Fifth Year Class Reunion at Wellesley "'Topic A' was women's liberation, which most of the alumnae seemed to embrace wholeheartedly."[50] Under these circumstances, then, we are seeing women undergraduates in a reversal of positions, acting as role models to their seniors who graduated a few years earlier. Clearly, middle-class college women who initially sought to transform society, transformed themselves in the process and in turn will transform society.

FOOTNOTES FOR CHAPTER I

[1]Patricia M. Reinfeld, *Woman: Yesterday, Today, Tomorrow* (Sewell, N.J.: Eric Document Reproduction Service, ED 091 254, 1974), p. 6.

[2]Judith Hole and Ellen Levine, *Rebirth of Feminism* (New York: Quadrangle/The New York Times Book Company, 1971), p. 14.

[3]Betty Friedan, "Up from the Kitchen," *The New York Times,* 4 March 1973, sec. 6, p. 9.

[4]Ibid., p. 30.

[5]Betty Friedan, *The Feminine Mystique* (New York: W. W. Norton and Company, 1963), p. 19.

[6]Ibid., p. 29.

[7]Ibid., p. 44.

[8]Ibid., pp. 56-57.

[9]Ibid., p. 60.

[10]Ibid., p. 74.

[11]Ibid., pp. 103-125.

[12]Ibid., p. 215.

[13]Ibid., p. 305.

[14]Ibid., pp. 314-316.

[15]Ibid., pp. 329-330.

[16]Ibid., p. 364.

[17]Ibid., pp. 360-361.

[18]Ibid., pp. 365-366.

[19]Ibid., pp. 231-232.

[20]George Orwell, *Animal Farm* (New York: The New American Library, 1946), pp. 15-16.

[21]Lynn White, Jr., *Educating Our Daughters* (New York: Harper and Row, 1950), p. 36.

[22]Alice S. Rossi, "Equality Between the Sexes: An Immodest Proposal," *Daedalus* 43 (Spring 1964): 610.

[23]Joan N. Burstyn, "Striving for Equality: Higher Education for Women in the U.S. Since 1900," *University College Quarterly,* January 1973, p. 29.

[24]Lucy Komisar, "The New Feminism," *Saturday Review,* 21 February 1970, p. 28.

[25]Gladys E. Harbeson, "The New Feminism," *AAUW Journal,* January 1970, p. 53.

[26]Rossi, "Equality Between the Sexes," p. 614.

[27]Komisar, "The New Feminism," p. 29.

[28]Hole and Levine, *Rebirth of Feminism,* p. 187.

[29]Margaret Mead, *Male and Female* (New York: William Morrow and Company, 1949), p. 14.

[30]Norma Raffel, "The Women's Movement and Its Impact on Higher Education," *Liberal Education* 59 (may 1973): 248.

[31]Caroline Bird, *Born Female* (New York: Pocketbooks, 1975), p. 175.

[32]Hole and Levine, *Rebirth of Feminism,* p. 303.

[33]Rossi, "Equality Between the Sexes," pp. 631-632.

[34]Harbeson, "The New Feminism," p. 54.

[35]Burstyn, "Striving for Equality: Higher Education for Women in the U.S. Since 1900," p. 22.

[36]Ibid.

[37]Rossi, "Equality Between the Sexes," p. 613.

[38]Catharine R. Stimpson, *What Matter Mind: A Theory About the Practice of Women's Studies* (Bethesda, Md.: ERIC Document Reproduction Service, ED 068 078, August 1972), p. 16.

[39]Hole and Levine, *Rebirth of Feminism,* p. 159.

[40]Mary C. Howell, "Professional Women and the Feminist Movement," *The Journal of the National Association for Women Deans, Administrators and Counselors* 37 (Winter 1974): 86.

[41]Ibid., p. 84.

[42]Florence Howe and Carol Ahlum, "Women Studies and Social Change," in *Academic Women on the Move,* eds. Alice Rossi and Ann Calderwood (New York: Russell Sage Foundation, 1973), pp. 419-420.

[43]Hole and Levine, *Rebirth of Feminism,* p. 108.

[44]Jessie Bernard, "You Can't Destroy This Movement," *U.S. News and World Report,* 8 December 1975, p. 72.

[45]Jo Freeman, "Women's Liberation and Its Impact on the Campus," *Liberal Education* 57 (December 1971): 469.

[46]Ibid., p. 470.

[47].Harbeson, "The New Feminism," p. 53.

[48]Rose M. Somerville, "Women's Studies," *Today's Education* 60 (November 1971): 35.

[49]Judy Klemesrud, "Barnard's New Alumnae Tell What They Now Want Out of Life," *New York Times,* 2 June 1971, p. 36.

[50]Judy Klemesrud, "After Wellesley, Women's Liberation," *New York Times,* 7 June 1971, p. 28.

Chapter II

SOCIALIZING THE AMERICAN FEMALE

While the family remains the cornerstone of American society, it is the middle-class family which especially concerns us. This seeming qualification is dwarfed in significance when it is remembered that America is largely a middle-class society in mores if not always in fact.[1]

Certainly the structure of the family unit through history has witnessed such traumatic changes that even the immediate precursor to our own family is unrecognizable by contemporary standards.[2] In the past, motherhood entailed a very active career: the woman was responsible for much of the food, clothing and assorted products without which humankind could not have survived.[3] While feminine liberation from domesticity was gradual, it accelerated abruptly as women moved to the cities and were given access to the most modern conveniences. Unfortunately, however, in "progress" women lost more than their bondage—they lost a profession and with it the last vestiges of dignity.

It is true that many contemporary women have found employment to supplement the household budget. But even these "fortunates"—and they are numerous—typically were first obliged by their young children to remain at home in virtual isolation from other adults and the outside world. By contrast, their less-educated female ancestors enjoyed an extended family to assist them in the activities of everyday life. In addition, the extensive mobility of the American family has wrought considerably more havoc on the employed female than the male, for when the male moves he merely trades one "office" for another but a woman must give up her friends and associates, help her children to readjust and look for some new "temporary" employment while yielding any modest seniority she may have acquired.

18

Still another problem with the middle-class arrangement is that it provides an intoxicant for the woman not to work. A husband is confronted with strong societal supports and may even be censured if he fails as a provider. Since a woman may be considered as an extension of the man, his success can be vicariously interpreted as her success. To compound matters, since one of the symbols of success for the man is the nonemployment of his wife, a husband may look with disfavor upon his working wife.[4] A woman who attempts to establish a career outside of the home is often stigmatized with the "scarlet letter" of disapproval. To her family she may be seen as disloyal while to her neighbors her gender integrity will be subjected to scrutiny. Not surprisingly, many women opt to remain with their offspring for an extended period of time, a practice which is confining to both the mother and child.[5]

As an even further inducement, she faces the future threat that any malady her child might encounter in later life could be blamed on deficient maternal upbringing. Accordingly, if she assumes a career during the so-called formative years of her child—which, incidentally, are also the crucial years for her own career development—and the child does suffer difficulties, she may very likely be held culpable. To make things even worse, the American woman is made to feel that she must perform the role of housewife regardless of the extent of her outside commitments. She is told through popular myth that the normal woman enjoys doing such work and is made to feel guilty about delegating it to others.

As if this were not enough, a woman must not only be prepared to face stiffer professional obstacles in the form of antipathy from the masculine work world, but she must be stronger if she is not to be enticed into giving up her professional aspirations. At every stage in a woman's career, she is given the face-saving option of abandoning a potentially unpleasant confrontation or assignment altogether.[6] A man is not afforded this luxury and society, through its supports, gives him the determination to succeed when success seems so elusive. This is one reason why the argument that a woman should be given the choice between housework and a career is self-defeating: once she is awarded a choice, her incentive and productivity may well be diminished. Lotte Bailyn puts the matter succinctly:

> The fact that a woman functions in a situation in which she may or may not work decreases the likelihood that the choice to work, when made, will be definitive. Commitment may be seriously undermined. All serious work entails drudgery and unrewarding effort, and there are times when anyone—regardless of sex—would welcome a legitimate excuse to stop. Such excuses are near at hand for the professional woman. When faced with discouragement in her work it is not difficult for her to discover that her children really do need her all of the time.[7]

While many authorities suggest that a woman's family life may be made compatible with her professional ambitions, this places a woman at a severe disadvantage vis-a-vis men. For if a woman is permitted to "drop-in" and part-time study is given added respectability, it is, in effect, an inducement for a woman to take an excessively long time to complete her training. If the meritocratic market is to be maintained, how can women seriously contemplate competing with men who are steadfastly committed to their professions on a full-time basis from the time they enter graduate school until the time of retirement, with little extraneous distraction to deflect them from their purpose or dilute their expertise?

That societal attitudes are so effective in deterring talented women from pursuing a career course is depicted by the Radcliffe Study which expresses surprise at the lack of vigor on the part of their graduates.[8] This paucity in productivity, despite evidence of encouragement from educational institutions, is an i..dication that academe is not an entity unto itself but should be viewed as an appendage attached to the societal universe that must also be changed if women's academic status is to be uplifted.

THE SOCIALIZATION OF THE AMERICAN GIRL

At the heart of the woman's problem is the intense and intricate socialization process by which all people as mem-

20

bers of society are affected. From an economist's perspective, we may not be a cradle to grave society, but from a psychological outlook, what we are told in the cradle governs our entire outlook until we are liberated by the grave. Even from early childhood, well before the new citizen of the world can reason, she or he is made to understand that there are sexual roles that should not be transgressed. The illustrations are abundant. In compliance with societal expectations, parents will stress the education of their sons over their daughters.[9] Young girls soon come to realize that their success will be measured in terms of their husbands' worth and not in their own ability or muted accomplishments. Throughout early life, girls are guided toward the role of wife and mother and conditioned to accept this as natural. Vocational training is encouraged if it complements this fixed role orientation but discouraged if it is incompatible.

The consequences of these socializing tendencies are repeatedly confirmed by the statistics. For example, while women generally receive higher grade-point averages in high school, usually considered the best indicator of college potential, they are nonetheless discouraged from college attendance; they are told that they need not go, and if they matriculate, that they need not stay. In light of this it is not surprising that Patricia Cross notes that many more males than females report parental encouragement as a reason for attending college.[10]

The very contemplation of her future marriage obligations will have a severe impact on a girl's ultimate career selection and commitment.[11] Thus while the male is trained to regard his career accomplishment as a measure of his personal worth, the female who embarks on the same course is frequently made to believe that she will use her career only if she is a failure: if for some reason she cannot assume her proper, more traditional role.[12] The consequences of this attitude on the career development of the young female are apparent: college-bound girls are reluctant to take out college loans because they may not expect to make full use of their education and might not wish to enter the state of matrimony with a negative dowry.[13]

It is interesting to consider that the lower-class child,

enduring a poor life-style and aspiring for a better one, may reject the traditional role model of her struggling mother while the

> middle class girls whose mothers are housewives see modeled exactly the pattern they should be taught to avoid. More often than not, their mothers are nearly as well educated as they themselves will be.[14]

Middle-class girls, of course, are especially victimized. Not only do they have negative role models in terms of home-making mothers, but they have smaller families. In effect, there is more chance for a girl to be an only child. Few studies have been done, but it may be worthwhile to research whether a large family composed of many boys and girls automatically leads to a deglamorization of the sex roles since sisters have opportunities to give orders to their younger brothers and to refuse the edicts of their older male siblings.

In the middle-class homes and in schools, too, girls are discouraged from participating in such activities as organized sports, debating clubs and other similar events.[15] As a result, they are not socialized as boys are into the idea of good sportsmanship or to the need for accepting defeat gracefully. Their egos are protected but they do not mature and they are less prepared to face a truly meritocratic world where any minor setback may take the form of a crushing defeat. Alternatively, lower-class children do not have the problem of avoiding success since their parents are preoccupied with the problems of survival.[16]

It is clear that women are really faced with a "no win" situation whatever their economic station: if they come from a lower-class background they will not have the funds or the parental encouragement to pursue a college degree; yet if they are of the middle class, they will be confronted with a homemaker role model that they may be more likely to emulate. Whatever their social class identity, then, by adolescence most girls come to identify what is considered to be the proper feminine pursuits while shunning those commonly thought of as masculine. Unfortunately, the educational world has been a willing accomplice in this sexual categorization. As an illustration, in their early high school years students were characteristically given vocational aptitude tests that were frequently differentiated according to sex. It was not until recently, as a result of pressure from the American Personnel Guidance Association, that this practice was discontinued.[17] Strangely, Helen Astin writes how even subtle changes in the high school environment can have a dramatic effect on future career orientation.[18] Accordingly,

> girls who attended larger high schools were more likely to plan careers in the professions and sciences, whereas the girls who attended smaller high schools were more likely to aspire to teaching or office work.[19]

In various other high schools, too, it appears that girls are discouraged from entering the masculine fields such as industrial arts and are encouraged instead to enter the domestic home economics courses.[20] Certainly to the young woman, college is not an institution where she can explore new horizons, but a place where she can settle on a prearranged curriculum determined in large measure by primary and secondary school teachers and counselors.

Daryl and Sandra Bem sum up the consequences of the process and the concomitant tragedy that is perpetrated upon females in America:

> When a [boy] baby is born, it is difficult to predict what he will be doing 25 years later. But if that same newborn child happens to be a girl, we can predict with almost complete confidence how she is likely to be spending her time 25 years later.
> ... Her individuality is irrelevant.... In our society, being female uniquely qualifies an individual for domestic work—either by itself or in conjunction with typing, teaching, nursing, or (most often) unskilled labor. It is this homogenization of America's women which is the major consequence of our society's sex-role ideology.[21]

This ideological orientation is begun at birth.[22] Not only is a little girl dressed in pink to signify her sex, but educators have found that the pink-clad baby is touched more and spoken to more frequently by fondling mothers than are little boys and this can be witnessed when the babies are only two days old.[23] Could we speculate and say that this conditioning may be a reason for the later differentiation in verbal ability between boys and girls? That if boys were treated more like girls their verbal ability might actually be enhanced? We know, of course, the deleterious effects of conditioning on girls in the scientific fields, but this could be an unnoticed form of negative conditioning on boys. In both cases the sexes mutually suffer to the detriment of society as a whole.

In some instances it is blatantly obvious that the specialization process goes against the iron laws of nature. In America, little girls are handled in a more fragile manner despite the fact that they are sturdier than their brothers. As they grow older, studies report that parents allow boys to cross streets with heavy traffic at a younger age than girls—again despite the fact that the girl's motor development is considerably more advanced than a boy's.[24] Also, research undertaken by the Fels Institute disclosed that the more intelligent girls actually like baseball whereas many bright boys may have a tendency toward orientations that people have hitherto regarded as feminine.[25] Finally, although girls are made to feel more dependent than their brothers, they actually mature faster and have fewer physical and emotional ailments than males.[26]

Not surprisingly, the artificially contrived sexual differences encouraged at birth soon begin to emerge and polarize: by the ninth grade only 3 percent of the girls but 25 percent of the boys indicate that they are considering a career in the sciences. Later on, as they prepare for college, girls score significantly lower in mathematical aptitude. Suspiciously, the effect of conditioning on mathematical aptitude is demonstrated by the fact that when the mathematical questions deal with domestic chores, girls generally improve their test scores.[27]

The indoctrination of females affects their classroom performance in many other ways. Researchers generalize that girls are more "socialized" than boys. Various studies tend to support this assertion. In one survey, 35 percent of high school males but 55 percent of the females believed that it was very important that their teachers held a favorable opinion of them.[28] We know, too, that girls are more peer-oriented and less independent than boys. Since girls are encouraged to be people-oriented, it is not surprising that they are inclined to enter the "caring" professions in favor of the "independent" field of abstract thinking.[29]

It is obvious that were the academic world to treat women and men equally, the women students would be handicapped, given their prior social indoctrination; for many women, through no fault of their own, simply cannot think of themselves in terms of being successful in career endeavors.[30] As historian Gerda Lerner explained a few years ago at the University of Pittsburgh:

> We assumed that equality of opportunity was sufficient, and disregarded the heritage of injury to self-esteem, the lack of self-assurance, the confusion about conflicting demands made by the girl upon herself and by society upon the girl. We have learned in the past few years that the damage to girls has been great indeed, but I do not think that we have fully realized how greatly it has affected the performance of college students. Girl students in the crucial years from 18 to 22 enter college with all the tensions and conflicts which sexual role indoctrination has imposed upon them, and the battlefield on which these conflicts are fought out is the intellectual performance in the classroom. Most girls, by the time they reach college, have been accustomed to failure. . . .[31]

In sum, in primary school girls are taught to go into the doll's corner while boys are encouraged in more active pursuits.[32] The early learning of the toddler gets progressive reinforcement. What makes this indoctrination so effective and so difficult to counter is its intrinsically "unconscious" nature.[33] As a small girl begins to read, she is successively bombarded first in children's stories and then in textbooks regarding her preordained role.[34] The effects of education take their toll and, while education is supposed to enlighten, its effects are to "endarken." Starting from the ignorant

25

"state of nature" where male and female are equal, as boys and girls become increasingly civilized, the boys acquire progressively lower opinions of girls while girls' grades show a steady and unremitting decline suggesting a progressively lowering opinion of themselves. If we judge education by its results, we may say that the prejudicial aspects of our publicly subsidized educational system has no equal. Already by the fourth grade it is demonstrated that girls generally see their available options to be teacher, secretary, nurse, or mother.[35] The contributory role of the mother in enforcing these educational beliefs serves to seal her daughter's fate. Thus when the mother of a nine-year-old girl was told how bright her child was in mathematics, she was reported to have said "How terrible! Why didn't it happen to one of the boys instead?"[36]

THE SOCIALIZATION OF THE AMERICAN COLLEGE WOMAN

Paralleling our primary and secondary schools, America's institutions of higher learning have been similarly culpable in helping to solidify the woman's domestic, nonintellectual role. Instead of attempting to pioneer new thought patterns they have acted to cement the old. This is truly reprehensible, especially in view of the tremendous expense incurred in receiving a higher education. Accordingly, a girl subsidizes research facilities through her parents' tax levies and her tuition expenses although she has been socialized not to make full use of them. Indeed, the situation in higher education may actually be worse than what she experienced in her earlier years. Then, a female was expected to take the same curriculum as her male counterpart; however, in college, while her tuition remains the same, she has been subtly coerced into going into separate and coincidentally less expensive feminine disciplines rather than to transgress and subsequently compete with males in the more lucrative scientific areas.

The confusion of the American college woman quite predictably affects her performance and outlook in an intricate

26

variety of ways, inescapably undercutting her professional development.[37] For example, women are susceptible to the mischievous notion that in order to succeed they must be better than men. This type of philosophy can be deleterious in that it provides an ego-saving rationale for failure. Actually this idea is not only hurtful but frequently untrue: "It isn't that they must be better than a man which causes girls to despair, it's that they think they must be better."[38] Another misleading concept that college-bound women should dispel is that marriage is necessarily incompatible with serious career expectations. Since our society encourages marriage, and since the female is called upon to make the supreme sacrifice to sustain it, women fear that adherence to a career orientation frightens away prospective mates. If college women were made to realize that the mating-dating game continues in professional school as well, they might be less reluctant to see the career life-style not as an either-or option but one that can exist in harmony within a revised marriage system.[39] Also, because of the accelerating divorce rate, there is further argument for preparing women to be self-sufficient professionally. In addition, the impermanence of the marital arrangement means a continuing rotation of available mates and correspondingly, women need no longer be as fearful of the need for a marriage deadline.[40]

To both women and men, a latent function of feminine college attendance is the acquisition of a husband. Cross notes that approximately 25 percent of female high school seniors openly admit that the pursuit of a husband remains their primary collegiate objective while 37 percent of the men interviewed concur. Cumulatively then, much too many college-bound youth hold that women are not primarily concerned with education, the manifest function of the college and university system, but with other motives.[41] These figures may even be understated in that about three-fourths of the college women who were surveyed said that there was a chance that they would marry within one year of graduation.[42] It seems apparent that Americans send their middle-class daughters off to college with the objective of finding

suitable mates.[43] These data are substantiated by other findings. Friedman's Vassar study in 1956, echoing the identical
theme, showed the seemingly desperate determination of
most women to be married within a few years of graduation.[44] Certainly, on some campuses, not to be engaged by
the senior year was regarded by many as a stigma.[45]

Various collegiate subinstitutions have arisen to fulfill
this mate-procuring latent function of academe. John Scott
lucidly describes the most famous. The sorority as an organization, especially during the 1950s, served as a structure
similar in function to the fatting houses of other societies.
That is, it gathered a group of preselected females from particular backgrounds and through careful if not formal guidance, dictated their choice of a mate. Sororities are much
more important for a woman than fraternities are for a man
in that the early selection of a mate is accorded much more
priority by the female.[46] This is because a woman's "market
value" diminishes with age, giving urgency to quick mate
selection. Characteristically the sorority system is essentially
composed of identifiable groups that seek to guarantee
through the maintenance of specifically prescribed norms that
the young girl's social environment will be carefully monitored in order that she may have the opportunity to "randomly" fall in love with the "right" boy.

Recognizing the function of sororities, it is not surprising
that they are especially important for the woman in that, in
American society, she is obliged to yield the status of her parents for that of her future husband. Since one of the reasons
Americans go to college is for status enhancement, and since
a woman receives her greatest status rewards through proper mate selection, it is natural that the woman, and certainly her parents, are duly concerned over her ultimate
choice. The process by which a woman can move up socially
as a result of marriage is known as hypergamy and has become effectively institutionalized in our society, especially
through the sorority system. Since status in America is in a
constant state of flux, and since marriage represents a new
status arrangement, it is no wonder that with the influx of
many minorities, sororities have assumed such importance to

28

parents and their children.[47] Moreover, a lower-status woman has an added advantage in her quest for finding a higher-status man in that a woman's status is not easily transferable to her future husband.[48] Consequently a man is not as likely to scrutinize the status background of his potential wife. Recognizing that American society operates under the guise of unarranged marriage, it is the function of the sorority to make certain that the opportunity to fall in love is carefully screened.[49] Testimony to its function can be discerned through any cursory examination of where it is thriving: in large state universities where there is a great mixing of the population, the sorority system is also found "most fully developed."[50]

The sorority is organized to perform its role well. Recruiting often starts when the girls are still in high school. To those students who may be fearful of an awesome academic work load in an unknown environment, the sorority offers the prospect of the familiar and the friendly. When the young recruit arrives on campus she will become a "pledge" and have all her free time so thoroughly consumed by the sorority's demanding social engagements that she will have little chance to stray from the pact into the wider collegiate wilderness. Typically, the sorority may be paired with a fraternity of similar class and ethnic background.[51] Once matriculated, scholarship is minimized to the extent necessary to allow the young woman to continue her matriculation.

The recruitment process is carefully regulated. Generally a prospect may be recommended by alumnae or have a mother who was a member. Furthermore, activist, excessively enterprising young girls are discouraged from applying since they may exercise a disquieting influence on the established mores of the group.

In accord with their function, sororities give special attention to the male-female relationship, "codifying" its progress through "pinning" and other ceremonies. By institutionalizing each of the stages leading to marriage, the sorority makes it especially difficult for the young woman to rescind her involvement.[52]

Elizabeth Almguist and Shirley Angrist support the general views of Scott concerning the role of the sorority as a family surrogate on campus. Interestingly, career-oriented women tend to be less amenable to sorority membership, precisely because of its mating function.[53] An intriguing fact noted by Rossi is that many sorority women seemed to be strangely unfulfilled. When she asked a selected group of college-educated women which females they admired most, the vast majority selected those who had distinguished themselves in a career despite the fact that the interviewed women had personally opted for the sorority ideal of wife and mother.[54]

Is the sorority system today just as strong as it was in past decades? Probably not. Ethnicity must break down to some extent as a result of the assimilation process. Furthermore, as a probable consequence of the women's liberation movement, women have something to offer other than their ephemeral beauty. If professions continue to be an important measure of status in America, and as more women enter the masculine professions, they will have status and currency to give their husbands. No longer will women have the incentive to marry young. Indeed, if they wait until they complete their professional training, they might increase their value in the marital marketplace.

Finally, it could be argued that the chief latent function of colleges for the female population—that of marriage broker—was dysfunctional to the manifest function of academe—that of learning. For as we saw, not only did the sorority system not encourage educational learning, but saw it as a threat to its purpose, and correspondingly sought to minimize its overall implications.

In conclusion, the importance of the husband and the image of the proper female role in marriage prove to be impressive guiding forces for the female student. Since few young women anticipate spinsterhood, and most view the prospect of marriage as either imminent or inevitable, they naturally opt to prepare in a "generalist" fashion knowing full well that their education must be forever compromised to their husbands' career needs.[55] Clearly, excessive specialization in the present may be rewarded by intense frustration in the future if they are expert in a field which they can never hope to practice.[56] Steinmann observes that while they might prefer a more active life, they see men as desirous of the subordinate, affable female who invariably places her family obligations above her own inclinations and development.[57] Many other problems abound which are considered by the career-oriented woman. Thus when she enters college she may feel constrained from performing to the full level of her abilities out of fear that her very success will spell failure in acquiring a mate, or, if she is already married, will highlight his inadequacies.

THE CONTRADICTORY DEMANDS OF THE FEMALE ROLE

Given the socialization process that a woman must endure, it is not surprising that she is confused. Perhaps no two people better summarized the incompatibility of the female's earlier socialization with her subsequent life-style in college than Mirra Komarovsky and Matina Horner.

Mirra Komarovsky

To Komarovsky, in childhood, females are indoctrinated to succeed but as they mature they are abruptly told to forego this type of success in favor of marriage. She categorizes these two orientations as the "feminine" and the "modern." The "feminine" philosophy defines the woman in her sexual role as comforter (supportive) while the "modern" notion ignores sexual roles in place of the general, asexual normative demands of contemporary society.[58] The problem is that both roles exist simultaneously throughout the life of the female, although one may appear more dominant at a specific stage in her life cycle. The seeds of this conflicting pattern are sown early in the girl's life, lying dormant only to blossom much later.[59] Hence, whereas in childhood sexual roles are not as significant, and the girl will be encouraged to perform on the basis of her innate ability, as she grows older the sexual role will begin to emerge. Upon reaching college the woman may be startled by seemingly abrupt and obviously contradictory values requiring a transformation from one expected mode of behavior to a contradictory alternative.

> It seemed to some of them that they had awakened one morning to find their world upside down: what had hitherto evoked praise and rewards from relatives, now suddenly aroused censure.[60]

According to Komarovsky, 40 percent of those women surveyed who as young girls were conditioned to produce good grades now "indicated that they had . . . concealed academic honors. . . pretended ignorance. . . ." Yet parents still expected their daughters to succeed in both the "modern" and "feminine" roles, demanding that they capture the academic honors while simultaneoulsy subduing the most masculine male on campus.[61]

Clearly, society tells the young girl that what she may be warmly applauded for as a child will be the very behavior most often condemned when she reaches her majority. It is tragic to consider the tremendous plight of the young woman embarking upon a college career with innocent excitement. For in the act of leaving home for college a male faces the apprehensions of a new environment for which he has been carefully prepared, while a woman must face this same newness but unexpectedly confront a world where the only values she has to guide her have become suddenly invalidated.[62] Strangely, the girl who has no strong commitments appears least victimized; the female of genius aptitude who has fostered a passion for academic success will have a rude awakening at the gates of higher learning.

In a later study, Komarovsky observes that males, too, face a conflict, albeit not as serious to their development or happiness.[63] We know from early infancy, for instance, that male children are subtly trained to believe in masculine superiority. This idea has hitherto remained unchallenged in the typical all-male college and university. However, as more talented women begin to seek and gain admission to college, the young male is confronted as never before with an elite

32

core of intellectually gifted females who may be superior. Understanding that "mere equality with a woman may be defined as a defeat or a violation of a role prescription," the new realities must be startling.[64] This hardship nothwithstanding, the dilemmas facing the female are incomparably more serious in magnitude and character. For the male's development is not thwarted nor is his future happiness endangered—though his ego may be temporarily impaired. Furthermore, the male is confronted with this seeming contradiction because his ill-conceived but carefully nurtured prejudice against the female sex does not conform to his present experiences. In a sense, his prejudice has been placed in question. Positive learning has taken place.

Of course, not all the college males reported significant conflict in the dating relationship. Some may have regarded themselves as intellectually superior without relevance to the facts while a few others may actually have been superior. Another group may have regarded the intellectual standard as irrelevant. A number of girls, who might have been intellectually superior, may have been emotionally dependent or plain looking, or in some other way offered suitable ego compensation for their male dates.[65]

In another series of questions, it was found that the typical males were insensitive to the aspirations of the females and while they agreed with the statement that "It is appropriate for a mother of a preschool child to take a full-time job," they quickly modified it upon closer scrutiny to mean "provided, of course, that the home was run smoothly...."[66] The male contradiction between stated liberalism and actual prejudice may cause some discomfort when the young man is confronted with these self-evident contradictions; nevertheless, it is the female who remains the victim.

Reviewing Komarovsky's statistics on college males, 24 percent of those interviewed said they wanted their wives to remain in the home while an additional 16 percent, although they claimed to accept the idea of women's work in principle, laid down so many impractical qualifications as to put them in the former category as well. The largest group, 58 percent, did endorse the notion of women's employment according to a "sequential pattern" so that the needs of childrearing could be accommodated. Only 7 percent of the males questioned were willing to alter their roles so that their own wives could have meaningful careers. The remainder felt ill-prepared to venture any views on marriage.[67]

Unfortunately, for the woman, even if she acquiesces to the sentiments of her husband she is still doomed to unhappiness; for among those men who stanchly favored the traditional wifely role to the exclusion of anything else, they still reiterated that "a woman who works is more interesting than a housewife." In effect, men desire women to be placed in a role that men regard as contemptible and unrewarding. As an illustration, referring to the woman's destiny, one male reflects: "Life ends at 40. The woman raised her children and all that remains is garden clubs and that sort of thing unless, of course, she has a profession."[68]

Even among those males who do profess to admire women involved in pre-med or pre-law programs, the promulgated ground rules effectively create a double standard to the detriment of the female.[69] Furthermore, in an apparent contradiction, a male student who proclaims his support of equal professional opportunities for women also stresses:

A woman should not be in a position of firing an employee. It is an unpleasant thing to do. Besides, it is unfair to the man who is to be fired. He may be a very poor employee, but he is still a human being and it may be just compounding his unhappiness to be fired by a woman.[70]

That college men bare the inconsistencies is apparent; that women are made to reap the consequences is clear. What is the solution? Komarovsky indicates that the woman's role will not radically change until society provides new supporting structures to encourage the adoption of new roles and the abandonment of old thinking.[71]

Matina Horner

Certainly, the college years can bring a woman's abilitites to either fruition or frustration. For on the one hand the emphasis on finding a mate will be increased, yet if a woman is to develop to her full potentiality, her college years represent her best hope—especially given her prior training and future prospects: for these are the years, away from home and independent of any man, when she is afforded the opportunity of knowing herself.

To Matina Horner, however, there are many pitfalls that confront the academically inclined female on the college campus. The freshman woman, she says, must abandon her own standards of success if she is to live up to her environment's expectations of her as a female. Horner's thesis is that a woman is conditioned not to succeed and therefore the more she does succeed, the more she will feel apprehensive over her success. To a woman then, success brings tension; to a man, success yields societal rewards.[72] Since men are socialized to feel threatened by equal women and constantly will avoid them, this will have a predictably negative impact on the woman's behavior. Unequivocally, a woman's socially induced need to be liked acts as a virtual time bomb, placing her at a severe disadvantage in competition against the independently socialized male.[73] Since competition almost automatically produces interpersonal friction, it is naturally discomforting for women.

Horner's study is illuminating from many vantage points. Women, she says, "get higher test-anxiety scores than do the men."[74] She notes what Margaret Mead has previously observed, namely, that the pursuit of intellectual fortitude can be synonymous with "competitively aggressive behavior."[75] A contradiction is therefore created in the woman's mind: the more intellectual she is the less feminine she has become. The problem is particularly keen for the brightest woman in that

> she worries not only about failure, but about success. If she fails, she is not living up to her own standards of performance; if she succeeds she is not living up to societal expectations about the feminine role.[76]

To Horner, a woman logically desires to avoid success that will mean a loss of popularity while concurrently endangering her femininity.[77]

The implications of the Horner study are profound: her theories indicate that precisely those talented women who are career oriented need feel threatened. Only those few women who can succeed in an independent, isolated and less publicized framework appear undeterred.[78] Her writings suggest another reason why the women's liberation movement has the united support of most intellectual women transcending political affiliation: they are, after all, the ones who are most victimized by the old order.

That men and women are conditioned differently is obvious. That academe is structured to benefit the man at the expense of the woman has only recently come to light. Clearly, in higher education, competition is necessary if success is to be realized. What Horner found out is that while men perform better in a competitive situation than alone, the exact opposite is the case for women. To Horner, the more women feared success, and these were invariably the brighter women, the worse they performed in the competitive situation. Certainly the college learning environment, as now constituted, has a detrimental effect on the lives of the nation's most talented women.[79] The psychological burden that they have had to endure is considerable and will not be ameliorated by eradicating only the legal and educational restraints to feminine equality.[80]

THE SOCIALLY ACCEPTABLE FEMALE ATTRIBUTES

Are Sex Traits Innate?

If women are chastised for behaving in a certain manner as suggested by Komarovsky and Horner, and are confused over determining which behavioral patterns they should properly assume, are there any "universal" sexual attributes generally regarded as exclusively belonging to the feminine domain?

Functionalists in the past have argued the traditional "woman's role" as compatible with nature's "law." That functionalists have not applied their craft consistently is obvious. They assert that the intrinsic nature of feminine

36

characteristics sets them apart from men making certain roles mandatory to their sex. Yet since women are as intelligent as men but also weaker, would it not be functionally advantageous for men to undertake most of the physical activities while women's work should be limited to intellectual pursuits? Furthermore, since women are generally held to be more sensitive and personable, should they not occupy all the management and administrative positions in society? And since they are more "emotional," would it not be natural that they should constitute the nation's poets and composers?[81]

In America, females are supposed to be more emotional, sensitive, and deferential than their masculine counterparts.[82] Independence and assertiveness are regarded as masculine characteristics. Moreover, anything that is regarded as feminine is generally deprecated—by women as well as men.[83] In effect, women are supposed to assume qualities which, if adopted, make it impossible for them to succeed. To Cross:

> the only traits on which more women than men rated themselves above average were artistic ability, cheerfulness, understanding of others, and sensitivity to criticism.[84]

Indeed, the very myths about women are harmful to society in many ways. For example, it was held for years that it was foolish to educate women since they are unalterably less rational than men.[85] The assumption was that only "rational" beings could reap the full benefits of education, preferably in the rational subjects. Such a myth could be held to account for what some have called the rise of the "mass man."[86] For we have escalated the rational to the supreme altar of humanity and dubbed it masculine, but in the process we discarded the philosophical and ethical, relegating it to feminine status where it was forgotten. If society is to realize its full potential it must rediscover its feelings. But what would such an awakening do vis-a-vis men's relationship with women?

Moreover, even though emotion is characterized as dysfunctional to managerial employment, employers see nothing wrong when a man "loses his cool." It is perceived differently, as a rational reaction against a somewhat desperate situation. Therefore when a man loses his temper it is justified as proof of the gravity of the situation; when a woman loses her temper it is judged as verification of the woman's inability to handle a routine task.

That traits are universal only to a particular society in a particular time is well illustrated by Edward Hall who notes that in Iran it is manly to be emotional and womanly to be rational.[87] The important point is that as new conditions arise old preconceptions must be altered or the society will be imperiled. While the universality of a trait does not establish its naturalness, the lack of universality makes a good prima facie case for arguing the arbitrariness of masculine and feminine differentiations. In addition, even if statistical differences do emerge between the sexes, they are easily overshadowed by the similarities. Professor Dwight Chapman reiterates that

> the study of possible differences or specialities in the education of men and women is really also an examination of differences among people in general, that where there have been demonstrable differences between populations of women, there are still highly overlapping populations.[88]

As we shall contend in this discussion, even the subtle differences that do emerge could easily be more the product of psychological conditioning than of intrinsic differences. Nowhere is this clearer than in the sciences. For given the attributes internalized by females, it is not surprising that they find science distasteful. As Rossi elaborates, a scientist is supposed to be highly "mathematical," manifest extreme independence, and be to some extent a social isolate—characteristics considered unwomanly.[89] Also, women are said to lack the resolve or need to achieve that is so necessary if there is to be scientific advancement.[90] Since achievement orientation is marked by competitiveness and since women are taught to shun activities which may make them disliked, people have used this socially contrived lack of competitiveness as proof of women's innate inability to succeed in the scientific arena.[91] In fact, if women are to succeed, they must do so in a somewhat surreptitious manner. Not only are the means to achieve denied a woman but also her will to succeed is dissipated. For in internalizing the "universally" accepted female attributes, she adopts a negative self-image, loses confidence in herself, and prefers instead to seek vicarious fulfillment through the accomplishments of the man closest to her.[92] Thelma Alper succinctly states the problem:

> In our culture, men are not only expected to achieve, they are also expected to want to achieve. Women, on the other hand, have neither been expected to achieve, nor do they want to do so.[93]

As we said, women as presently socialized are more people-oriented, and as a result, their abrupt inclusion in the scientific community could mean a radical departure of emphasis as well as approach. For example, the technical and fiscally cold efficiency of the medical partnership could give way to a more personal albeit less mercantile formula in medicine. Truly, if women were to dominate the medical environment, it might become less austere and more friendly. Since women are "more emotional" and "sensitive" and perhaps less prone to the overriding "monetary incentive," they may be less inclined to recommend medically extreme though lucrative surgical remedies. Turning to the campus, the impact of women could be equally dramatic. Rossi writes:

> Women are more often found teaching science than doing science. Women college teachers mention as most satisfying about their campus jobs "good students" and "desirable colleagues," whereas men teachers stress "opportunities to do research" and "freedom and independence."[94]

Recognizing that male science students are taught by few female professors, masculine socialized attributes will dominate to the overall detriment of society as a whole. Since it is considered "masculine" to be a researcher, even the incompetent male must apply his energies to research to the detriment of his students and himself. If we abandon the sexual role identification, allowing individuals to follow their own abilities instead of their socially contrived inclinations, we may have less-frustrated scientists and better-educated students. If the prestige of "research" is subdued, then only those who are truly dedicated will invest their time and society's money in an effort to extend the frontiers of knowledge.

EXPECTATION AND PERFORMANCE

Is Prejudice Self-Fulfilling?

Women must live and work in "a climate of unexpectation."[95] Even in higher education, the prevailing assumption is that females are not expected to be career successes.[96] The faculty member, embracing these notions as well, reaffirms the young woman's self-doubts by communicating these sentiments to female students.[97] Put another way, women (and their parents) subsidize higher education in order that they may have their conviction reaffirmed that they are inferior.

The socialization process is subtle but effective. "Are you really serious?" is a question frequently asked of females that is value-laden with insinuations concerning the integrity of the woman's commitment.[98] There is, of course, an abundant array of data to prove that expectation is correlated strongly with performance. In various studies of different educational levels, it was found that when the teacher expected more of a particular student, no matter how vague the encouragement, the student's academic performance improved markedly.[99]

Turning specifically to higher education, many authorities report that women graduate students usually concur that faculty members will not "take female graduate students seriously."[100] A vicious cycle is formed: if women perceive that they are not regarded as seriously by the faculty they will become less serious in fact, thereby fulfilling

40

the erroneous impression of their mentors.[101] Other studies confirm these findings.[102]

Since people perform according to the expectations of those around them, it is not surprising that women have such a low self-image. Rossi cites studies showing that college women seek mates whom they regard as more intelligent than they believe themselves to be. The significance of this is clear: if women seek out someone whom they regard as superior, they will continually be treated as inferiors—the contagion of intellectual deference finds an all-too-ready acceptance remembering the male socialization background.[103] Since almost all women eventually seek a marital bond, they inevitably place themselves in an intellectually subordinate position.

Perhaps one of the more frequently cited and intriguing studies concerning women's unconscious and unconditional deference to male authority was recorded by Philip Goldberg. In his experiment, he asked randomly selected college women to read and evaluate certain articles. Unknown to them, the name of the author was altered.

> An example: If, in set one, the first article bore the name John T. McKay, in set two the same article would appear under the name Joan T. McKay.[104]

What Goldberg found was that the college women were consistently anti-feminine "even in the traditionally female fields," uniformly selecting male "authored" articles as superior.[105] Conclusively, by being prejudiced against female professionals, these women inadvertently were prejudiced against themselves and the fulfillment of their own potential. Goldberg reiterates: "Women seem to think that men are better at everything—including elementary-school teaching and dietetics."[106]

College women are subjected to many related problems brought about by their lack of self-respect. For one thing, they have considerable difficulty maintaining "a sense of identity."[107] It is interesting that women who succeed do manage to maintain or acquire this identity as a sustaining force which contributes to their professional fulfillment. According to Phylis Frankel, such women think of themselves in positive terms and have a high degree of "self worth."[108] Mary Richardson agrees: "Self-esteem operates as a positive influence on the development of career orientation and as an inhibiting influence on the development of a homemaking orientation."[109] Moreover, Frankel's view that "goal-oriented undergraduates viewed the feminine role as basically active and dynamic in nature" has intriguing implications.[110] For this positive view of the feminine posture goes against the very socialization which depicts a woman's role as passive and subservient. Hence it might be that those who are most ignorant of what is expected of them—the Don Quixotes— have the stronger prospects for success. Since adequate self-image is basic for a healthy goal orientation, and since women are conditioned to maintain a lower opinion of themselves, it would appear that only those who "escaped" their upbringing would have the best chance for developing an eclectic career outlook.

FOOTNOTES FOR CHAPTER II

[1]In this discussion, then, middle-class connotes more than an economic classification—it is a state of mind. People are middle-class if they believe themselves capable of realizing many of the rewards of an affluent society.

[2]Barbara Sicherman, "American History," *Signs*, no. 2 (Winter 1975), pp. 465-480.

[3]Lynn White, Jr., *Educating Our Daughaters*, pp. 28-29.

[4]Thorstein Veblen, *The Theory of the Leisure Class* (New York: The Viking Press, 1945), p. 81; Alice S. Rossi, "Women in Science: Why So Few?" *Science*, 28 May 1965, p. 1198.

[5]Cynthia Fuchs Epstein, *Woman's Place: Options and Limits in Professional Careers* (Berkeley: University of California Press, 1971), pp. 108-110.

[6]Lotte Bailyn, "Notes on the Role of Choice in the Psychology of Professional Woman," *Daedalus* 93 (Spring 1964): 707.

[7]Ibid., p. 703.

[8]*Graduate Education for Women: The Radcliffe Ph.D.*, A Report by a Faculty-Trustee Committee (Cambridge: Harvard University Press, 1956), pp. 34-35.

[9]Helen Astin, *The Woman Doctorate in America* (New York: Russell Sage Foundation, 1969), p. 4.

[10]Patricia K. Cross, *College Women: A Research Description* (Chicago: ERIC Document Reproduction Service, ED 027 814, 5 April 1968), p. 4.

[11]Mabel Newcomer, *A Century of Higher Education for American Women* (New York: Harper and Row Publishers, 1959), p. 133.

[12]Epstein, *Woman's Place: Options and Limits in Professional Careers*, p. 64.

[13]Ibid., p. 126.

[14]Diana Baumrind, "From Each According to Her Ability," *School Review* 80 (February 1972): 166-167.

[15]Ibid., pp. 174-175.

[16]William J. Goode, ed., *The Contemporary American Family* (Chicago: Quadrangle Books, 1971), p. 33.

[17]The Carnegie Commission on Higher Education, *Opportunities for Women in Higher Education: Their Current Participation, Prospects for the Future, and Recommendations for Action* (New York: McGraw-Hill Book Company, 1973), p. 44.

[18]Helen S. Astin, "Career Development of Girls During the High School Years," *Journal of Counseling Psychology* 15, no. 6 (1968): 538.

[19]Ibid., p. 539.

[20]Gail T. McLure et al., "Sex Discrimination in Schools," *Today's Education* 60 (November 1971): 33.

[21]Darly J. Bem and Sandra L. Bem, "On Liberating the Female Student," *The School Psychology Digest* 2, no. 3 (1973): 10-11.

[22]Lois Wladis Hoffman, "Early Childhood Experiences and Women's Achievement Motives," *The School Psychology Digest* 2, no. 3 (1973): 20.

[23]Bem and Bem, "On Liberating the Female Student," p. 13.

[24]Hoffman, "Early Childhood Experiences and Women's Achievement Motives," p. 21.

[25]McLure, "Sex Discrimination in Schools," p. 33.

[26]Ibid., p. 35.

[27]Bem and Bem, "On Liberating the Female Student," p. 14.

[28]Cross, *College Women: A Research Description*, p. 6.

[29]The Carnegie Commission on Higher Education, *Opportunities for Women in Higher Education*, pp. 48-49.

[30]Phylis M. Frankel, "Sex-Role Attitudes and the Development of Achievement Need in Women," *Journal of College Student Personnel*, March 1974, pp. 118-119.

[31]Marcia Landy, "Women Power and the Word," *College and University Journal* 2 (September 1972): 20.

[32]McLure, "Sex Discrimination in Schools," p. 33.

[33]Ann W. Engin, Iris Fodor, and Jean Leppaluoto, "Male and Female— The Mutually Disadvantaged: The School Psychologist's Role in Expanding Options for Both Sexes," *The School Psychology Digest* 2, no. 3 (1973): 2.

[34]McLure, "Sex Discrimination in Schools," p. 34.

[35]Engin, Lappaluoto, and Fodor, "Male and Female—The Mutually Disadvantaged," pp. 5-6.

[36]Virginia Pfiffner, "The Needs of Women Students?" *Community and Junior College Journal* 43 (August/September 1972): 13.

[37]Cynthia Epstein, *Woman's Place: Options and Limits in Professional Careers*, p. 51.

[38]Rita Lynne Stafford, "Do Women Believe the Inferiority Myth?" *AAUW Journal* 61 (January 1968): 58.

[39]Ibid.

[40]"1974 Divorces Were at Nearly 2% Rate," *New York Times*, 21 April 1976, p. 18.

[41]Cross, *College Women: A Research Description*, p. 9.

[42]Ibid., p. 10

[43]Epstein, *Woman's Place: Options and Limits in Professional Careers*, p. 48.

[44]Ibid., p. 63.

[45]Paul Heist, "The Motivation of College Women Today: The Cultural Setting," *AAUW Journal* 56 (January 1972): 55.

[46]John Finley Scott, "The American College Sorority: Its Role in Class and Ethnic Endogamy," *American Sociological Review* 30 (August 1965): 515.

[47]Ibid., pp. 518-520.

[48]Ibid.

[49]Ibid., p. 521.

[50]Ibid., p. 522.

[51]Ibid., pp. 523-525.

[52]Ibid., p. 526.

[53]Elizabeth M. Almguist and Shirley S. Angrist, "Role Model Influences on College Women's Career Aspirations," *Merrill-Palmer Quarterly* 17 (July 1971): 269-270.

[54]Rossi, "Women in Science: Why So Few?" p. 1198.

[55]Epstein, *Woman's Place: Options and Limits in Professional Careers*, p. 127.

[56]Shirley S. Angrist, "Counseling College Women About Careers," *The Journal of College Student Personnel* 13 (November 1972): 494.

[57]Anne Steinmann, Joseph Levi, and David Fox, "Self-Concept of College Women Compared with Their Concept of Ideal Woman and Men's Ideal Woman," *Journal of Counseling Psychology* 2 (Winter 1974): 372.

[58]Mirra Komarovsky, "Cultural Contradictions and Sex Roles," *American Journal of Sociology* 3 (November 1946): 184-185.

[59]Ibid.

[60]Ibid., pp. 185-186.

[61]Ibid., p. 187.

[62]Ibid., p. 189.

[63]Mirra Komarovsky, "Cultural Contradictions and Sex Roles: The Masculine Case," *American Journal of Sociology* 78 (January 1973): 873.

[64]Ibid., pp. 874-875.

[65]Ibid., pp. 875-876.

[66]Ibid., p. 878.

[67]Ibid., p. 879.

[68]Ibid., p. 880.

[69]Ibid., pp. 880-881.

[70]Ibid.

[71]Ibid., p. 883.

[72]Ann Scott, *The Half-Eaten Apple: A Look at Sex Discrimination in the University* (Bethesda, MD.: ERIC Document Reproduction Service, ED 041 566, May 1970), pp. 3-10.

[73]Thelma G. Alper, "Achievement Motivation in College Women: A Now-You-See-It-Now-You-Don't Phenomenon," *American Psychologist* 29 (March 1974): 195.

[74]Matina S. Horner, "Fail: Bright Women," *Psychology Today* 3 (November 1969): 36.

[75]Ibid.

[76]Ibid., pp. 36-38.

[77] Ibid.

[78] Ibid.

[79] Ibid., p. 62.

[80] Ibid.

[81] Goode, *The Contemporary American Family,* p. 11.

[82] Mary S. Calderone, "New Roles for Women," *School Review* 80 (February 1972): 273-276.

[83] Baumrind, "From Each According to Her Ability," p. 161.

[84] Cross, *College Women: A Research Description,* p. 15.

[85] Catherine Stimpson et al., *The Women's Center* (New York: ERIC Document Reproduction Service, ED 063 913, 1971), p. 1.

[86] Jose Ortega y Gasset, *The Revolt of the Masses* (New York: W. W. Norton and Company, 1957), pp. 81-82.

[87] Epstein, *Woman's Place: Options and Limits in Professional Careers,* p. 21.

[88] *Report of Conference on the Undergraduate Education of Women* (Allentown, Pa.: ERIC Document Reproduction Service, ED 043 283, 8-10 July 1969), p. 3.

[89] Rossi, "Women in Science: Why So Few?" p. 1200.

[90] Lora Robinson, *Women's Studies: Courses and Programs for Higher Education* (Washington D.C.: ERIC Document Reproduction Service, ED 074 997, 1973), p. 4.

[91] Florence Howe, "Women and the Power to Change," in *Women and the Power to Change,* ed. Florence Howe (New York: McGraw-Hill, 1975), pp. 142-143.

[92] Frankel, "Sex-Role Attitudes and the Development of Achievement Need in Women," p. 114.

[93] Alper, "Achievement Motivation in College Women: A Now-You-See-It-Now-You-Don't Phenomenon," p. 202.

[94] Rossi, "Women in Science: Why So Few?" p. 1201.

[95] Audrey C. Cohen, "Women and Higher Education: Recommendations for Change," *Phi Delta Kappan* 53 (November 1971): 164.

[96] Barbara Sicherman, "The Invisible Woman: The Case for Women's Studies," in *Women in Higher Education,* eds. Todd Furniss and Patricia Albjerg Graham (Washington, D.C.: American Council on Education, 1974), p. 159.

[97] Paul L. Dressel, *College and University Curriculum,* 2nd ed. (Berkeley, Calif.: McCutchan Publishing Company, 1971), p. 205.

[98] Ann Sutherland Harris, "The Second Sex in Academe," *AAUP Bulletin* 56 (September 1970): 285

[99] Ibid.

[100] Arlie Russell Hochschild, "Inside the Clockwork of Male Courses," in *Women and the Power to Change,* ed. Florence Howe (New York: McGraw-Hill, 1975), p. 53.

[101] Saul D. Feldman, *Escape from the Doll's House-Women in Graduate and Professional Education* (New York: McGraw-Hill, 1974), p. 12.

[102] Naomi Weisstein, "Woman as Nigger," *Psychology Today* 3 (October 1969): 22, 58.

[103] Alice S. Rossi, "Barriers to the Career Choice of Engineering, Medicine, or Science Among American Women," in *Women and the Scientific Professions,* eds. Jacquelyn A. Mattfeld and Carol G. Van Aken (Cambridge, Mass.: The M.I.T. Press, 1965), p. 54.

[104]Philip Goldberg, "Are Women Prejudiced Against Women?" *Transaction* 5 (April 1968): 29.

[105]Ibid., p. 30.

[106]Ibid.

[107]Patricia K. Cross, *Beyond the Open Door* (San Francisco: Jossey-Bass, 1972), p. 148.

[108]Frankel, "Sex-Role Attitudes and the Development of Achievement Need in Women," p. 117.

[109]Mary Sue Richardson, "Self Concepts and Role Concepts in the Career Orientation of College Women" (Ph.D. dissertation, Teachers College, Columbia University, 1972), p. 110.

[110]Frankel, "Sex-Role Attitudes and the Development of Achievement Need in Women," p. 117.

PART TWO

THE TRADITIONAL COLLEGE, THE TRADITIONAL WOMAN, AND THE UNTRADITIONAL MOVEMENT

Chapter III

SEXISM ON CAMPUS

STATISTICS ON WOMEN IN ACADEME

The socialization process permeates its mischief throughout the societal structure, and academia, reflecting this bias, is no exception. Indeed, while women's participation in higher education was rarely equitable, proportionally women seemed to have fared better academically in the early twentieth century than they were to do fifty years later.[1] The figures are irrefutable: In 1900 women approached 50 percent of the student population at Oberlin College, and 22 percent at Michigan, and by 1930 they constituted 43.3 percent of the national college student body. Nevertheless, during the reform years of 1969-1970, their ratio dipped to 41.3 percent.[2] Incontrovertibly, then, the highwater mark in women's educational involvement appears to have been about 1930.[3] This decline in relative student participation has been attributed to many factors. The Depression naturally reaped its greatest havoc on women since men were automatically given preference for the limited number of available positions; there was a rapid expansion of what were generally regarded as masculine fields such as engineering, and the conclusion of World War II also left women the chief victims, as returning men decreed that women were to leave their work rooms and classrooms and go back to the nursery room.

At the University of Wisconsin the picture is illustrative. On the Wisconsin campus there was considerable feminine attrition between the bachelor and doctoral levels: as undergraduates, women comprised 43 percent of the student body, diminishing to 36 percent at the masters level, while only 19 percent were listed as pursuing the doctorate.[4] A similar narrative could be written of Berkeley.[5]

Turning to faculty representation, the picture is similar. Ann Harris sums up the dictum for women. "The rule is a simple one: the higher the fewer."[6] Even in such fields as art history, where there seems to be a preponderance of women, Harris' rule is unflinching: They appear to hold fewer higher ranked positions and conspicuously less hold the department chair.[7] She observes in the years 1969-1970 that women constituted only 2.3 percent of the professors at Berkeley; 2 percent at the University of Chicago; 2.2 percent at Columbia; 4.3 percent at the University of Michigan and 1.6 percent at Stanford. With instructorships, on the other hand, women were 18.9 percent at Berkeley; 12.2 percent at Chicago; 7.2 percent at Columbia; 40 percent at Michigan and 30 percent at Stanford.[8]

A Harvard Report confirms the aforementioned trend. As of 1970 women were 17 percent of the lecturers, 13 percent of the research associates but only 6 percent of the assistant professors.[9] The low level at which a woman is usually appointed helps to forestall any expectations that she may entertain of a truly rewarding career. The Harvard Report relates:

> The prospects for women obtaining regular staff positions are certainly not good, here or elsewhere. They are more likely to end up in research positions where academic tenure is not an issue.[10]

According to estimates based on 1960s data, while the production of women scholars is far from adequate, those who do graduate are nonetheless seriously underutilized. Certainly the popular notion regarding the scarcity of women doctorates, while true, clouds the fact that among these few women who have demonstrated superior stamina and ability, fewer still are sought out for employment.[11] When viewing specific disciplines, the picture becomes suspicious. In English, which is known to attract women both at the undergraduate and graduate levels, there is "an availability pool of 24% women, and only 6% women among the faculty members with doctorates."[12] Reaffirming the earlier data, not only are women underrepresented according to their own market availability, but those actively retained on the faculty tend to coalesce toward the bottom ranks of the teaching ladder. In Lucy Sells' 1960-1969 survey, she found that whereas 3 percent of full professors in the humanities were women, 7 percent were associate professors, 12 percent assistant professors and a whopping 30 percent were instructors or lecturers. Similarly, in the social sciences 2 percent of the full professors and 27 percent of the instructors-lecturers were women. The biological sciences, too, had the same imbalance: 2 percent of the full professors were women while 33 percent remained at the lower levels.[13]

The employment tendencies relating to women were carefully scrutinized by Helen Astin as well. Indeed, in reviewing her conclusions one might readily assert that Sells was actually overrepresenting women's influence in academe. For Astin observes that women have a tendency to coalesce in the small college setting.[14] Since it is the prestigious research institution that has power, women are clearly excluded from important disciplinary positions.

Turning to the problem of feminine attrition, the Harvard Report is equally castigating. The common argument has been that because women have a higher drop-out rate, graduate schools are more reluctant to accept them, and consequently require a more formidable academic background than male peers must offer. Without question, women generally leave the graduate school to a greater extent than males. Yet a male who leaves an institution generally leaves the profession for which he was preparing to enter. Correspondingly, while women have a higher drop-out rate, they also have an impressively higher "drop-in" rate. Thus one institution's loss is another's gain. Looked at in this way, a woman may be a poorer risk for a particular institution, but a better risk for the discipline at large. Thus while graduate schools are forever bemoaning their losses they are quite silent about their prospective gains in the steady flow of advanced, sophisticated graduate students they receive from other institutions.

Also, women are a good investment when viewed in terms of professional commitment. What is often overlooked is that while many men get their doctorates, they may move on to other callings, thereby squandering the public funds invested in their education. Women, however, have a tendency to remain loyal to their original educational aspirations. Moreover, according to the Carnegie Commission, and contrary to public myth, females have an impressive rate of labor participation. Of those married women who have received their doctorates within the last nine years, and who have young children, 59 percent were engaged in full-time activity while 25 percent had part-time positions. Viewing other categories, 96 percent of women who were not married were employed full time and 87 percent of those married but with no children continued in full-time activity.[15]

In spite of this impressive and demonstrated ability, women suffer more than rank discrimination. Particularly irksome is the salary differential. In academe, married men tend to make more than those who are single, although viewing the female sample, single women appear to do better than married women. It appears that the perception of financial need rather than merit is the determining factor in governing a faculty member's financial remuneration.[16]

There are a number of other reasons why women are poorly paid. Primary among them is the fact that salary connotes worth. Since women's work is regarded by society as demeaning, anything approximating financial parity would be a slight to the masculine ego. In addition, if salary were paid on a meritocratic formula, then in many instances the married woman subordinate would very likely have a greater combined income than many of her superiors, enabling her to adopt a superior life-style. Since, in America, economic wealth is regarded as a crucial element in the prestige formula, a chairperson might find it difficult to allocate greater prestige to her/his junior staff associate. For all these reasons, then, it is not surprising that sex is one of the best determinants in estimating future salary and rank within the academic establishment.[17]

THE COOLING OUT OF WOMEN IN ACADEME

The appalling statistics on student women betray the fact that something very unusual is happening: While wo-

52

men generally have better records than men, they nevertheless have a higher attrition rate. In short, as they progress through the academic maze, women are, in effect, being "cooled out" of education.

The term "cooling out" was popularized by Burton Clark to show how less-qualified students are allowed to "fail on their own" rather than by telling them of their inability to pursue college-level work. The failure of these students "takes place within the college instead of at the edge of the system."[18] As it was originally applied, the "cooling out" process was the "soft" response to failure: "never to dismiss a student but to provide him with an alternative."[19] Viewing women, the analogy is apparent: Given their impressive performance in elementary and secondary school, they could not be told abruptly that they should not have a career despite their prior academic accomplishments. Rather, they are accepted into college but then encouraged to segregate themselves within certain disciplines. While they may not be dismissed from the academy as some of the "cooled out" males would be, they are nonetheless "dismissed" from any meaningful competition.

In the classical sense of the "cooling out" process, the male may be given counseling in order that he may be gently channeled into the appropriate area of study.

> Of the common case of the student who wants to be an engineer but who is not a promising candidate, a counselor said: "I never openly countermand his choice, but edge him toward a terminal program by gradually laying out the facts of life."[20]

So, too, the woman is told repeatedly not only by her counselor but by her boy friends and teachers of the "facts of life." Clark continues: "Substitute avenues may be made to appear not too different from what is given up."[21] Similarly, like her brother, the woman goes to college and must endure term papers, exams, and comprehensives designed and graded by professors who are nevertheless convinced that she will and should not have the opportunity to use her talents. Women, it seems, can pursue their fields with dignity if not with purpose. Through the course of her four years, she is persuaded through a mutually reinforcing environment to revise her original goals downward: The budding chemist might become an elementary school science teacher while the woman biology major may pursue a career in home economics.

The symptoms of the "cooling out" process are suspiciously apparent in the observations of Cross.

> The interviewers reported that while freshmen and sophomore women were giving serious thought to their educational and professional futures, by the time they were interviewed as seniors, they expressed less intensity of commitment to future education.[22]

Strangely, in an institution which is supposedly designed to instill intellectual pursuits and interests, women appear to be less concerned with academic priorities when they graduate (12 percent) than when they first arrive as freshmen (21 percent).[23] Many other authorities report what is actually an aspect of the "cooling out" process. Joan Roberts suggests that "women students are not taken seriously by academe. This leads to a higher drop-out rate."[24] Paul Heist indicates

> Most freshmen and sophomore girls of superior ability, having given very serious thought to their educational and professional futures, expressed less intensity of commitment to future education by the time they were interviewed as seniors.[25]

The significant point is not that these women had less seriousness of purpose by the time they were seniors, but that they believed they reached this attitude on their own. In college the woman is made to "discover" her limitations. She is encouraged by her environment to doubt her own ability and purpose. Symptomatic of the "cooling out" process, then, women are not told of their "inadequacy," but are made to "find" it for themselves.[26]

As proof of this process, Cross relates that almost 50 percent of those college "freshmen" surveyed expected their greatest fulfillment to come from their course work. Yet, by the time they were seniors, only 20 percent reiterated this view.[27] In addition, she notes that while women who come into college with the intention of selecting "feminine" fields generally "stay in them," those who originally opted for the masculine subjects soon found themselves changing "into 'feminine' ones."[28]

The "cooling out" process of gently lowering ambitions seems to be peculiarly applicable to all women in academe regardless of their original commitment or overall ability. In sum, the ingredients of the "cooling out" formula are simple: It must not be understood by those who are to be "cooled out." Individuals must come to their conclusion seemingly through their own initiative.[29] Stress is minimized.[30] Parents play an active role as "coolant," especially for their daughters. The mother may influence her daughter to opt for a "feminine career"; alternatively, the father may serve as coolant by refusing to subsidize his daughters in what he perceives as nonsocial objectives.[31] Finally, to confirm the "cooling process," the women tend not to view "the college in which they were enrolled as an obstacle or a hindrance" and are grateful for the opportunity accorded them of a college education.[32]

It is truly a deplorable state that women must pay massive tuition and spend many thousands of hours studying only to be rewarded with a lowered opinion of their own worth. In the forthcoming sections we will explore various aspects of the "cooling out" process that discourage women from enrolling in colleges, from staying there, from pursuing graduate work and from becoming academic professionals.

ADMISSIONS AND WOMEN

Clearly, many women are prevented from even having the opportunity of being "cooled out" of academe. For a woman's problems start when she first submits her admissions application. As an illustration, since women usually acquire better high school averages and are therefore in a stronger competitive advantage vis-a-vis men for college places, the institutions have compensated for this "deviation" by implementing what has become known as the "equal rejection" philosophy.[33] In effect, instead of allowing each individual to compete according to her or his abilities, a sexual quota is imposed. As a result of this system, women are judged relative to their performance with other women. One may well ponder whether such a policy would have been inaugurated had the sexual performance been reversed: in other words, had men scored higher than women. Coincidentally, this "equal rejection" theory, created by the academic meritocratic establishment, bears a striking resemblance to the present affirmative action policies, the scorn of academe, which as its antagonists describe, allocates "numbers" for each group and then allows the meritocratic system to work within the confines of that group.

The "equal rejection" theory was baltantly antimeritocratic in that it was a system devised to allow males with poorer credentials to be accepted in favor of superior females while steadfastly maintaining the fiction of a merit standard. For example, in the past

> women medical applicants generally have the same acceptance ratio as do men; thus if 5 percent of the total number of applicants to a particular medical are women, then 5 percent of those admitted are women.[34]

This practice is even more unfair than it appears on the surface when one remembers that, given the massive socialization process, those women who eventually do apply for medical schools will be considerably superior to their male competitors and consequently should enjoy a higher acceptance ratio.

Such admissions policies were openly acknowledged even at publicly supported institutions. At Penn State University the sex balance for undergraduate admission stood for a long time at 2½ to 1.[35] Similarly, at private Stanford University, a sexual quota of two males for every female was implemented. Indeed, Mrs. Leland Stanford was so fearful of Stanford becoming a female institution that she placed a limit of 500 females who could "be enrolled" at any one time. This ceiling remained until the 1930s when Stanford's edict

56

was reinterpreted to mean that she wanted a ratio that existed at the time she announced the 500 female maximum.[36]

Even the College Board Scores of the Educational Testing Service can be viewed as a "trap" to assist the male population at the expense of females. Since the grade point average in high school is considered to be such a reliable indication of how well an individual will perform in college, one can properly wonder why the College Board Scores assume such overriding importance. Since women achieve roughly equal scores on the College Boards, and these scores are taken as the chief indicators of ability, then women are discriminated against in that the proper significance of the grade point average loses importance.[37] Moreover, the rationale for the College Board score is that it is a reliable predictor as to how well the individual should perform in college. However, if an individual performs well in high school, yet does poorly on the College Boards, is he or she a better risk than the student who does well on the College Boards but poorly in high school? For high school grades measure not only aptitude but also perseverance, organizational ability, and study technique, along with ability, whereas the College Board measures the ability to perform well in a tense situation. Finally, "studies going back as far as 1929 have shown better grades for females from elementary school through college."[38] It would certainly appear that if the academy were true to its meritocratic contentions it should consider weighting the College Board scores in favor of women in order to get a more reliable indicator of future college performance.

GRADUATE FELLOWSHIPS

The competition the girl faces to get into college is analogous to the struggle of the graduate woman in procuring graduate assistance. Only a few years ago, the overwhelming majority of prestigious fellowships were given to men.[39] Fellowships, of course, are important not merely for the financial assistance they provide but also for the practical contacts and specialized knowledge gained as a direct consequence of being a fellowship recipient. For when an individual's resume can boast the reward of a particular fellowship, that person is generally placed in a more marketable situation relative to the student who fails to hold an equivalent distinction.[40] As an illustration, it is well known that the holder of the Rhodes has a conspicuous advantage despite the fact that as of 1975 a woman was automatically disqualified from even applying by virtue of her sex.[41] The tremendous advantage for the Rhodes winner is in being a Rhodes winner, and not necessarily in any scholarly achievements gained while in England. Thus, in eliminating people because of their sex, and by giving those who are accepted an unnatural advantage in the academic job market, the effects of the entire Rhodes competition are antimeritocratic.

There are many additional obstacles that women are obliged to overcome in the fellowship competition. For one thing, as a result of their social conditioning, they appear to be less motivated even to apply for an award.[42] Also, a prevalent "myth" that is strong among fellowship committees is that they are poor risks.[43] Furthermore, women themselves may perceive discrimination even where there may be none and consequently fail to consider the fellowship option.

That many qualified women do not apply for fellowships out of the conviction that their candidacy will not be accorded equal consideration is apparent. Certainly the English Rhodes may have done more harm than ever imagined in fostering a masculine connotation for prestigious fellowships. Unfortunately, the blame for encouraging such an attitude is not exclusively that of the British. The American government, too, is culpable. For example, the Smithsonian has described its Woodrow Wilson International Center for Scholars as "a place where men of letters and men of public affairs might. . . work together. . . live, dine, study, and rub shoulders—and ideas—with each other."[44]

The perception of women—that they will not be accorded equal treatment in the fellowship competition—is confirmed by the historical statistics. The stated purpose of the John Simon Guggenheim Memorial Foundation was, from its inception in 1925, to promote the advancement and diffusion of knowledge and understanding and the appreciation of beauty, by aiding without distinction on account of race, color, or creed, scholars, scientists and artists of either sex in the prosecution of their labors.[45]

However, it is curious that in 1971 women had received only seven out of a total of 312 Guggenheims awarded. Speaking for the Guggenheim Foundation, Gordon Ray stated that it "makes its rewards through annual national competition solely on the basis of demonstrated accomplishment as judged by leading professionals in each field."[46] Who are these "leading professionals" and how did they arrive at their prominence? For the most part, a person becomes a "leader" by being granted research fellowships in graduate school, being encouraged to attend the best institutions in the country and being free to settle wherever the working conditions are most propitious.

The practices of various fellowship committees were readily visible regardless of the field or profession surveyed. The Nieman Fellowships, for instance, are regarded as prestigious awards in the field of journalism. They enable established practitioners to take a subsidized year off and study in the contemplative atmosphere of Harvard University. Like many other highly coveted awards, the amount of wisdom absorbed may be debated, but the future value of such recognition in job advancement cannot. Thus in 1968, 1969, and 1972 there were twelve, thirteen, and twelve recipients, none of whom were women. In 1970 and 1971 women temporarily increased their representation 100 percent—one woman for each year.[47] Certainly if such awards are the cornerstone of a successful career and women received only two fellowships over a five-year period, then their impression of journalism as a male-oriented profession is confirmed and their entrance is impeded.

Historically, the White House Fellowship Program also appears to have discriminated against women applicants. Created in 1964 and inspired by John Gardner, its stated rationale was

To provide gifted and highly motivated young Americans with the same first hand experience in the process of governing the nation and a sense of personal involvement in the leadership of the society.[48]

From 1969 to 1973 there were 18, 17, 16, 17, and 18 recipients respectively. Of that number, women received two fellowships each in 1969 and 1971, one fellowship each in 1970, 1972, and four fellowships in 1973.[49]

Reviewing the Alfred P. Sloan Fellowship awards, which were designed for talented people in such fields as economics and mathematics, the figures are equally disconcerting. In a five-year period, from 1968 to 1972, there were 378 recipients of whom only four were women.[50]

One may interject that there are few women interested in such fields. Yet the fellowship process helps to initiate, cement, and institutionalize the maleness of certain disciplines. The argument that women have a distaste for the "hard" sciences where many of the fellowships are to be found is circuitous; for if women were encouraged to apply for such fellowships, they might be attracted to such fields.[51] Certainly there is little evidence to support the notion that females by definition do not make good scientists, but there is a preponderance of information to indicate that anyone receiving the conditioning that the typical American woman is subjected to would find science distasteful and unfeminine.

Turning to graduate financial support, much of the statistics do not reveal discrimination in the awarding of such assistance even when it may in fact exist. One authority reports that:

> With respect to financial assistance during graduate study, it appears that women receive as much financial aid as men; 57 percent of all the women doctorates of 1957 and 1958 had held either assistantships or fellowships during graduate training, as compared with 58 percent of the men doctorates of 1955.[52]

While these data may be totally accurate, they do not reflect the entire story. Harvard, for example, found that women tended to be discriminated against in the awarding of the first-year fellowships but that this imbalance was usually rectified in later years.[53] However, to many women who are indecisive about whether to enter graduate school, the first-year stipend could be crucial to their decision in that it not only provides them with money, but perhaps more importantly, with much-needed encouragement.

Finally, we know that one of the arguments against giving fellowship support to women rests on the notion that they are a bad investment. The higher attrition rate of the Woodrow Wilson Fellows is frequently cited as supporting testimony to that fact.[54] Yet the importance of fellowship support for women can be demonstrated not in the Wilson statistics but in the study by Michelle Patterson and Lucy Sells. For all the Wilson data tell us is that women have a higher drop-out rate than male recipients. They do not tell us how many women were saved for academe by virtue of the Wilson program nor do they relate how many men probably would have gone on to receive their degrees regardless of the Wilson award. Patterson and Sells, on the other hand, suggest that "the presence of fellowship support for women in their second year of graduate school reduces their drop-out rate by more than one-fourth."[55]

PROBLEMS OF WOMEN STUDENTS

In sum, it is clear that regardless of the institution the woman student attends she will have problems. What type of school is best equipped to cope with her requirements may be debated, but her unique disability, long unrecognized by most of academe, is now recognized as an unassailable fact. Most schools now concede "the problem." The controversy centers over its resolution.

What are some of the other common difficulties a woman must face by virtue of her being a woman in academe? We saw the consequences of academe's attitude toward women in observing the progressively deteriorating feminine performance in higher education. We noted that in high school, girls achieve a higher grade point average than boys; yet by the time of college graduation, women's performance generally deteriorates to the level of men.[56] We also saw how females have difficulty believing that they can succeed as students.[57] Since an adequate self-image is necessary for continued good performance and the maintenance of career ambitions, the consequences of this debilitating attitude are sadly predictable.

But perhaps one of the greatest "sacrifices" imposed upon the academically serious woman is in the need for her to forego marriage.[58] Women, who have been told since childhood that they will find fulfillment through marriage, now find that they must seemingly choose between a career and a husband. Bernard relates the special injury for such groups as Irish Catholic women because

> Irish Catholic men are somewhat more patriarchal and less willing to marry women of higher academic aims than men of Jewish or liberal Protestant backgrounds. Catholic college girls, like other college girls, want to get married.[59]

Women in pursuit of a career certainly face the prospect of social isolation. Even that rare breed known as the married female graduate student is handicapped in that most of those with whom she will associate socially will be her husband's friends, not her student colleagues. Alternatively, marriage does not notably influence the social relationships of men students with their academic peers.[60]

Other assorted abuses abound. When a woman entered graduate school in the past, she was often disadvantaged in terms of the housing arrangements. For example, at Harvard it was considered normal for the graduate woman to pay considerably more for identical dormitory accommodations than her male colleague.[61] After being settled in her more expensive room, she received printed greetings, explaining the graduate routine, that made her feel more like an invisible intruder than a student. Women were continually bombarded with "Dear Sir" letters and at times were asked to bring "your wife" to particular gatherings.[62]

In the following sections we will survey the impact of the marital institution in the career development of women students, in the unfair competitive advantage that the husband enjoys in the form of wifely services, in its effects on the professional aspirations of the faculty wife, and finally in its impact on female administrators.

Any obstacle that the career-bound woman faces, from admission to scholarship assistance, is dwarfed in magnitude when contrasted with the hubby problem. It is not accidental that in most studies the husband may emerge either as chief villain or sole savior. He is a villain because his marital role is by definition that of superior whose inclinations his wife will carefully consider. Not unusually, his preferences and career expectations must be supported by the wife to the frequent detriment of her own personal advancement. Yet a carefully considered marital choice for the professional woman can be the cause for considerable rejoicing.[63] Since a woman has been socialized to exist within the family, if she elects to live outside the conjugal bond, she has to accept the enormous personal cost of living the life of a social isolate in couple-oriented America.

One of the recurring problems for the professional wife is that her own accomplishments may trigger feelings of incompetency in her mate. This may be especially true in the case of an academic couple where many Ph.D. marriages occur in the same field.[64] Also, the husband may feel that since his wife's salary may not be essential, she is depriving their children of a mother during the creative years. As Rossi observes, men are considerably more traditional than women with respect to women's place in the home. She stresses that although women are cognizant of this discrepancy between themselves and their husbands, nevertheless "most women do as they say most husbands would prefer."[65] Still another hurdle is that the husband will invariably place his career above that of his wife.[66]

It should be recognized that it is not only men who are the enemy in the career advancement of women but most particularly men in their role as husband. For example, Rossi reflects what at first glance appears to be an enigma: that fathers are much more tolerant of their daughters' career goals than they are of their wives' ambitions.[67] This inconsistency is apparent, not real, and is due in large measure to the nature of the man's role: If the daughter becomes a successful professional the father can justifiably feel pride; but if the wife seeks similar attainments, the husband at the very least will be forced to undergo considerable constrictions of his wife's services.

The importance of such "services" cannot be underestimated. As Joan Abramson relates:

> In universities such a career—almost always a male career—often finds the marriage partner spending enormous amounts of time researching, editing, and helping to write the grant proposals, articles, and books of the other partner.[68]

By now it should be recognized that it is not the family which is the asset to the husband but his wife. She is the one who prepares his meals, cleans his clothes and sometimes writes, usually edits, and almost always types his manuscripts while simultaneously making certain that the children are quiet so that he may devote his full time to the furtherance of his career endeavors. Since the rewards are based on relative achievement, the advantages of the married family man are enormous. Certainly, one could argue that the university value structure is so constructed as to ensure the perpetuation of the married male's hegemony, for the single male or female has to compete "with the heads of small branch industries." Arlie Hochschild relates that "It is a familiar joke in women's circles to say, 'What I really need is a wife.'"[69]

THE WIFE AS ADVOCATE FOR HER PROFESSIONAL HUSBAND

Upon receiving her terminal degree and contemplating the pursuit of a professional academic career, the woman soon realizes that she must not only compete with men and with her women peers, but she must also suffer frequent though perhaps inadvertent sabotage from other women on the fringes of the academy. For example, we already saw that the values of wifely services are considerable and the woman, by virtue of not having a wife, is placed at a competitive disadvantage. Indeed, one thing often overlooked in the functions of a wife is that she provides an emotional outlet for the strains of the work day.[70] The career male can talk out his daily hurts to a sympathetic companion in much the same way that a patient releases his accumulated tensions to a therapist. To single people, the agony of having to retain the hurt of the day is imperative lest they confide in an individual who might violate their confidences and imperil their careers. The woman, whose fortune is intricately bound to that of her husband, and who has been socialized to play the role of listener and soother, is indispensable in providing an often forgotten but nevertheless important emotional function even aside from her intellectual assistance.

The married woman who happens to be professionally employed does not enjoy the advantages of her mate. As her husband's job is assumed to be primary, and as it is she who has been socialized to console him, the professional advantages accrued to the man are not reciprocated. As Diana Baumrind reports:

> The professional woman not only does not have such a helpmate but frequently is expected to be one to her husband even when she has her own professional responsibilities.[71]

Emile Durkheim supports the general thesis of the important emotional effects accruing to men in marriage. Saul Feldman, while he concurs that marriage reduces strains for men, also notes that it exacerbates conflicts for women, especially those who wish to pursue a career.[72]

> Divorced men are less committed to remain in graduate school, and they are unhappier with the graduate-student role than single or married men. Of all students, divorced women are most content with the graduate-student role.[73]

The female faculty member, like the female student, must undergo the same social penalties modified only by her particular circumstances. Admittedly, she is no longer constrained by such considerations as the dating relationship, as there are fewer eligible men for her to consider. As Mead observed: "The academic world is fundamentally hostile, by tradition. . . to those aspects of feminity which involve child rearing."[74] There are some who maintain that academic women are single because the very nature of academe attracts those who are inclined to the celibate life.[75] However, it is strange that this tendency is not also discernible in the academic male.[76] Certainly there are grounds for asserting that the educational screening process limits the available pool from which women may draw prospective mates while the men's options remain thoroughly open.[77] Also, because a woman needs a sympathetic husband, she must be more careful not to marry someone intellectually at a lower level. If her husband does not understand the role of the academician, her career could be shortlived. In addition, and as we have previously hinted, even if the academic woman is married to an understanding husband, she is still obliged to fulfill her familial roles unlike the "free" academic man.[78] To be truly competitive requires a supporting spouse, not one who demands services.[79]

Men and Women Faculty Compared

At the present time, the woman faculty member devotes considerably more time to student-related services while men claim to be more involved in research.[80] While women's activities are concrete—they are seen and measured by all—a man is on his "honor" in the privacy of his own study to do research. Moreover, if all the male faculty who considered themselves "scholars" would produce only modestly, we would be deluged by such an explosion of words as to denude the forests and cause a bitter reaction by the environmentalists. Fortunately academe has been spared the productivity if not the boastfulness of its male "scholars." If males do not produce according to their pretensions, and do not "teach," the question might be posed as to what services do they perform? It is clear that when any cutbacks are proposed, women are more reluctant "to suggest . . . curtailment in services to students."[81] When queried, women seem more to favor the personal satisfaction they get from their academic relationships with students, whereas men are more inclined to prefer the opportunity for research which they rarely do.[82] Since few men avail themselves of this scholarly alternative one might suspect that men like the appearance of being a scholar and the status and compensation it provides rather than the pursuit of scholarship in its own right.

Yet while male research claims fall far short of actual accomplishments, it does appear that proportionally more men are involved in research endeavors.[83] This is due to many factors. To a certain extent, of course, scholarship entails a necessarily all-encompassing commitment with an accompanying desire to succeed. However, whereas men are singularly self-contained in the world of work and thereby isolated from any distractions, women, whatever else they might do, are intricately integrated into the life of the family. This means that they have less time to devote to the scholarly realm and, as we previously saw, that they "have so many outs for failure."[84] For men, failure is equated with failing to achieve recognition in one's profession; for women, society allows the claim of success on many fronts. Put another way, men have both a powerful negative as well as a positive inducement to succeed intellectually; women, not having the fear of failure, are not so fortunate.

Women have many other disadvantages in the research competition. For example, many women are bearing children at an age when the enterprising male is busily establishing his professional reputation. In addition, a woman who interrupts her study to raise children usually finds that the discipline has changed radically in the interim.[85] Thus it is difficult for her to be one of the pioneers at the frontiers of knowledge when she is unable to determine where the frontiers actually are. This could be one of the major reasons why women are usually condemned to teaching the basic unchanging aspects of their disciplines. Naturally, as women start to coalesce in such branches, the myth arises that women are incapable of entering or prefer not to enter the more controversial aspects of their fields, when in fact they are induced by their social circumstances to accept this alternative if they wish to remain in the academic profession.

If a woman overcomes all these obstacles to research and does manage to write a book or article, she is then subjected to the politics of publishing:

> men have an advantage because almost all publishers and editors are men and there is much to be gained by the easy social contact possible for men at meetings of learned societies and elsewhere.[86]

Women, knowing that they will have difficulty publishing their work, may accordingly decide never to write it!

The Radcliffe Study

A Radcliffe study disappointingly surveys the dearth of scholarly productivity among its graduates. Strangely, even though the Radcliffe degree is among the most coveted in the world, the Radcliffe graduate seems to behave more like her sisters in the coeducational institutions than her brothers at Harvard.

> As a group, they give the impression of having performed their obligation as teachers with devotion and competence. As scholars, the majority have at some time or other published the results of research. Their record in this respect, however, is not spectacular. . . . And few have achieved a position of commanding distinction and leadership. It is not possible to know what are the reasons for this failure to rise to the top. Apparently many of the women themselves would give as one explanation the frequently expressed belief that, in order to get ahead, "a woman has to be twice as good and work twice as hard as a man." The record of their work in publication does not suggest that they work twice as hard, or even as hard, as male competitors. . . .[87]

An attitude, of course, has a way of becoming self-fulfilling. As we already saw, simply because a woman feels she may have to work twice as hard to achieve half as much may prevent her from trying at all. Indeed, since the training of the Radcliffe women is regarded as superior, it is reasonable to place her meager productivity on environmental constraints which exercise a disquietingly uniform influence on all women regardless of aptitude or level of preparation. Bernard seems to confirm the importance of environment when she stresses that those women employed at the university level are in the main more productive scholars than male college professors.[88] The Radcliffe study, too, suggests that the reason for the paucity of research, despite the abundance of talent, may be explained by their graduate's propensities for coalescing around the smaller institutions rather than the large universities.[89]

The study makes other observations. While the single female can usually be content with her salary and the married woman may regard her salary as secondary, the male has the compelling need to provide for a family on the basis of his earnings alone. Since scholarship is usually rewarded with increased salary compensation if not with royalties, there is an added inducement for the male to remain productive.[90] Also, those Radcliffe women who do publish tend to write for a more highly specialized audience than their male counterparts. Very few Radcliffe alumnae, for instance, write reviews for the *New York Times*. The Radcliffe study conjectures:

> Women professors are not asked to write book reviews and articles for the quasi-popular periodicals because they are not known, and they are not known because they do not write. . . semi-popular books which would establish their reputations among the literate public to which the magazines appeal.[91]

The interrelationship between society at large and professional success is again confirmed. To achieve, one must be known, but the only way to become known is to achieve. Men seem to have multiple avenues to publishing success while women have few. In addition, given the generally higher prestige and validity accorded to a male author by society, it is not likely that a competitive free press will voluntarily encourage women to establish themselves at the company's expense and risk. Finally, how do the editors of the public journals know who is "expert" if not by the recommendations of the male academic establishment? Certainly, for women the written word, difficult as it is, is not as difficult as getting that word published.

THE FACULTY WIFE

While the woman who happens to be married to a professor is often cast in the role of the villain, especially in her relationship with the academic women around her, it should not be forgotten that she is in turn a victim. In some instances the situation is confused when a woman serves in a dual capacity as full-time academic professional and faculty wife. In such a situation, her role strain is exacerbated.[92] Indeed, her status as professional colleague is often subordinated to that of faculty wife.

Many faculty wives with impressive academic credentials, characteristically working in a part-time capacity, enjoy only "fringe benefit" status at their husband's institutions. Because financially they do not have to work, they are grateful for the opportunity to pursue their professional calling no matter how compromised. In fact, they tend to be compensated at a much lower rate and afforded considerably less recognition than men of similar achievement.[93] This "fringe benefit" woman is also satisfied because her status has been lifted in relation to the nonworking women of the community. These (usually part-time) faculty women are also more readily accepted by faculty males in that they present fewer sex-role conflicts for men than the full-fledged faculty women.[94] In effect, a faculty wife may be regarded as "vocation—rather than career-oriented." Her ambition is solely to be able to practice her craft and not to "rise within some organizational or professional structure."[95] In this context, one may duly speculate whether the part-time faculty wife is a real hindrance to the career ambitions of the full-time woman in that her lower status may be generalized to include all women working within the academic community.

The situation is further muddled because the part-time

faculty wife often assumes the status of her academic husband. As a result, the faculty wife has "ascribed" status by virtue of being married to a faculty member. The faculty career woman has "achieved" status exclusively. Since the promotion rate is much lower for women than for men, this means in many instances that the faculty wife will enjoy higher and higher status relative to the career woman as her husband steadily progresses up the power structure. To the faculty wife working part-time, her sex can be construed as an advantage in her particular predicament.[96] Not unexpectedly, she provides unflinching support to the cause of her husband's professional advancement at the expense of the full-fledged career woman.

The Plight of the Faculty Wife

The faculty wife is not perceived as a nuisance whose presence male academe begrudgingly recognizes, but is enthusiastically viewed as a convenient source of cheap labor to be abused at will. She is available under such conditions as to, in effect, subsidize the academic male. She teaches courses that no one else will accept—all in good-natured gratitude. If a male faculty member desires to go on leave, she is the indispensable "security blanket" who will in actuality pay for his leave by being willing to take up any available courses at small expense to the institution.[97]

One frustration some faculty wives experience is that they may gain valuable knowledge working for their husbands which cannot be transferred into academic recognition. Thus only through their husbands' work can they find intellectual satisfaction. In effect, they become total captives of their mates since they may not be properly "credentialed" either to write a book or to receive a faculty appointment.[98] An illustration of this comes from the example of Jane Spock who helped to write her husband's famous works in exchange for a gratuitous acknowledgment in the preface. "The book," she says, "was written half by me." Despite her background, she "said she wished she had a career because she feels she is really not trained to do much of anything." Indeed, parts of the book were actually her own such as the section on layettes, how to make a formula, all of the research from the Academy of Medicine, going to the nutritionist to find out how much cheese is the equivalent of a glass of milk, things like that."

Furthermore, she describes how:

> I was at the typewriter from 9 PM to 1 AM every night for a year while he slowly dictated to me. . . . Sometimes I'd say: "That's not clear," and I did quite a lot of changing of expressions and other things that weren't clear. And I did endless medical research. . . .[99]

Jane Spock reflected that her husband had failed to publicly recognize her contribution

> because he saw me only as a wife and mother. I was expected to have a good dinner ready when he came home. I don't think he realized what he was doing to me.[100]

It is no wonder that Dr. Benjamin Spock stressed the importance of a woman remaining in the home.

The Nepotism Debate

Perhaps no university regulation has subjected intellectual womankind to such abuse as the ill-considered nepotism provisions.[101] The origins of the antinepotism impetus can be traced to the "Progressive" Movement. Then public institutions were properly fearful that they would become receptacles for patronage slots.[102] Another motivating force behind the imposition of antinepotism regulations was to discourage families from collectively securing employment at the same institution. Naturally these regulations have had a devastating impact on married women who are obliged to follow their husbands to their places of professional employment and are therefore arbitrarily precluded from pursuing their careers.[103] The academic woman married to a faculty member is more affected by this than perhaps any other woman in any other walk of life in that, because of her heavy specialization, the college that employs her husband may be the "only business in town" as far as she is concerned.

As these regulations have evolved, they have manifested peculiarly sexist overtones. Harris reports that "Harvard. . . will employ and has employed father and son but not husband and wife in full-time tenured posts." Furthermore, nepotism regulations can lead to absurd consequences. She relates the story of Dr. Maria Gaeppert, a Nobel Prize winner in physics who was denied employment at her husband's school because he also happened to be a physicist.[104]

Without doubt, antinepotism policies seem to have a particularly adverse effect on women.[105] To many women students their selection of an educational institution at which to study may be dictated entirely by geographical considerations.[106] Furthermore, the rationale of these anti-inbreeding regulations, that it prevents stagnation of ideas from developing since graduate students usually reflect the attitudes of their mentors, is fallacious since inbreeding exists and is given academic license among and between similar institutions. Departments are noted for seeking out like-minded practitioners and it is not uncommon for one department to be viewed as empirical and another normative. Certainly while the purpose of anti-inbreeding regulations may be commendable, it has rarely been effective except in excluding women from practicing their professions.[107]

THE PROBLEMS OF WOMEN ADMINISTRATORS ON CAMPUS

Women administrators share many of the same problems of their teaching sisters by virtue of sameness of their sex which overrides differences in career callings. Like their faculty counterparts, they perceive the chances for happiness and success as almost hopelessly weighted against them. This perception of reality, although quite accurate, serves to further deter many women from pursuing an academic-administrative career.[108]

Yet the differences in callings have created different obstacles as well. For example, an argument frequently advanced for not hiring female administrators has been that neither men nor women respond enthusiastically to orders issued by women. This is faulty reasoning. Prejudice,

73

whether it emanates from men or women, should not be condoned but resolutely condemned. Furthermore, academics have argued that women simply do not have the administrative background to become successful practitioners.[109] However, we know this to be an excuse since in academic administration many men initiate their management careers with only a classroom background. Indeed, academic administrators are almost totally trained in a discipline and for a variety of reasons seem to "stumble" into administration.[110]

With the demise of the sororities and the atrophy of the Office of the Dean of Women in the cult of sexual togetherness, women have yielded the meager authority they once held. Hence the Office of the Dean of Women has generally been replaced by the Dean of Students who invariably is a man.[111] It is not surprising then to find Jacqueline Mattfeld writing that the professional representation of women in administration deteriorated even further during the early 1970s. Referring to the 1972-1973 situation in the Ivy League:

> women accounted for: one part-time president of the remnant of a coordinate college, four special assistants to the presidents, one vice-president, two assistant vice presidents, one associate provost, one assistant dean of the faculty, one assistant dean of a college of liberal arts and sciences. They average nine months in their positions and six of the eleven have been appointed only this current fiscal year.[112]

Clearly, neither the numbers nor the positions women held within the hierarchy, nor the length of time they held it, is impressive. Administrative titles aside, Mattfeld notes, fully 75 percent of those women enumerated were essentially limited to student services.[113]

As a result of all this, one of the many problems that a contemporary woman administrator has to confront is that she is given titles without authority.[114] Whatever the grievance, it is obvious that the job is exasperating. All too often, a woman is thought of as limited to the role of female advocacy both by the students and the administration.[115] The pitfalls of her position are considerable, for one cannot sponsor the cause of women and students and the administration concurrently without losing whatever credibility one has with each. For the woman in administration the seeds of role conflict are inescapable. She is part of and paid by an administration which her "natural" constituency regards with hostility. Suspected by all, supported by few, the task of a woman in administration is not an enviable one.

To make matters worse, the woman administrator was coerced into the same celibate life-style as her academic counterpart. Marriage and administration were considered incompatible. When, early in Wellesley's history, President Alice Freeman opted for marriage, she yielded her Wellesley post.[116] Perhaps reflecting on such realities, when the former president of Bryn Mawr was asked "How many of your graduates marry?" she replied, "Our failures only marry."[117]

Still another problem, like that of the faculty woman but more so, is that the female administrator is in need of a wife. In the competitive bidding this is especially important because the school that recruits a married male in effect gets two for the price of one. It secures the services of a hostess along with that of a male administrator.[118] The problem is graphically illustrated by Barbara Deinhardt. She observes that when a college hires a male administrator, it is largely assumed that the institution will also acquire the social services of his wife. If a woman is hired, however, no such assumption is made concerning her mate's services.[119] This societal expectation, of course, not only perpetuates an injustice upon the woman administrator but also—and much more often ignored—upon the male administrator's wife as well. For as a consequence of this societal decree, she must forfeit any career ambition of her own in exchange for the opportunity to do unsalaried work in an unacknowledged but often full-time capacity. Even during her free time she must be forever mindful of whom she associates with and what she says, thereby placing added restraints on her own freedom of action.[120] The university, in effect, tells the administrator's wife not only what functions she is obliged to perform but also what activities she must refrain from undertaking as well. Evidence of the woman's plight is glaringly supported in a news article by James Braunn. In describing the common reactions of these women to their jobs he quotes them as saying: "It's like being God's older sister. . . . You are always watched." Such comments as these were uttered in a descriptive, noncomplaining manner at a seminar for men who had recently ascended to academic presidencies. While the husbands of these women were busily engaged in discussing the typical academic problems, their wives were herded together and lectured on such topics as the "strategies for declining invitations."[121] The assumption of the conference, of course, was that the presidents had wives who would automatically fulfill specified functions. Accordingly, the wives were forewarned that they had to choose their friends with care and that their conduct would be monitored: "The public," they were told, "will view your behavior as part of the institution."[122]

Perhaps the situation should be remedied by acknowledging the need for the administrator's wife function and separating it from that of the administrator. Deinhardt recommends this solution:

> The person who fills the job, whether administrator's wife or not, should be interviewed for it, and, when hired, provided with title, office space, secretarial help, and budget.[123]

FOOTNOTES FOR CHAPTER III

[1]The Carnegie Commission on Higher Education, *Opportunities for Women in Higher Education*, p. 88.

[2]Burstyn, "Striving for Equality: Higher Education for Women in the U.S. Since 1900," pp. 23-24.

[3]Elizabeth Duncan Koontz, *Plans for Widening Women's Educational Opportunities* (Racine, Wisc.: ERIC Document Reproduction Service, ED 067 990, 13 March 1972), p. 1.

[4]*An Affirmative Action Program to Redress Past Inequities and to Establish a Policy of Equal Treatment and Equal Opportunity at the University of Wisconsin for All Women* (Madison, Wisc.: ERIC Document Reproduction Service, ED 067 982, 10 May 1972), p. 26.

[5]Feldman, *Escape from the Doll's House—Women in Graduate and Professional Education*, p. 9.

[6]Harris, "The Second Sex in Academe," p. 284.

[7]Barbara Ehrlich White and Leon S. White, *Women's Caucus of the College Art Association Survey of the Status of Women in 164 Art Depart-*

ments in *Accredited Institutions of Higher Education* (New York: ERIC Document Reproduction Service, ED 074 901, January 1973), pp. 2-5.

[8]Harris, "The Second Sex in Academe," p. 290.

[9]*Report of the Committee on the Status of Women in the Faculty of Arts and Sciences* (Cambridge, Mass.: ERIC Reproduction Document Service, ED 057 714, April 1971), p. 1.

[10]Ibid., pp. 6-7.

[11]Lucy Sells, *Availability (sic) Pools as the Basis for Affirmative Action* (Scottsdale, Ariz.: ERIC Document Reproduction Service, ED 077 461, 5 May 1973), p. 3.

[12]Ibid.

[13]Ibid.

[14]Astin, *The Woman Doctorate in America,* p. 72.

[15]The Carnegie Commission on Higher Education, *Opportunities for Women in Higher Education,* pp. 21-23.

[16]Marianne A. Ferber and Jane W. Loeb, "Performance, Rewards, and Perceptions of Sex Discrimination Among Male and Female Faculty," *American Journal of Sociology,* January 1973, p. 1000.

[17]Barbara Larson, *Affirmative Action and Academic Women: A Crisis in Credibility* (Bethesda, Md.: ERIC Document Reproduction Service, ED 084 585, November 1973), p. 3.

[18]Burton R. Clark, "The 'Cooling-Out' Function in Higher Education," *American Journal of Sociology* 65 (May 1960): 571.

[19]Ibid.

[20]Ibid., p. 572.

[21]Ibid., pp. 574-575.

[22]Cross, *College Women: A Research Description,* p. 11.

[23]Ibid.

[24]Joan Roberts, "Problems and Solutions in Achieving Equality for Women," in *Women in Higher Education,* eds. Todd Furniss and Patricia Albjerg Graham (Washington D.C.: American Council on Education, 1974), p. 52.

[25]Heist, "The Motivation of College Women Today: The Cultural Setting," p. 56.

[26]John W. Gardner, *Excellence—Can We Be Equal and Excellent Too?* (New York: Perennial Library, Harper and Row, Publishers, 1971), p. 82.

[27]Cross, *College Women: A Research Description,* pp. 12-13.

[28]Sandra Acker Husbands, "Women's Place in Higher Education?" *School Review* 80 (February 1972): 270.

[29]Kathryn M. Moore, *The Cooling Out of Two-Year College Women* (Bethesda, Md.: ERIC Document Reproduction Service, ED 091 021, April 1974), p. 3.

[30]Ibid., p. 4.

[31]Ibid., p. 5.

[32]Ibid., pp. 6-7.

[33]Pamela Roby, "Institutional Barriers to Women Students in Higher Education," in *Academic Women on the Move,* eds. Alice Rossi and Ann Calderwood (New York: Russell Sage Foundation, 1973), p. 43.

[34]Carol Nadelson and Malkah T. Natman, "The Woman Physician," *Journal of Medical Education* 47 (March 1972): 176.

[35]Roby, "Institutional Barriers to Women Students in Higher Education," p. 43.

[36]Aimee Dorr Leifer, *When Are Undergraduate Admissions Sexist? The Case of Stanford University* (Bethesda, Md.: ERIC Document Reproduction Service, ED 095 740, 18 April 1974), pp. 1-2.

[37]Patricia K. Cross, "The Woman Student," in *Women in Higher Education*, eds. Todd Furniss and Patricia Albjerg Graham (Washington, D.C.: American Council on Education, 1974), p. 36.

[38]The Carnegie Commission on Higher Education, *Opportunities for Women in Higher Education*, p. 51.

[39]Cynthia Attwood, *Women in Fellowship and Training Programs* (Washington, D.C.: ERIC Document Reproduction Service, ED 081 371, November 1972), abstract page.

[40]Judith Niles, *Women and Fellowships* (Washington, D.C.: ERIC Document Reproduction Service, ED 091 970, April 1974), p. 3.

[41]Ibid., p. 4.

[42]Jessie Bernard, *Academic Women* (University Park, Pa.: Pennsylvania State University Press, 1964), pp. 60-61.

[43]Attwood, *Women in Fellowship and Training Programs*, p. 7.

[44]Niles, *Women and Fellowships*, p. 5.

[45]Ibid., p. 1.

[46]Ibid., p. 2.

[47]Ibid., p. 9.

[48]Ibid., p. 13.

[49]Ibid.,

[50]Ibid., p. 21.

[51]The Carnegie Commission on Higher Education, *Oppportunities for Women in Higher Education*, p. 95.

[52]The Carnegie Commission on Higher Education, *Opportunities for Women in Higher Education*, p. 95.

[52]Astin, *The Woman Doctorate in America*, p. 103.

[53]*Report of the Committee on the Status of Women in the Faculty of Arts and Sciences, Harvard University*, p. 47.

[54]Michelle Patterson and Lucy Sells, "Women Dropouts from Higher Education," in *Academic Women on the Move*, eds. Alice S. Rossi and Ann Calderwood (New York: Russell Sage Foundation, 1973), p. 85.

[55]Ibid., p. 88.

[56]Cross, *College Women: A Research Description*, p. 5.

[57]Saul D. Feldman, *Escape from the Doll's House–Women in Graduate and Professional Education*, p. 95.

[58]Ibid., p. 18.

[59]Bernard, *Academic Women*, p. xxii.

[60]Feldman, *Escape from the Doll's House—Women in Graduate and Professional Education*, p. 132.

[61]*Report of the Committee on the Status of Women in the Faculty of Arts and Sciences, Harvard University*, p. 15.

[62]Ibid., p. 16.

[63]Nine Rees, "Panelist," in *Wmoen and the Scientific Professions*, eds. Jacquelyn A. Mattfeld and Carol G. Van Aken (Cambridge, Mass.: The M.I.T. Press, 1965), p. 38.

[64]Eli Ginsberg et al., *Life Styles of Educated Women* (New York: Columbia University Press, 1967), p. 114.

[65]Rossi, "Women in Science: Why So Few?" pp. 1198-1199.

[66]Donna Martin, "The Wives of Academe," *Change*, Winter 1972-1973, p. 68.

[67]Rossi, "Barriers to the Career Choice of Engineering, Medicine, or Science Among American Women," p. 91.

[68]Joan Ambramson, *The Invisible Woman: Discrimination in the Academic Profession* (San Francisco: Jossey-Bass, 1975), p. 85.

[69]Hochschild, "Inside the Clockwork of Male Careers," pp. 67-68.

[70]Epstein, "Women's Place: Options and Limits in Professional Careers," pp. 112-113.

[71]Baumrind, "From Each According to Her Ability," pp. 165-166.

[72]Feldman, *Escape from the Doll's House—Women in Graduate and Professional Education*, p. 136.

[73]Ibid., p. 131.

[74]Bernard, *Academic Women*, pp. 206-207.

[75]Ibid., p. 208.

[76]The Carnegie Commission on Higher Education, *Opportunities for Women in Higher Education*, p. 112.

[77]Rossi, "Barriers to the Career Choice of Engineering, Medicine or Science Among American Women," pp. 74-75.

[78]Elaine B. Hopkins, "Unemployed! An Academic Woman's Saga," *Change* 5 (Winter 1973-1974): 49-53.

[79]Bernard, *Academic Women*, p. 223.

[80]Ruth Eckert, "Academic Women Revisited," *"Liberal Education,* December 1971, p. 483.

[81]Ibid., p. 484.

[82]Ibid.

[83]Ibid., p. 483.

[84]Bernard, *Academic Women*, p. 156.

[85]The Carnegie Commission on Higher Education, *Opportunities for Women in Higher Education*, p. 139.

[86]Beatrice Dinerman, "Sex Discrimination in Academia," *Journal of Higher Education* 62 (April 1971): 258.

[87]*Graduate Education for Women: The Radcliffe Ph.D.*, p. 34.

[88]Bernard, *Academic Women*, p. 154.

[89]*Graduate Education for Women: The Radcliffe Ph.D.*, p. 45.

[90]Ibid., pp. 45-46.

[91]Ibid., p. 49.

[92]Abramson, *The Invisible Woman: Discrimination in the Academic Profession*, p. 12.

[93]Bernard, *Academic Women*, pp. 99-101.

[94]Ibid.

[95]Martin, "The Wives of Academe," pp. 68-69.

[96]Bernard, *Academic Women*, pp. 104-105.

[97]Abramson, *The Invisible Woman: Discrimination in the Academic Profession*, pp. 14-15.

[98]Ibid., p. 86.

[99]Judy Klemesrud, "The Spocks Bittersweet Recognition in a Revised Classic," *New York Times,* 19 March 1976, p. 28.

[100]Ibid.

[101]Margaret Dunkle and Adele Simmons, *Anti-Nepotism Policies and Practices* (Bethesda, Md.: ERIC Document Reproduction Service, ED 065 037, January 1972), abstract page.

[102]Rita Simon, Shirley Merritt Clark, and Larry L. Tifft, "Of Nepotism, Marriage, and the Pursuit of an Academic Career," *Sociology of Education* 39 (Fall 1966): 344.

[103]The Carnegie Commission on Higher Education, *Opportunities for Women in Higher Education,* p. 127.

[104]Harris, "The Second Sex in Academe," p. 291.

[105]Martin, "The Wives of Academe," p. 68.

[106]Abramson, *The Invisible Woman: Discrimination in the Academic Profession,* p. 6.

[107]Martin, "The Wives of Academe," p. 67.

[108]Mary Ann Carroll, "Women in Administration in Higher Education," *Contemporary Education* 63 (February 1972): 214-215.

[109]Ibid.

[110]Jacquelyn A. Mattfeld, *Many Are Called, But Few Are Chosen* (Bethesda, Md.: ERIC Document Reproduction Service, ED 071 549, 6 October 1972), p. 2.

[111]Carroll, "Women in Administration in Higher Education," p. 214.

[112]Mattfeld, *Many Are Called, But Few Are Chosen,* p. 6.

[113]Ibid., p. 3.

[114]Mary Elizabeth Reeves, "An Analysis of Job Satisfaction of Women Administrators in Higher Education," *Journal of the National Association for Women Deans, Administrators, and Counselors* 38 (Spring 1975): 135.

[115]Lisa Hammel, "We Are the A's: Associate, Assistant, Adjunct, Acting," *New York Times,* 26 October 1973, p. 48.

[116]Bernard, *Academic Women,* p. 207.

[117]Liz Schneider, "Our Failures Only Marry: Bryn Mawr and the Failure of Feminism." eds. Vivian Gornick and Barbara K. Moran (New York: Basic Books, 1971), p. 426.

[118]Elizabeth Tidball, "Women on Campus—and You," *Liberal Education* 61 (May 1975): 291.

[119]Barbara Deinhardt, "Mother of Men?" in *Women in Higher Education,* eds. Todd Furniss and Patricia Albjerg Graham (Washington, D.C.: American Council on Education, 1974), p. 145.

[120]Ibid., p. 148.

[121]James W. Brann, "An Introduction to Life at the Top," *Chronicle of Higher Education,* 12 July 1967, p. 1.

[122]Ibid., pp. 1, 3.

[123]Deinhardt, "Mother of Men?" p. 150.

Chapter IV

THE FEMALE COLLEGE, COEDUCATION, AND THE AMERICAN WOMAN

PHILOSOPHY AND HISTORY OF WOMEN'S EDUCATION

Initially, education for women was discounted in America. In his history of American education, Frederick Rudolph describes the colonial outlook: "The colonial view of woman was simply that she was intellectually inferior. Her faculties were not worth training."[1] Perhaps reflecting differences in disciplinary orientation, Thorstein Veblen offers a somewhat different explanation. To him, learning was a function of the leisured class and to admit women would be tantamount to lowering the overall prestige of those associated with education.[2] Such self-debasement could not be voluntarily expected of any group. Whatever their respective explanations, however, most authorities come up with the same conclusion: Women were summarily dismissed from having a valid place in the educational world.

The attempt by women to shatter the male educational citadel met with repeated frustration. One of the earliest recorded incidents, in December 1783, documents a Lucinda Foote who at the age of twelve had an excellent comprehension of Greek and Latin and was "fully qualified, except in regard to sex, to be received as a pupil of the freshman class of Yale University."[3] She was declined admission. Not surprisingly, the beginnings of formal higher education for women could begin only as an innocent facade. Perhaps as a necessary first step, early seminars were established in some places that made no pretense about modeling themselves after superior male institutions.[4] In 1821 the Troy Seminary was created. Later, the Mount Holyoke Seminary, which was the forerunner of the modern-day prestigious college, was opened.[5]

Simultaneous with the expansion of the female

seminaries, the idea gained credence, popularized in New York, that women power could be harnessed for secondary school teaching—a vocation that held little attraction for men but was essential if the nation's burgeoning colleges and universities were to be fed with a continuous supply of students. As Conway depicts: "The goal of educating women was the utilitarian one of securing a pool of trained teachers to staff the school system at a minimum of cost."[6] Also, not to be forgotten, the ravenous appetite of the colleges of the day for qualified students contributed significantly to the reluctant acceptance of women as college students.[7] Academe, then, gained considerably through the education of women. For by increasing the pool of eligible teachers they eventually would increase the number of qualified males who could pursue college work, and in feminine matriculation they were offered the proceeds from added tuition payments. Women, in effect, paid the male colleges for the opportunity to acquire credentials in order that they might assume a demeaning nonlucrative vocation that would ensure the well-being of the colleges through an expanded supply of male secondary students from which to draw.

An important landmark in the education of women came in 1837 when Oberlin College permitted four women to matriculate. However, the Oberlin experiment, while of considerable symbolic importance, could not be characterized as a major breakthrough. Caroline Bird describes the life of these coeds. They "were given a watered-down literary course and expected to serve the men students at table and remain silent in mixed classes."[8] It is one of those interesting historical footnotes that of these four pioneering students, "two married classmates, one married a professor, and one married the President of the College."[9] One could hardly characterize these women as the prototypes of the later-day women reformers. Nevertheless, to Oberlin's credit, it was still the first "regular" institution to grant women the traditional baccalaureate. While some other contemporary colleges permitted women to attend courses and otherwise perform the duties of a student, they were nonetheless prohibited from acquiring the degree.

The Oberlin experiment, profound as it was then,

showed the extent to which women had to go to receive educational parity with their brothers. Allowances were made to dispense with Monday classes so that the women could do the college's laundry. Other required chores, such as repairing the men's clothes, were arranged so as not to interfere with class recitations.[10] One need not speculate as to the type of woman Oberlin hoped to produce!

Before surveying the major impetus to women's education, the founding of the prestigious women's colleges, it may be useful to enumerate the various female schools as they evolved in American history.

As we already saw, there were first the seminaries, which emphasized a finishing-school education. These institutions were the forerunners of the famous women's colleges and are still flourishing, especially in the South.[11] Parallel but not identical to these schools, Catholic education was responsible for the construction of a vast network of community-based religious academies throughout the nation. Finally, we have what was to be perhaps the most important advent in women's education—the prestigious women's college.

Whatever the motives, and there were many, the experiment of top quality education for women was an idea whose fulfillment was inevitable. Matthew Vassar was a wealthy businessman who owned a brewery in Poughkeepsie, New York. Although he originally decided to donate his $400,000 estate for a hospital, his niece, Lydia Booth, prevailed upon him to invest in women's education instead. Perhaps as a tribute to his niece, who died prematurely, Vassar decided to fulfill her wish.[12] Vassar College began operations in 1865.

Smith College was created in 1875, with a determination to be as strong as the best men's colleges. Established on the wealth of Sophia Smith, it is noteworthy that the original trustees were all male who specified that its admission standards should be as stringent as the best male institutions in the country.[13] Similar to Smith, Wellesley College was founded

> for the purpose of providing for women a liberal arts
> education of the same high standard as that offered at

the best colleges for men in the latter part of the Nineteenth Century.[14]

In 1880 Bryn Mawr College came into being under the austere directorship of the now legendary Cary Thomas. She, too, was convinced that for women eventually to take their place as equals, a curriculum would have to be devised "just as stiff as Harvard's."[15] To President Thomas, women were destined to live as "pathological invalids" unless they could establish by the weight of their accomplishments that they were in fact, if not in myth, equal. This was the way through which centuries of prejudice against women, adopted as Gospel truth, could be finally eradicated. Thomas describes how she was a humiliation to her family because she chose to study at Leipzig.[16] Truly, the singular dream and ultimate contribution of these early women educators rested not in permitting women to take their place beside men but in proving that intellectually they could do so.

Later in 1891, Radcliffe College was authorized to grant the traditional academic degrees bearing the seal of Harvard and the co-signature of its president. Harvard was also to permit Radcliffe students to enroll in certain graduate-level courses of the University, thereby conferring additional status to the cause of women while concurrently allowing them to pursue work that would eventually lead to the doctorate.[17]

Not unexpectedly, in the beginning the women's colleges met with considerable societal scorn. A contemporary *New York Times* editorial wrote:

> What do you think of the idea of a women's college? And why not? After Allopathic, Homeopathic, and patient pill colleges, universities, and all that sort of thing, why not let the girls have one.[18]

Nevertheless, it was a notion that could be quelled, the *New York Times* notwithstanding. The Movement had begun. Along with Harvard, Brown and Columbia were to found parallel women's colleges in 1891 and 1893 respectively.[19] Unfortunately, even with the women's educational successes, the notion that they should make use of this newly acquired education in a manner identical to that of men remained socially unacceptable.

A second generation of prestigious women's colleges was founded in the 1920s. Thought to be every bit as competitive as their earlier counterparts, these schools were especially designed to reflect women's unique experience in society. The new experimental institutions stressed areas such as the performing arts, which were continually shunned by the male academy. Further, they committed the blasphemy of emphasizing pedagogy rather than research.[20] While such programs seemed to be tailor-made for assisting the present generation of women in better coping with their traditional lives, their strength was also their weakness. For the unsettling question must at least be asked as to whether the program is more practically designed to make women comfortable with a biased status quo. All this is not to say that the experimental schools do not make a profound contribution in higher education. However, they should have introduced their curriculum as an alternative for all, not as a panacea for women. Indeed, by emphasizing women and their relationship to a particular mode of studies, inadvertently they may have made it even less acceptable to the male world.

Unfortunately, whether the school was Progressive or traditional, after World War II social reform seemed to have dissipated. Women, regardless of the institution they attended, were now more concerned with finding an appropriate mate and catering to the changing needs of the business and professional husband. Caroline Bird describes the new curriculum as an adjustment to the "New Masculinism." Instead of serving men by performing the standard domestic duties, women were now obliged to respond

> to the changing needs of business or politics. New Masculinism produced such women as Mary Lindsay (Vassar '47), who devotes her considerable talents to providing whatever ambience is needed by John Lindsay (Yale '44).[21]

This new attitude affected the entire curriculum and for a

time the study of children attracted more Vassar students than any other area.[22] Even the control of women's schools was fast becoming a male preserve. Masculine dominance not only permeated the administration but engulfed the faculty as well. Hence, whereas Vassar could boast thirty-five women at the rank of full professor in 1958, this number dwindled to sixteen by 1970.[23] Similar trends were discernible throughout the women's colleges.

This situation prevailed through the 1950s and well into the mid-1960s. Then for a variety of reasons, things began to change. The advent of the "pill" signalled a new freedom. Children were no longer the "act of man" but an act of forgetfulness. The social movements of the 1960s rekindled within women their own sense of inequality. As women became sensitized they saw how they were being treated as second-class citizen in the coeducational school environment. It is more than coincidental that the new women's movement was given an early impetus on the coeducational campus where discrimination was overt.[24] The women's colleges, precisely because sexual discrimination was not so blatant, were not as responsive to the sexual renaissance. For, as we observed, throughout the 1950s and 1960s these schools were busily expunging themselves of female control. The new men recruited were now quite established and desirous of raising their own prestige through research and lobbying for the eventual admission of young men. During this period, even Bryn Mawr College fell prey to the masculine ideology:

> Bryn Mawr has capitulated utterly to society's regressive view of women and is actually producing intellectual decorations, women of "sensitivity," who are rising to the challenge of "managing career and family."[25]

Some, of course, have argued that President Thomas was particularly at fault for attempting to lay the framework of a masculine curriculum at a feminine school without first examining the assumptions implict in that curriculum—that the elitism she advocated was irrelevant to the woman's purpose.[26] There is much truth in this account. However, given the time and the circumstances, President Thomas could have done no more and could and did do a great deal in laying the groundwork for challenging the credibility of masculine oppression. In proving that women were intellectually equal and could do the work of men, she categorically proved that the old system was unjust in assigning women to socially contrived (not biologically ordained) roles.

Perhaps Jean Grossholtz understood the root problem of contemporary women's education. When asked why she abstained on a faculty vote at Mount Holyoke concerning the adoption of coeducation she exclaimed, "What matters is that this college should devote itself to being a woman's college. Something it is not now...."[27] Clearly, a woman's college can in fact be a "man's college" if it is dominated by the prevailing assumptions implicit in a masculine curriculum. The ideal institution, then, should be a woman's college in form as well as in spirt.

THE MARCH TO COEDUCATION

In hindsight, it was perhaps inevitable that because women's colleges were no longer catering to the education of women, their educational raison d'etre was made forfeit. Accordingly, finding no advantage to a woman's college, young females began to seek alternative coeducational institutions. Never before had the survival of all-women's colleges been in such peril of extinction.[28] The statistics are dramatic. For example, in 1968 there were approximately 248 women's colleges; by 1970, that number was down to 150.[29] Many women's colleges abandoned their philosophy, opting for coeducation as the panacea through which they could maintain needed student enrollments.[30] Vassar and Yale, for example, began to talk of togetherness—Vassar would merge with Yale, and become Yale. Wellesley, which eventually decided against coeducation, announced an experimental plan of cross registration with M.I.T.[31] Women's institutions, as a distinct species in the educational world, were endangered. The prevailing ethos induced many women's academies into the irreversible decision of coeducation. The homogenization of academe had accelerated.[32] Finally, of course, the pendulum of public tastes began to swing back and a reawakening of the importance of women's colleges took hold, too late to undo the mischief that had already taken place, but in time to prevent the total disappearance of the women's college.

THE ARGUMENT AGAINST WOMEN'S EDUCATION

Those who lent fuel to the drive against the maintenance of women's colleges suggested that they were harmful to the healthy development of the young woman.[33] Authorities such as Christopher Jencks and David Riesman, while they deplored the social contagion that adversely infects a woman's confidence and curtails her ambition, argued nonetheless that women were most malleable during their last years of high school, and that if sex segregation were truly necessary it should be implemented at the secondary school level. Also, the critics add, do not women's colleges merely accentuate the socializing tendencies of society? In this respect a woman who attends a woman's college will endure the same disadvantages she would expect in a coeducational setting with none of the concomitant advantages. Supporting this thesis, a NOW study confirms that many women's institutions generally provided a curriculum weak in science, stressing child-related areas instead.[34] Furthermore, in a comparative analysis of the academic facilities and offerings at women's colleges as contrasted with those exclusively for men, the Report concluded that regardless of the educational indices, men's colleges were uniformly superior.

Recognizing the problem of inequality, the issue is raised as to whether women's colleges can be upgraded to take advantage of the latest curriculum offerings while simultaneously allowing their young charges to learn in an unbiased female environment. Conway thinks not:

> Given the scarcity of resources available for the support of education and research, it is clear that with

one or two exceptions it is not possible to develop parallel women's institutions which will offer levels of support for research activity comparable to those available in male controlled institutions.[35]

Lynn White adds to this chorus by asserting that women's colleges will inevitably be poorer than their male counterparts precisely because females outlive their husbands. He suggests that on the death of their husbands, women have a tendency to memorialize them by giving to their mates' colleges to the detriment of their own.[36] Also, men's colleges are more likely to find their graduates conveniently placed in the top circles of government and business thereby being in a position to provide their alma maters with invaluable assistance.[37] Moreover, so the antagonists maintain, the argument that women's colleges are necessary because they are tailored to meet the unique needs of women is not entirely correct. For as we saw, in the past women's colleges were founded on the male model and even today are "dependent on the national (and predominantly male) graduate schools, both to define their objectives and to train their faculty.[38]

Aside from all this, women's colleges themselves impose stringent "protective" rules on their students, effectively sheltering them from the realities of the outside world.[39] Understanding that the young woman's college choice may have a decided bearing on her ultimate success, should not the career-bound woman, given the choice, prefer Harvard or Yale rather than one of the better-known women's colleges? Also, if young women require special shelter where they will be treated as "first class citizens," what happens when they must enter the outside world—"What if sheltering breeds dependence on sheltering?" A graduate of Bryn Mawr writes of her alma mater:

> I think about the gracious living as I move across campus. Hadn't I bought it all—lock, stock, barrel?... I doubt if the genteel tradition has ever been useful to women. I suppose at first gentility was thought to protect women from the ferocities of men, but the men somehow got on with the ferocities anyhow and women were left holding the dry end of gentility, their own ferocities pent up.[41]

A 1972 College Research Center Survey of achieving high school students reported that after academic integrity of the school, coeducation was accorded top priority as to what college-bound youth most desired.[42] Since male schools are considered academically superior and since many of the male schools have now converted to coeducation, it would appear that the new generation of women can have their cake and eat it too! They can have the best education available to them and in the preferred coeducational environment. In light of such arguments, then, the Jencks-Riesman statement that "women's colleges are probably an anachronism" originally received wide acceptance.[43] Certainly, as long as women do not have genuine equality with men, those who attend the prestigious male schools will be at a tremendous advantage not only in terms of the education they will receive but also in the contacts they will make and in the husbands they may eventually acquire.[44] Since the selection of a husband may influence her career pattern and life-style more than any other variable, is it wise to sacrifice utopian ideals for practical reality? In addition, if coeducation is considered harmful, why is it that the women's studies movement seemed to make its greatest headway among sexually integrated instititions? One could argue that this women's studies surge is a response to a discriminatory environment, yet it is nevertheless responsible for sensitizing the woman to a new awareness of the feminine condition. Alternatively, when women live together in the absence of men, they are deprived of knowing the extent of their impending difficulties. One can, of course, read about discrimination, but "living discrimination" in a coeducational setting might be the best teacher. In addition, a woman's college is not necessarily synonymous with a feminist college since men may control an inordinate amount of the administrative-faculty positions. Under such circumstances, the discrimination might be much worse, given the fact that it goes on unrealized and unchecked. Also, since the general population seems to prefer coeducation, what makes educators believe that they have any divine right to reject the democratic urge?[45]

The Coeducational Dormitory

A case in point concerning the advantages of a common education can be illustrated in the effects that the coeducational dormitory arrangement has had on women students. It may be recalled that in the colonial past, women went directly from the homes of their fathers to those of their husbands. With the advent of women's education, they were provided with a "break" in the form of a few intervening years at college. For the most part the young woman was carefully regulated and protected to preserve and reinforce the socializing tendencies of her early childhood through an institution known as the women's dormitory—a system that had effectively created a double standard on a single campus.[46] Under this arrangement, women were subjected to extensive regulations imposed under the ever-watchful eye of a house mother. Hence the inconsistency—women who were emotionally more mature and sophisticated than their male counterparts, had to endure restraints on their movements while the 'adolescent" male could roam and ravage at his pleasure. Yet in the 1960s things began to change and change brought about unexpected ramification. Initially, women started to live with men as part of a new phase in their life-style.[47] Since they were still free from the restrictions of matrimony, and since they were sharing an identical status as students, they were on an equal footing with their male friends. A seemingly inevitable compromise, more socially acceptable than having women living with men off-campus, was in the concession of allowing women to live in the same dormitories with men on the campus. Unpredictably this "coeducational living system has created a family camaraderie among dormitory occupants of the opposite sex. . . ."[48] Women, according to this observation of the Yale situation, have the unique opportunity to view men in their dormitories as brothers, rarely as romantic partners. Naturally, the brother-sister relationship is based on equality. Consequently whether on or off-campus, women are confronting a new life-style that is bound to have an effect both on academe and later in society.

91

The socialization process of their youth, instead of being reinforced by the collegiate environment and the peer culture as it was heretofore, is now shattered.[49] Certainly this is a development which could not easily have occurred at an all-women's college. After all, so the proponents of coeducation maintain, what could be more sensitizing than to come to college, experience a breakdown in the sexual role pattern, and concomitantly come to suspect the arbitrarily assigned sexual functions altogether? Looked at in this perspective, women's colleges are not only passively useless but rather actively destructive to the goal of female equality.

The detractors of the women's college often point to the life these institutions provided, especially during the 1950s, as proof of their chronic inadequacies. Indeed, many women have publicly deplored the condition and mood that then prevailed. In this context, John Bushnell's "anthropological" study of life on the Vassar campus is supportive of the coeducationists' contentions.

Vassar: A Case Study

As many observers may acknowledge, the women's colleges in toto cannot be generalized from a study of one institution taken at one point in time. Nevertheless we may discern some important insights by examining Bushnell's exploration of a prestigious school at the height of the "Feminine Mystique." Hopefully, we may gain an added understanding of its function in educating women and of its perception of its overall contribution to American society.

Between 1954 and 1958, Bushnell undertook to record life at Vassar College.[50] At that time, the characteristics of the student body displayed considerable homogeneity with the great majority of young women coming from very comfortable backgrounds.[51] Furthermore, since the dress code was simple, and the bicycle was the only mode of student transportation allowed on campus, any differences in the financial strata had little practical significance.

From an extracurricular perspective, the college was vigorous: "It is only the highly marginal student. . . who foregoes this area entirely."[52] By contemporary standards, the Vassar students appeared highly sheltered. Dinner was served at a prescribed time followed by a coffee hour. Typically the student on "'coffee girl' duty pours demi-tasse size cups."[53] After allowing some time for library study, the students were locked up in their dormitories at 10:30 during the week days and 11:30 on Fridays. Authorization was needed to get the time extended.

The student concensus was that the workweek belonged to scholarly activites while the weekend was the exclusive domain of social pursuits. This polarization appeared absolute. Even if a Vassar student had no personal commitments for the weekend she would publicly curtail her studying "by Friday afternoon."[54]

Peer group pressure was considerable and "the individual who seeks occasional respite from her fellows must make a deliberate effort to isolate herself."[55] While there was a small minority of students primarily committed to their academic work, they were commonly dubbed "the science-major types." At the other extreme were those known as the "good-time Charlies" who would use Vassar merely "as an address" but "lived" in other areas.[56] Not surprisingly, one could expect to find the "typical" student zealously allocating her time between "work" on the week day and "play" on the weekend. In the confines of this work-play combination, academic achievement was duly recognized.[57] Bushnell seems to depict the overall philosophy of the "typical" Vassar student as one of fatalistic passivity.

> Vassar students. . . are. . . convinced that the wrongs in our society will gradually right themselves with little or no direct intervention on the part of women college students.[58]

He goes on to characterize the Vassar student in ways that could be described only as the very embodiment of the "Feminine Mystique":

> Not to marry is almost inconceivable and even the strongly career-oriented girl fully expects someday she too will be a wife and mother. Not only is spinsterhood viewed as a personal tragedy but offspring are considered essential . . . . In short, her future identity is largely encompassed by the projected role of wife-mother.[59]

93

To the Vassar student, then, the female role is viewed as a "help mate" who immerses her identity in the lives of others. The aims of the women's movement of a generation before is neither favored nor condemned; it is forgotten. The importance of becoming an indissoluble and subordinate part in the family structure assumes uppermost primacy.[60]

Given this philosophy, and understanding the intimate structure of the Vassar community, a woman who came to Vassar with the intentions of pursuing a professional career apparently had to surmount a truly hostile environment. Yet, a note of caution should be added. To cast Vassar as an arch-villain, frustrating and sabotaging the cause of women, would be erroneous. For Vassar merely reflected societal values, and depended upon that society for its survival. Few institutions can prosper in direct contradiction to the prevailing mores of the world at large. If Vassar's manifest function was to provide "help mates" for the future leaders of society, it performed its task in a quality manner. An institution should be measured by its day. The Vassar story is a reaffirmation of the indivisible relationship between society as a whole and its member parts.

WOMEN SUCCEED BEST IN WOMEN'S COLLEGES

Conceding for the sake of argument that women's colleges were not always synonymous with women's rights at a particular time in history is not to concede that they were always unresponsive to feminine causes or that they might not still be the best hope for women in the future. Indeed, what we could have been narrating in the Vassar description was the dismal condition for women generally in the age of the "Feminine Mystique" regardless of the institution they chose to attend.

The counter argument, that women's institutions performed a truly vital function that only they could have undertaken, is impressive. If the integrity of a woman's institution is characterized by how well it performs its manifest function, and such a function is here defined by how

94

many women students eventually embark on a professional career, then the accomplishments of the women's colleges are far superior to anything the coeducational colleges or universities can muster. The interesting Elizabeth Tidball study is a case in point. Tidball randomly selected a number of women's names from editions of *Who's Who of American Women*. She was clearly assuming, as we are, that the express function of higher education is to produce "achievers." In her extensive survey, covering the period from 1910 to 1960, she found that there was considerably more likelihood of a woman becoming recognized if she graduated from a woman's college.[61] If Tidball's statistics are persuasive, so are her arguments. She emphasizes that the coeducational environment helps to reinforce the woman's earlier socialization indoctrination regarding the primacy of finding a mate. The consequences of this unrelenting goal are that she may be unable to remain as committed to her studies as she might otherwise be. However, at a woman's college the environment is different. There the impressionable student will more likely have positive role models in the form of women teachers and administrators.[62] To Tidball this is essential— "the development of young women of talent into career-successful adults is directly proportional to the number of role models to whom they have access."[63] Furthermore, not only do women career adults provide a positive influence, but, equally important, the presence of male students seems to act as a serious impediment with respect to the eventual career fulfillment of women students.[64] Tidball concludes that a woman who graduated from a woman's college has a two and one-half times greater chance of recognition than those who studied at coeducational institutions. In a further profile of this achieving woman, she notes that the young woman has an even greater chance for success the longer she remains single, a condition that is more easily maintained in an all-female environment.[65]

One of the chief arguments leveled against the women's college is that because it exists in a contrived environment, it poorly prepares the young woman to adjust to and cope with the external world she must inevitably enter. Despite the wide currency that such a contention enjoys, the proponents of all women's education find it specious. Why should women be expected to emulate a discriminatory world model on the undergraduate level as well? Is it the objective of education to reinforce the defects of society or to correct them?

Without question, the Tidball thesis provides an important cornerstone in the dialogue for separate women's education. Authorities such as President Barbara Newell of Wellesley College concur with her findings:

> the research we have clearly demonstrates that women's colleges produce a disproportionate number of women leaders and women in responsible positions in society; it does demonstrate that the higher proportion of women on the faculty the higher the motivation for women students.[66]

Chatham's President Edward D. Eddy echoes: "Until women are really equal there will be a need for a separate educational experience."[67] Women's institutions, then, are the necessary medicinal remedy for a sick society and may expire only when our twentieth-century society becomes a truly natural society not by man's decree but by nature's law.

That the coeducational institution functions in America with the male as chief client is incontrovertible. In extracurricular activites, subsidized in large measure by the student body, women have their money allocated in a way conducive to the glorification of their male counterparts. Since masculine activities are taken as the norm, this differentiates women to their disadvantage. In other activities, too, the resources of women and their parents are used to sustain masculine enterprises. Hence the career counseling services offered by academic institutions have been typically oriented to encourage the man but dissuade the woman. Certainly, in view of the career patterns of American college women since World War II, one could well speculate that the career office was as useful to their development as the football stadium. Finally, as we shall see later in another context, the male faculty member usually caters to the needs of his budding masculine proteges, ignoring women whom he regards as future kitchen scholars. Quite obviously, by these arguments the women's colleges need not be perfect to justify their existence, for the coeducational institutions are rationale enough for some kind of alternative.

Since the typical educational institution is geared to the young single male, the argument is advanced that the all-female college is necessary for at least the following reasons: (1) in just being there, it is diminishing the number of students at coeducational schools thereby encouraging the coeducational world responsively to revise their ideology and modify their structure if they are to get a healthier share of the ever-decreasing pool of available students, and (2) in providing a tailor-made education for young women, it is preparing them with the necessary incentives to succeed in the career world.

Also not to be forgotten is the fact that, by their mere existence, women's schools are inevitably providing an alternative model for emulation by all. Certainly with the return of middle-aged and retired men and women coupled with the shortage of traditional male students, the experimental nature of many women's schools may very well contain the ideal formula for curing academe's current woes. Finally, it could very well be that as a result of the coeducational trend of the 1960s, women could have hurt their own cause through the unintentional subsidization of male-oriented institutions. As President Newell observed in the early 1970s:

> The current trend toward coeducation has increased rather than lessened male domination of American higher education, I fear.
>
> It is naive to believe that any movement for educational equity for women can come out of such colleges and universities. This leadership will have to be sustained by colleges like Wellesley which not only resist the trend toward coeducation but affirm the need for equal education for women.[68]

What constitutes an "equal education" for women, and why cannot the "established" schools willingly conform to the new realities? The answer is easier than the solution. Those who comprise the traditional academic community have been so imbued with a fixed and unconscious pattern of behavior that any change in the campus life-style requires the community to undergo a profound reappraisal of its identity both individually and collectively. Certainly both in getting women to realize that they are treated as "second-class" citizens and in getting men to acknowledge the abuses leveled upon women while willingly relinquishing what may properly be construed as a favored position is a major undertaking. Not surprisingly, a student at Wilson College, in describing her experience, gives a defense of women's institutions:

> On the campus of a college for women, of course, women students are never second-class citizens. They hold all major offices on campus. . . . They have unlimited opportunity to develop interests. . . . Through self-determination of lifestyles, the Wilson student gains insight into herself. . . and a consciousness of her friendship to other women, and self assurance that enables her to become an independent mature woman.[69]

In a statement of a few years ago, the Southern Association of Colleges for Women provided a succinct summation regarding the rationale for the maintenance of women's institutions.

> Most women never experience first-class citizenship because they never elude the male-dominated society long enough to discover themselves as persons. Coeducational campuses have yet to prove that they regard coeds as much more than social conveniences for men and financial necessities for the college. . . .[70]

The Association is, in effect, making a biting attack against the erroneous assertion that since male schools are superior, females should prefer them. For even though, as the NOW survey states, coeducational institutions may have superior equipment and more distinguished professors, it does not necessarily follow that women have access to the commodities that go into the ratings. Thus

> Dollar for dollar, women's colleges give more for your money because every dollar is spent for your develop-

ment—the development of a woman. You do not have to wait in line behind men to use expensive scientific equipment, computer terminals, studios, the pool, the tennis courts, or the gymnasium. . . . Your money is not used to support expensive intercollegiate athletic programs that benefit you little, if at all.[71]

The Assembly on University Goals and Governance of the American Academy of Arts and Sciences in 1971 further cautioned academe against the apparent coeducational trend in reiterating what others had often stressed, that coeducational institutions all too often are male dominated.[72] Lynn White, too, adds to this theme by elaborating upon the inequities in female extracurricular activities.[73] Sadly, he suggests that perhaps the only women to practice limited self-government are in the traditional sorority: it is clearly the height of irony that this sytem, designed as a "fatting" institution to marry women off to proper young men, should be the seemingly exclusive organization offering women any semblance of sovereignty.

Men at institutions with a student population of over 10,000 held 92 percent of the top elected positions during the years 1967-1970, and on all but women's campuses, men are likely to hold "all positions with much power and influence," whether elected or appointed.[74]

Unfortunately women are discriminated against not only in the extracurricular setting. A

recent study of career choices among women at Stanford University and San Jose State College conducted by Joseph Katz and Associates indicated that a critical factor in determining career choice was the approval of male contemporaries.[75]

Mount Holyoke's David Truman, among others, confirms these findings. He notes that the selection of courses by women in women's colleges seems to be markedly different from that of their female counterparts in coeducational environs. The reason for this appears unequivocal. At a woman's college, there is little diminution in status for them to elect what otherwise would be considered a masculine course of study, the exclusive criterion being what it should be—whether the woman feels comfortable with the major she selects.[76] President Truman neatly sums up the problems of "a woman on a coeducation campus...who feels that she must both compete with men and for men" and who consequently yields to the temptation "to become a pom-pom girl."[77]

Also, while some surveys have questioned the comparative integrity of the best women's colleges, we would be remiss in allowing these assertions to go unchallenged. After all, the prevailing norm to which women are affixed is that anything having to do with women is automatically inferior. Therefore is it axiomatic that women's colleges are automatically classified as inferior?[78]

Perhaps Truman presents what could very well be the strongest rationale for the necessity of the women's college:

> The ten year olds today who will be forty in the year 2000 have been exposed now, most of them, to 10 very important years of conditioning...this conditioning process, if our past experience is any guide at all, is likely to change much less rapidly than the character of the adult environment itself. The experiences to which women will be exposed will change....The conditioning that is given to the young girl, particularly the preadolescent girl, is not likely to change with anything like the same rapidity.[79]

In effect, we are moving into the twenty-first century but training women as if they are still in the nineteenth. Since conditioning is so subtly passed on from generation to generation, society must utilize its institutions in order to redress the balance. Half the population of the country cannot be socialized to be automatic anachronisms! Given this state of affairs, the women's colleges remain society's only conveyance suited to challenge the former conditioning of women. Even Jencks and Riesman, while they tend to favor the coeducational environment, seem nevertheless to acknowledge that because of the conflicts women face in college, there are definite "advantages" to educating women sepa-

100

rately from men.[80] To President Newell the "conflicting signals" that young women receive are an important justification for the maintenance of the single-sex institution.[81] The problem in coeducation is not only the male attitude but the male presence. For the mere physical proximity of males triggers the notion in the woman that her primary function is to become a wife and mother.[82]

Only in a woman's college, then, can the young student freely articulate her ideas and become involved in extracurricular activities and social causes.[83]

Reviewing the extensive history of discrimination against women, there seems to be no viable alternative other than the feminist institution.[84] For not only does society treat and regard women as unequal but they themselves have adopted the image of that society of which they are an intrinsic part.[85] Accordingly, there is the necessity for the implementation of an "artificial" environment to act as a "counter-balance" to the prevailing ethos.[86]

In considering the prospects of coeducation, the Mount Holyoke Trustees Report concluded that there are very important "cultural reasons" for women to have a sex-segregated institution of their own.[87] As President Truman observes, many women feel that they are under the compulsion to become either attractive females, with all that that entails, or to seek the lonelier goal of fulfilling themselves as human beings through the realization of career objectives. The choice is that of finding satisfactions in their own accomplishments or through those of their husbands.[88]

The counter-argument of President Alan Simpson's of Vassar that coeducation is "natural" because "the world is coeducational" is anathema to many proponents of women's education.[89] If it is natural for the world to be bigoted, should the academic institution logically reflect and sustain that bigotry so as to better prepare the bigot and the victim for their respective roles in society? Could a German university under the Nazis use Simpson's arguments to justify anti-semitism at the university? To the Nazis, after all, the Jewish place and function in society were predetermined and "natural" as is the traditional role of women in contemporary America to us. While a woman's physical existence is in no way endangered, her emotional existence and fulfillment as a human being are nonetheless impaired. Viewed in this extreme, not only is Simpson's argument incorrect but seems immoral as it perpetuates and gives license to an unethical status quo.[90]

As we previously emphasized, even conceding that certain women's colleges may have abused their trust in the past, it does not necessarily follow that they are abusing their trust now or that other women's colleges ever lost sight of the "true" nature of their original assignment; or that, just because they wavered in the past, they are still not the best hope for the future. As Chatham's President Eddy remarked:

> One need not embrace the Women's Liberation Movement to subscribe to the notion that there is indeed a barrier against women in many channels of opportunity.[91]

Diversity, then, should be defined not only according to sexual enrollment but also according to prevailing philosophy.[92] Society seems to view women's institutions as they formerly viewed the Blacks: all of one color and identical in appearance. The differences, however, were quite real; it was society that had the illusions.

The question soon emerges: granted that women's education has an important role to play, are college-bound women prepared to consider single-sex education in preference to a coeducational academic environment? While admitting that coeducation has a strong appeal, a Princeton University survey taken in 1972 (at the height of the coeducational fervor) suggested that "the key to success for women's colleges lies in high academic standards and innovative programs. The students realize it, and the colleges emphasize it."[93] Hence while many women may not be cognizant of the special value inherent in attending all-female schools, they are still willing to go to women's colleges that are of indubitable intellectual integrity. Furthermore, that they do not know why these institutions are best for their needs is not an argument for abandoning them for, like the Blacks of the past century, if the propaganda is all-encompassing and pervasive, people accept a derogatory view of themselves as correct and may not see the vital need of affirmative education to right the wrongs when in their eyes no wrong has been committed.

It is clear to many that women are so severely handicapped through an all-encompassing socialization process that only through determined countermeasures can they be assured of a productive life. Yet while the strong academic schools seem destined to survive there should also be a demand for the less competitive women's college. For, if the current trend goes on unabated, it appears that the less intellectually endowed woman will be obliged to go to a coeducational institution even though she is as much in need of a special curriculum as is her brighter sister. The injustice endured by the less talented woman is as real whether she is conscious of it or not, and regardless of whether she can make as meaningful a contribution to society as some of her female peers. Ultimately, all of society is benefited if each member of that society is functioning up to her/his optimum level. Moreover, to forego the education of these women is to say that their function should be what it always has been and not what it ought to be. All women, after all, should have the opportunity to be proud of being women, to better understand themselves, their function and their birthright.

Women's colleges are of course challenged by the male superstructure not only because they represent lost profits in terms of diminished enrollments, but also because their very existence is a tacit challenge to the status quo. For example, as we have already alluded, many women's colleges have represented more than women's liberation; they have also been cradles of innovative thought. Since many women's colleges are distinguished for their academic excellence despite the fact that they are small, they present what may well be regarded as a real challenge to the large multiversities that equate bigness with excellence. Looked at in this way, a woman's college, being small and with a specific constituency, might in fact be more responsive to change and represent a thorn in the side of an otherwise total monopoly. As all monopolies, almost by definition, set out to eliminate competition in order that they may pursue their policies uninhibited, so too might the male academy see a similar benefit in the final elimination of the female academy. For its existence invites comparison and comparison can be unfavorable. Certainly, "the great universities, with their dazzling array of scholars in absentia" are liable to severe criticism.[94] This is not to suggest that women should reject male academe in toto but rather only those aspects that have had a uniquely deleterious effect on the full potential development of women as well as men. Thus, like the early women's college movement that set out to prove that women were every bit as intelligent as men, it may now be practicable for women to consider the creation of a women's university not necessarily limited to women, but with the woman in mind. They could positively demonstrate that a woman-inspired university can take its place among the giants of academe, altering them in the process. Once the societal myth concerning women is dismissed, then the assumption upon which it is based will be dissipated and society will change. No woman or man wants the genius of a woman locked up collecting "X" stamps when she could be unravelling the mysteries of cancer or producing the great American novel. Once men realize that it is essential for women to flourish, then society will change. Benevolent feeling of men toward women is not the answer for benevolence breeds condescension while necessity ushers in equality.

THE VASSAR-SMITH REPORTS: A STUDY IN CONTRASTS

With the increase in the number of coeducational schools, some all-female institutions have moved substantially to provide a "coeducational environment" under the guise of a women's institution. If, according to Tidball's analysis, the major strong point of a women's institution is in the accessibility of professional role models, this is of serious concern lest it go too far. Indeed, perhaps in an effort to

further simulate the coeducational environment, many women's schools have actively sought to dimish the number of
females on their faculties in recent years.[95]

Two schools of considerably high caliber and recognized
prestige which agonized over whether they should become
coeducational were Smith and Vassar. These schools, of equal
reputation and identical constituencies, reached opposite
conclusions. The reasoning as well as the immediate consequences of their respective decisions may provide an added
dimension in the argument over the validity of separate education for women.

The Smith College Report

In 1965, the peak of the coeducational trend, Smith College undertook a study to explore the feasibility of admitting
men as students. Soon after, as perhaps a tentative first step,
a twelve-college exchange was originated that enabled males
and Smith students to study at the different campuses for a
period of up to one year.[96] At the time, many members of the
Smith community believed that this relationship would
eventually transform the college into a fully coeducational
institution.

The argument at Smith centered around the function of
the school as it was conceived and evolved. When Smith was
established, there was no crisis of purpose. Then, almost all
quality education was a virtual masculine monopoly and
Smith was to be the vehicle through which women could receive a quality education. Founder Sophie Smith hoped that
as a result of this type of education "What are called their
'wrongs' will be reversed, their wages [will be] adjusted, their
weight of influence in reforming the evils of society will be
greatly increased. . . ."[97] Unequivocally, the purpose that was
manifest to Sophie Smith, that of giving women a quality
education within a female environment, has been endangered by the founding and proliferation of coeducational
institutions. Yet the problem of social inequality prevails
and the ultimate goal remains unfulfilled. It seems, however,
that the solution lies not only in convincing men of women's

equality, but also in encouraging women to want to assume equal roles for themselves in society. For this to be achieved, a woman's college is deemed essential.

To Smith College the manifest function enunciated by Sophia Smith remains inviolable. The pervading question is how best to give modern-day meaning to the old founder's dream. Can women, given contemporary circumstances, receive the best education in a coeducational atmosphere or does the time-honored formula based on sex segregation still have credibility?

If Smith College were to go coeducational, the effects on the institution and on women would be traumatic. Many practical considerations would abound. For one thing, Smith would have to decide whether to decrease the number of women in order to compensate for the admittance of men or to physically increase the size of the institution. In either case, the consequences are deleterious to its mission. On the one hand it is decreasing the opportunity for young women to obtain a Smith education; if it opts for the other route of doubling the student body it will be partially destroying the small-college atmosphere that seems so conducive to innovation.[98]

The Smith Report emphasizes that sex segregation is essential especially during the college years in encouraging the young woman as a person and instilling career ambitions. At Smith, in the absence of men, she will be free to discuss and debate without the masculine eye monitoring her every stance.[99] Especially in this regard, the Smith authors are keenly concerned about the effect that coeducation would have on women in the physical sciences. Science is, of course, viewed as a male discipline by both men and women. In coeducational science classes men have been noted to dominate and women to acquiesce throughout the discussions and laboratory exercises. Certainly the problem is so widespread "that in several undergraduate surveys conducted at the College in recent years sentiment against coeducation was stringent among the students in the natural sciences."[100] Recognizing this social coercion, women feel intimidated at entering what is deemed to be a masculine field from which social decorum dictates their non-participation at the pain of ostracism.

The Smith Report is cognizant that women should be prepared to take their place in a coeducational world. Yet, they admonish, is it not better for the woman and ultimately for society as well if she first develops her intellectual potential?[101] If the whole is nothing more than the sum of its parts, is not society richer for having a more creative and less frustrated citizenry?

The coeducationists retort that one of the major weaknesses of the women's colleges lies in the paucity of available males to date.[102] However the severity of the mating-dating game has many consequences hitherto ignored. For example, as a result of the competition many women fail to develop friendships with other women, viewing them only as potential rivals. In addition, some women may not be successful in their relationship with the opposite sex and their accompanying frustration may cause permanent damage to their self-pride and cloud their relationships with men in the future while concurrently retarding the formulation of their own career objectives. Perhaps only through an artificially contrived environment, then, without any ephemerally intruding stimuli, can a woman see her true objectives in perspective.

We already saw that women will not compete with men to gain extracurricular offices. The ominous warnings of the Smith Report reaffirm this truism and may well have been heeded by Vassar.

> Coeducational undergraduate organizations tend to be dominated by men even when the proportion of men among their numbers is exceedingly small. This appears to occur not only because male students tend to assume that normally men will be elected to the chief positions of leadership and responsibility, but because women students by and large seem to act upon the same assumption.[103]

Moreover, to the authors of the Report,

> It is not at all clear that substantial numbers of highly

qualified men students could be found who would choose to come to Smith College as degree candidates during the next few years. Nor is it clear that any increase in the size of the student body could be accomplished at this time without a lowering of the average quality of those admitted.[104]

Another cause for concern with respect to coeducation is the problem of faddism which appears abruptly at irregular intervals only to dissipate just as unpredictably. How can a school identify change which is only temporary from that which is long lasting? In effect a school may be responding to a fleeting mirage and make implementations that are not easily correctable once the fad has been extinguished. Not surprisingly, like the nation at large, the Smith student body vacillated extremely. For example, in 1967 64 percent of those Smith College students interviewed were inclined toward coeducation and by the spring of 1969 the figure climbed to 72 percent. However by the fall of 1970, only 45 percent favored coeducation at Smith.[105] Quite obviously no institution can long survive if it follows the vagaries of a public opinion poll over its established long-range mission. Smith did not tie its fate to temporary passions but remained loyal to its original educational mission of providing quality education for quality women.

The Vassar College Report

Vassar College gave equally intensive consideration to the problems and prospects of coeducation as Smith but came to opposite conclusions. The Vassar Report stresses at the outset that any coeducational arrangement eventually implemented should take into account the special tradition of women at the College.[106] Unlike Smith, it dismisses the alternative of extensive semester exchanges as "unsuitable for a college which seeks to maintain any continuity in student faculty relationships" and warns that

should Vassar defer development of its own program for men too long, it might find itself at a serious disadvantage in admissions as more and more of the single-sex institutions of the Northeast adopt some form of coordinate or co-education.[107]

108

It would appear from the foregoing that Vassar responded to trends that the Smith authors were studiously cautious to avoid. For had Vassar stayed single-sex it would have remained in the distinguished company of Smith, Wellesley, Bryn Mawr and Mount Holyoke. Instead, in order to maintain its "marketability" it placed itself in contention for those coeducationally minded students who have the option of going to Amherst, Dartmouth, Princeton, or Yale. In apparently redefining its mission, Vassar lost its uniqueness. Obviously, marketability alone is a dubious reason for formulating or revising the institution's long-term purpose. Also, in its desire to pursue the coeducational alternative, Vassar seems to have hastily and strangely dismissed the option of student exchanges as a permanent solution to their coeducation debate—especially strange in view of Smith's apparent success with the program. Finally the student exchange program offers the enticement of reversibility: since the school's mission is maintained, the program can be abandoned without excessive cost.

Not only does the Vassar Report approve of coeducation, but its definition is all-encompassing. To its authors, "coeducation. . . is defined to mean the mixing of the sexes for both social and academic purposes."[108] The authors concede problems but are not unduly alarmed by the consequences.

> For most Vassar students living with these pressures will not be novel. Increasingly Vassar freshmen are coming from a coeducational secondary school background; separation represents a break with previous experience . . . . They regard the easy and informal mixing of the sexes as both natural and desirable.[109]

This Report appears to go against feminist thinking. Just because the pressures introduced to the Vassar student will not be new does not make them beneficial or necessarily easier to bear. Similarly, while sex separation for many freshmen represents a break from past experiences, that does not mean that the past experiences were good. Just because the freshmen may regard coeducation as natural and desirable should not be taken to mean that it is beneficial for them. The natural order, that which has always been, may be an unjust creation and the familiar, just because it is familiar, may take on the aura of desirability. In any event, should the mission of an institution be governed by the temporary preferences of high school seniors and college freshmen?

The Vassar authors recognize the problems of shyness and inhibitions that will be created by the introduction of men, and offer the consolation that "there is no satisfactory way of correlating chronological age with the end of adolescence."[110] Yet, while it is true that different women mature at different rates it is also true that since women as a group are generally more advanced than men, the innovation of coeducational classes is likely to have a deleterious effect on women.

The Vassar authors seem captivated by society's erroneous assumptions about females. They explain:

> Insofar as men tend to think more abstractly, valuing considerations of logic, verification, and clarity in statement more than those of form, feeling, and nuance, then their greater aggressiveness may cast the entire discussion in their terms. Women may be more tempted than they would be by themselves to let the character of discussion be shaped largely by male considerations and by a manner in discourse more congenial to the male mind.[111]

If this is truly a natural biological condition then the male by nature will dominate the female in class discussion, not allowing her to develop her full potential as an individual, and may be an argument for continued sex segregation. Moreover, the premise that men have a "certain mind" may lead educators to behave in a manner that confirms their expectations. Most poignantly, is it the function of a contemporary women's college to confirm societal values and help women to adjust accordingly or rather to assist them in understanding the inequities that exist, thereby acting as an agent for change? On the one hand, the educational institution is reinforcing the prevailing notions and, on the other, it is seeking to modify them.

Coeducation, the Report continues, is good because ac-

110

quaintance with the opposite sex will emphasize common interests rather than sexual attractiveness.[112] However, the Vassar Report earlier stressed as a reason for coeducation that more and more of their college freshmen came from coeducational secondary schools. Yet these students do not seem to have their sexual appetites subdued by their prior experiences.

Turning to extracurricular concerns, the Vassar Report dismisses as "myth" the notion that men tend to dominate such activities. This, despite the fact that the Vassar Study earlier acknowledged that men tend to be more "aggressive." Accordingly, they emphasize:

> Beyond the classroom, the argument for separation traditionally has held that women have fewer opportunities for leadership in college activities under coeducation. This argument seems less forceful than it once did. More and more in the best colleges and universities, those who do the work and assume the responsibility in campus enterprises hold the major office regardless of sex.[113]

That Vassar seemed to be unduly fascinated with the temporary student passion for coeducation appears self-evident. As an illustration, the Report urges that future dormitory and other construction should not be "suitable only for one sex."[114] Of course, building dormitory facilities to accommodate coeducational living means that there would probably be more pressure for coeductional habitation on those students who might otherwise prefer a segregated arrangement.

The authors emphasize the attributes of coeducation in the context of faculty development—more specifically, the added research opportunities afforded them by a larger and concomitantly wealthier institution. In a small school, they say, the faculty are obliged to teach extensively and are naturally discouraged from adequately pursuing the scholarly realm; hence, there may arise a "widening gap" between the scholarly attainments of the Vassar faculty as compared with those in the university colleges.[115]

Certainly the amount of research that the typical university professor engages in is meager. In addition, the value of research to teaching has long been debated—an inverse correlation might actually be the case. Vassar was small relative to the university world throughout its history yet maintained its first-class reputation. Also, what special value does the research-oriented professor have for the young woman who is precluded by virtue of her sex from eventually participating in the search for knowledge? Vassar, a first-rate college, in attempting to emulate the university world, may risk both its standing and its function. For no matter how Vassar tries, it cannot be a first-rate university; and no matter how much a university may desire it, it cannot be a first-rate college. A confusion of missions may lead to mutual deterioration.

It appears that the Vassar Report has lost sight of Vassar's heritage as an institution committed to the furtherance of women's education; for not only are they prepared to create an equal sexual ratio, but some would balance it if necessary in favor of males. Hence women are not only psychologically disadvantaged, as the Vassar Report concedes, but they may face the prospect of coming to Vassar and being numerically disadvantaged as well. The Report, in catering to men, seems to be ignoring its women.

> All consultants testified to the importance for the long run of approximating equality in numbers. Some recommended a slightly higher proportion of men, but in no case did the ratio suggested exceed 60-40. A permanent minority of men would reduce the amount and perhaps the value of coeducation in the classroom as well as limiting appeal in admissions. By thus accenting Vassar's primary concern with women's education, it might very well encourage a defensive minority-group attitude on the part of men.[116]

What then is Vassar's function if it should cease to accent its primary purpose of women's education lest it offend its new male clientele? Why should a woman, opting for a quality coeducational college, not prefer admission to Amherst or Williams? In catering to men, what does Vassar have to offer prospective women applicants that the male colleges do not?

The Report continues that it would be preferable to increase the number of places rather than to decrease the number of women:

> Since Vassar's historic mission has been the education of women, it seems questionable in principle whether the college should reduce the number who can benefit from its particular tradition and spirit.[117]

The Vassar authors, like their Smith counterparts, agree that coeducation could mean a lower caliber student. Since Vassar was largely distinguished more for the excellence of its students than for the renown of its faculty, it seems to be effecting a fatal exchange. Also since Vassar might well decline as a result of a less brilliant student body, and since a faculty member's prestige is intimately associated with her/his institution, then it might very well be that the general deterioration of Vassar's prestige would cause its more renowned faculty members to seek employment elsewhere. If the prestige of Vassar was centered in its student body, and if the faculty share the prestige of their institution, then the lowered student aptitude will mean lower prestige for the faculty as well. That there was a strong certainty that the caliber of the student, the cornerstone of the Vassar reputation, might be imperiled is clear:

> There is the danger of relying too heavily on a capacity to attract the solid, but undistinguished student who wants an Eastern prestige school but will not be accepted by Harvard, Yale, Princeton, Columbia, Amherst, Williams or Wesleyan. . . . By paying less attention to board scores and rank in class and relying more on interviews. . . the college can attract students whose motivation, talent, and achievement make them very promising, even though on paper, their quality may not be comparable to the students admitted by the most selective men's and coeducational colleges.[118]

In the past, Vassar's public mission was to provide a stringent education for the best of the country's women. The women who subsequently graduated had at least two advantages. They could go on to the nation's finest graduate and professional schools or they could have their choice of many of the most eligible males in the country as a result of their high Vassar status. In some instances, of course, they could have both.

The Carnegie Commission acknowledges that students can make the reputation of the institution.[119] In no small measure, the Vassar student of yore, the cream of American womanhood, was responsible for that institution's success. Thus Vassar concedes that "students and counselors alike agree that most of the well-qualified candidates for admission are concerned first with academic reputation. . . ."[120] Will not accepting lower College Board scores for admission have a decidedly negative influence on the bright woman's ultimate decision as to whether or not to attend the Poughkeepsie school? The Report mentions the prestige of a "Vassar education."[121] But Vassar got its prestige through educating the best women in the country. Prestige is not a birthright. In the Vassar case it was earned and what is earned can be lost. Quite naturally, as guidance counselors see a student with lower Board Scores accepted at Vassar they may encourage more with lower Board Scores to apply while rerouting the best students to consider schools which mandate the higher score.

The Vassar authors in their desire to approve coeducation a priori appear not to be reading what they are actually writing, for they state:

> Vassar must anticipate that in the early years a large proportion of the men who eventually come will not be coming as a first choice or, in many cases, even as a second or third choice.
>
> Fortunately, most students soon get over their initial sense of dismay at having been turned down by their preferences and—if the college they enroll in is interesting and attractive—soon identify with their college. But some sense of being personally inferior and of being part of an inferior student body may remain and there is no easy way for the college to overcome it.[122]

One need not ponder whether earlier Vassar students would have been attracted to Vassar had they thought they would have been part of an "inferior" student body.

It will be recalled that the Vassar authors did not envisage extensive student exchange programs as a meaningful alternative to full coeducation because such a "transiency" would have a decidedly negative impact on the faculty-student relationship.[123] Nevertheless, later in the same Report it is emphasized that:

> Advanced placement, multiplying opportunities for credit by examination, work-study programs... make it increasingly likely that many undergraduates in the future will not spend four sequential years in residence at the college of matriculation.[124]

Unequivocally, while the Vassar authors condemn the "transiency" of the exchange program as an alternative to coeducation because of the effects on intimacy, they nevertheless recognize its inevitability in any future environment. Finally, will not a larger student body to some extent impair the valued intimacy the authors seem to prize so highly?

The Vassar Report suggests that in the student demand for innovative courses, the faculty will be hindered by added preparations and will consequently not be able to pursue their disciplines adequately.

> If the college accommodates the greater demands of curricular flexibility on faculty time by deemphasizing scholarship, then the recruitment of faculty with a genuine interest in scholarship becomes more difficult.[125]

Yet the Report continues:

> If the college, on the other hand, emphasizes some scholarship... then the teacher who gives the fullest attention to his courses and advising is penalized. Shrewder faculty members save time for their research by cutting class preparation and discouraging students from seeking their assistance.[126]

Reiterating, given the size of Vassar, it will never rank among the greatest research institutions; but in striving to emulate the ideals of research, they may very well deteriorate as a teaching institution.

The sacrifice to greater scholarship, according to the Vassar Report, must be made to attract men. Certainly an insulting assumption of the "Feminist Mystique" variety is indicated. For the Report seems to suggest the possibility that the men initially attracted to Vassar might be "lower" than the Vassar women.[127] Thus the authors appear to be saying that their superior women are less in need of a research faculty than the intellectually inferior men whom they expect to matriculate. The Report continues:

> The Vassar ideal has been a teaching faculty... In the last decade, in an effort to strike more of a balance, increased attention has been given to scholarship.
>
> In seeking new teachers to educate men at Vassar, the nature of this balance may be even more important than in programs for women. Because of their more immediate preoccupation with a future career, men may be more concerned than women about the effect of their choice of college on their chances for admission to the best graduate and professional schools.[128]

Without doubt, the premonitions of the Association of Southern Women's Colleges concerning the tendency for coeducational schools to spend more money on men than on women seemed confirmed. For if the Vassar Report is correct, and men need more research facilities, who is to pay for these expensive additions? Are we not faced with the irony of the "quality" women being asked to subsidize a research faculty in order to attract inferior males?

This tendency is not seen only in academic subjects. It is suggested that athletic facilities should be built (where before there were none), to further entice the male students. Out of whose pocket is this to come? Who is meant to derive the chief benefit from these added facilities? Was the Vassar student of old deprived by the absence of these accommodations?

> When men are introduced to the Vassar campus in significant numbers, some provision for athletics will be

116

required. . . .In establishing an athletic program two issues require analysis.

The first is the need for facilities and opportunities
for intra-mural sports. Fields must be provided for touch
football, soccer, baseball, etc. . . . In estimating capital
costs, funds for a gymnasium are included in the projec-
tions listed in this report.[129]

Given the change of mission which a woman's college must
accept in its transformation to coeducation, it is problematic
whether it can survive or function as effectively as it did in
earlier days. After all, what is to be its new unique function?
How can it properly distinguish itself from the more established coeducational institutions and especially the prestigious male schools which recently opened their doors to women? Naturally, the extent of its difficulty may vary with
the degree of conversion. Thus Radcliffe, while it maintains
the fiction of a women's school, is for all intended purposes
coeducational while Smith and Mount Holyoke, even though
single-sex, are more "coeducational" than they were a few
years ago as a consequence of their numerous exchange programs.[130] The problems incurred also offer fresh possibilities
as well. Under new exchange formulas the women's colleges
may take on stronger meaning and identification since their
students by the very act of spending a "year abroad" in a
male-oriented institution may come to a greater appreciation
of the need for an all-female institution. Accordingly, the
weakness of women's colleges—that they do not sensitize
their students to the impending discrimination—is eliminated, while the strength of the colleges—that women can
come back and learn in a feminist, prejudice-free environment—is maintained.

Some authorities observe that the cooperative exchange
program is much cheaper for a single-sex institution than
the more radical transformation to coeducational status.[131]
Certainly the advantages of such an innovation would be
that the school could more easily retain a semblance of its
original purpose while never really abandoning its option of
returning to its former status. Moreover, the single-sex institution that maintains its unique atmosphere within an ex-

change arrangement might find unexpected strength. As students continually move from one school to another, they will be searching for alternative life-styles.[132] As a result, women who may have been reluctant to commit four years to a single-sex school may now find the idea of going to a place where women dominate an unavoidable temptation without the concomitant cloisterization that women's colleges formerly connoted. Clearly a new market may have been created with the inclusion of this educational innovation. Single-sex colleges, which a short time ago seemed destined for extinction, may find added strength in the exchange formula.[133]

That single-sex colleges face many imponderables when they transform their mission is obvious. Thus Vassar's mission, to educate the very best women of the land, had to be tacitly abandoned once the decision was reached to go coeducational. After all, no young male wants to go to a top woman's college. The consequences of Vassar's decision are well known.

> The college concedes it is having trouble attracting male students of high academic quality to its campus here. At the same time, overall applications to Vassar declined last year [1973] while many colleges that decided to remain all-women institutions are reporting increases. And, finally, Vassar has had to combat whispers that the men it has accepted have brought lower standards to the college, even though the college insists that just the opposite is true.[134]

Whether Vassar believes it has significantly altered its mission may be debated—at Vassar. In the public mind, however, the winner of the debate has been decided, and it is the public that supports the institution. Interestingly, in a *New York Times* dispatch, the Vassar Admissions Director in 1974 confessed in an interview that

> The College Board Scores of entering Vassar students are dropping faster than in the nation as a whole, and fewer students at the top of their high school classes are applying to Vassar than before.[135]

Without doubt, women who might automatically have been Vassar recruits are going elsewhere. Mr. Richard Stephenson defends the selectivity process, especially with respect to the male applicants, and observes that males are actually subjected to more strenuous admissions criteria. He supports this with the assertion that

> this greater selectivity for men shows up in the fact that proportionally more men than women graduated with honors.... While men comprised one third of the graduating class last summer, they made up 45 percent of the Phi Beta Kappas.[136]

What Mr. Stephenson does not say is that the aforementioned figures could also be taken as confirming some of the commonest fears of feminist educators—that brighter women, when they are obliged to compete with men, will naturally place a ceiling on their academic achievement out of fear of losing potential mates. Indeed, the Vassar Report itself may be used as refutation of the Stephenson thesis; for Mr. Stephenson observed that males made up only one third of the graduating class while constituting 45 percent of the Phi Beta Kappas. The Report ominously warns of the consequences of having too few men on campus:

> The greater the disparity in numbers between the sexes, the more likely it seems that their relationships will become exploitative. Competition between the girls for dates will increase. The overabundance of girls eager for dates is all too apt to encourage the men to take a contemptuous view of their eagerness and treat them more like objects of sexual conquest than companions.[137]

Hence the females, in an unfavorable sexual ratio, must compete for the favors of men, not compete with them.

Vassar cannot have it both ways. If it is thought of as a women's college, it will not attract the best men. Hopefully, so the argument goes, "after a while, the best men students will stop thinking of Vassar as a women's college."[138] If this hope is realized, Vassar will have traded the prestige of being numbered among the best of the women's colleges for being known as "a small liberal arts college." In its "league" as a women's college, Vassar had a reputation second to none; among such schools as Amherst, will it radiate the same appearance of excellence?

In his preference for coeducation, President Simpson stated, "I don't think it will be possible for colleges of the first distinction to remain single-sex colleges and be as distinguished as they have been."[139] Unfortunately, the reverse seems to be the truer axion: a women's college that changes its mission by converting to coeducation may well find its excellence imperiled—Smith and Wellesley among others seem to have remained colleges of the first distinction.

In the past, Vassar's manifest mission was to provide quality education for quality women. For a time in the 1960s Vassar, like her sister institutions, was experiencing trauma caused by the coeducational trend. Yet the quality of its product remained unchanged. Nevertheless, Vassar, in attempting to conform to new attitudes, abandoned its old constituency. By doing so, it eliminated the rationale for its special existence. Many schools can and do perform Vassar's present function, but few schools are prepared to perform the function of Vassar past.

If Vassar had to retrench in order to maintain the integrity of its mission, would that have been preferable to abandoning its historic mission? Mount Holyoke's David Truman cautions that while financial stability is obviously important, it may be excessively considered to the detriment of academic quality.[140] President Newell of Wellesley agrees. To her, many of the single-sex institutions that elected coeducation did so "because of financial reasons," not necessarily out of a concern for educational mission.[141]

The Vassar story provides a grim testimonial as to what can happen when the long-term mission of a school is abruptly changed. The lesson is an important as the tragedy is real and irrevocable. We can learn from the mistakes of others, but not necessarily correct the mistakes we make ourselves.

Postscript to the Coeducational Debate—
Sexual Integration at the Prestigious
Male Academy

In the foregoing sections we saw that when women's colleges debated coeducation, the argument usually focused on whether both sexes would mutually benefit through a common educational arrangement. Yet it is revealing that when the male institutions decided to integrate, they did not view the potential benefits of each sex upon the other, but often saw women as a marketable commodity designed to increase the institution's desirability to the male population. Women were rarely accorded the dignity of being considered as students in their own right. For example, while the motive of women in choosing such prestigious schools as Yale, Princeton or Dartmouth was educational, the rationale of these schools in accepting young women was sexual.

> Women were needed to attract the best male applicants, who increasingly were choosing coeducational colleges rather than spending four years in male monasticism. The "geisha girl theory of coeducation" did not mean that these schools recognized women's rights to the same kind of education and preparation for a lifetime career as men. It merely meant that the presence of women on campus would augment the daily regimen of male leaders-to-be by simplifying their access to women as companions and future wives.[142]

Thus when President Kingman Brewster of Yale discussed the merits of a proposed merger of Yale with Vassar, he reflected that in the past the Yale man was obliged to attend a "mass production mixer-type big weekend" which was the cause for considerable "frustration." John Hershey, who was then a Yale Master, stated the matter even more candidly, applauding "the speedy arrival of the young ladies. . . to save the Yale undergraduates from a continuing cycle of orgiastic weekends after monastic mid-week interludes."[143] Without question, at least to some, the coeducational drive was seen as a prescription to meet the sexual requirements of the young male Ivy Leaguers.[144]

Clearly, to women students Pepper Schwartz and Janet Lever, the Yale atmosphere was heavily biased in favor of men.[145] While Yale can truly boast that it heightened the sensitivity of its women, the problem remains whether a young female should be exposed to such an overpowering environment immediately upon leaving home, perhaps for the first time. Certainly, since young women and their parents have been so programmed to believe that the basic goal of every woman is to attract a man, girls might now be forced to attend these very institutions lest other females catch the prestigious male trophies. Formerly, while male-catching still received top priority, the game was often played in the confines of a desirable woman's school, where the woman had excellent opportunities for personal development without endangering her marital prospects.

Elga Wasserman recounts that Yale's lack of commitment and concern for the special needs of women was consistent, even before women arrived on campus. As an illustration, in viewing the mechanics of its admissions process, Yale made few accommodations—". . . two women were added to the admissions staff of thirteen men" and the "entire staff interviewed both male and female applicants. . . ."[146] Accordingly, when the new freshmen women arrived on campus, their backgrounds carefully screened by an admissions committee trained for accepting the "mentally attired" young man from the prep school or the promising male genius of less fortunate financial circumstances, they found an environment where of "the 407 tenured faculty, only 3 are women."[147]

Remembering certain aspects of the male conditioning, the presence of women in the male classroom can have a deleterious effect on men as well as women. Jencks and Riesman note:

> Girls may sometimes push their male classmates into exaggerated know-nothing postures, which they hope will dramatize their masculinity and help them escape the danger of subordination to "feminine" facts and reading lists.[148]

Moreover, the presence of women can lead men to become

anti-intellectual in order to prove their prowess as lovers and athletes.[149]

Alternatively, other authorities suggest that the intellectual level of the class is increased with the inclusion of young women—that the course standards have been raised. Yet, knowing how much young women feel intimidated by men, and realizing how men, out of machismo, might be more inclined to compete in the presence of women, could the intellectual level of the men be increased at the expense of the women? When some professors say that the intellectual caliber of the class is increased, are they talking about the men? the women? or both? At Harvard, where the climate may be more conducive to the intellect, masculine intellectual competition may be ameliorated with the addition of Radcliffe women at no particular advantage to these women.[150] Again, we see an illustration of the innovation of women on campus applauded because of its effect on men. The impact intellectually of men on women has scarcely been examined.

Yale women seem to be drawn to the prestigious academy in New Haven in spite of themselves. Thus, these women pay to enter an atmosphere where they

> must continue to depend on their own resources and form alliances with other women to combat the psychological and institutional barriers to their intellect and potential for achievement.[151]

Women are placed in the predicament of having to pay for an educational environment, the effects of which they must continually ward off lest their development be jeopardized. The argument that women should go to a school like Yale for the consciousness-raising benefits might be analogous to the suggestion that the best way to appreciate life is to be surrounded by death. Certainly the value of life might be enhanced, but at an emotional cost that may make life not worth living.

Originally, the Dartmouth admissions office echoed the Yale philosophy by emphasizing that they were looking for women of pioneering spirit: "girls who don't mind being in a minority, like the only girl in a class, at a table in Thayer

Dining Hall, or out on the track for phys ed. . . ."[152] Women, so intimidated by men, are now informed that they are tough enough to be the "only girl in class." We see another inconsistency where women are socialized to be weaker but expected to be stronger than their male contemporaries. Other prestigious schools also seem to expect their women to thrive amidst this "improved" atmosphere.[153]

How can the newly integrated Ivy League possibly perform the educational function for women when the coeducational schools have historically served them so inadequately?[154] Certainly, one of the recurring problems for women is that the academician has usually been concerned about them primarily in their relationships to and effects on men. Writing a long time ago on the spectre of coeducation, President Tappan cautioned "men will lose as women advance, we shall have a community of defeminated women and demasculated men."[155]

While academic standards may rise with the admission of women, females remain more subordinated than ever. For instance, in class "they find that their entry into the male debate is simply ignored."[156] The dominance of the male ethic at Yale was also indicated in many other ways. For example, when Yale first invited women students to matriculate as undergraduates they were obliged to pay a social activities fee to help defray the expenses of busing women to New Haven from other college campuses. To make matters worse, the attitude of the male undergraduates was poor. Thus Yale women were continually bombarded by such utterances as "it doesn't matter much what a woman studies."[157] It seems that before Yale set out to educate females it should have reeducated its males.

Not surprisingly, being human, the females at Yale accommodated themselves to their predicament by adopting the values of the dominant culture. Schwartz and Lever relate how the women "at Yale, like most women, accept the presumption of male leadership."[158] For women, then, the obstacle course called Yale is truly a harrowing experience. This destruction of female ambition is especially criminal at Yale which is attracting and anesthetizing some of the best minds in the country:

Their assumptions and interpretations concerning her behavior frequently become self-fulfilling. The student is encouraged to doubt herself, her work, and her suitability for creative effort, but she is rewarded for being "a cute young thing."[159]

A Yale coed describes the negative intellectual impact from one of the greatest intellectual citadels in the world:

> In the midst of all the pampering and publicity, a strange deterioration of the will took place. I was a poet when I came to Yale—I had won a national competition and felt sure that I wanted to continue writing. One of my roomates was a dancer and another an artist. As we were getting acquainted, we proudly performed for each other and supplied admiration and encouragement. When the telephone began ringing thirty times a day and there was a constant knocking at the door, Allison stopped painting, Jamie stopped dancing, and I stopped writing. Instead of saving secret time for self cultivation, we doled out our time to the curious, and became tourist attractions to our male classmates. Giving hours and evenings instead of autographs.[160]

That sexual integration might be dysfunctional to the development of the woman student can be illustrated by many other examples. For instance, some Dartmouth women were annoyed with "immature Dartmouth males."[161] It appears that those who emphasize the "naturalness" of integration forget that females at the freshman level are "naturally" more mature than their male contemporaries. Certainly, the consequences for a woman's scholarship in attending Yale or any other coeducational school are considerable. A young female reflects that since the social life of a woman assumes such importance, and since the man asks the women out at his convenience, a woman who has an exam the next day will be hesitant to turn down a date. Moreover, while she can control the dating pattern a little better if she "goes steady," all too often such an arrangement can lead to early marriage—to the detriment of the young woman's career development.[162]

The college woman, too, is much more likely to drop out in a coeducational setting if she regards her physical appearance as plain.[163] A man's physical appearance in a coeducational environment has no effect on his decision to remain in school. This could be especially true where a very plain-looking woman has to endure the extreme hardship of seeing her friends constantly "courted" while she is chronically ignored. The college women then, is placed in a position of being doomed if she does lead an active social life and doomed if she fails to do so.

Revealingly, it seems that the fear of success is dramatically heightened from 47 percent in the seventh grade to 88 percent at Radcliffe.[164] Since bright women are the chief victims and since the anxiety over success is likely to be triggered in an environment such as Yale's, it would seem that the extension of the coeducational arrangement by elitist male institutions is devastating to a woman's intellectual development. Looked at in this light, it is no longer an enigma as to why the women of Radcliffe, among the brightest in the nation, seem to vanish after graduation, without having the record of success of their female contemporaries in the all-women colleges.[165] The Yale experiment in coeducation has been tried at Harvard for years, with disheartening consequences for its women students.

An illustration of the intimidation felt by women can also be glimpsed at Princeton. In a course focusing on the "Feminine Mystique," where there were nine men and one woman, the woman did not participate in the discussion. Later she was asked for an explanation: "I generally feel intimidated being the only girl and therefore find it difficult to say what I'm thinking."[166]

That the male student needs a thorough resocialization in his attitudes toward women is obvious. For example, Sheila Tobias reports that the male treatment of female faculty in women's studies courses is frequently demeaning, with students establishing a first-name basis with the teacher and freely offering unsolicited advice as to how the class could be improved.[167] Male faculty, too, are biased in their academic relationships with women. Many research faculty avoid engaging women students in their work projects either from fear of their wives' resentment, or out of aware-

126

ness that their time could be better spent with a man who would eventually help to enhance the professor's reputation.

Without question there have been changes, but these have been modest and achieved in good measure through the efforts of the local women's organizations on a reluctant, inertia-bound campus. Mory's, a famous restaurant in New Haven that catered to the Yale male establishment, had to revise its exclusive practices.[168] However, while such a reform received excellent publicity, it in no way effected any fundamental change in the basic intellectual attitude at Yale. The women can eat at Mory's or at the "eating clubs" of Princeton, but still be ignored.

When women began going to Yale, Dr. Robert Arnstein, director of the Mental Hygiene Clinic, conceded that "of course there are inevitable problems with one girl to eight men. But you can't ever have a ratio that assures the absence of emotional problems. . . ." He stressed that the problems of young women existed long before they came to college.[169] While Yale may not be directly culpable for the immediate problem, does that give them license to accentuate it? Also, while you "can't ever have a ratio that assures the absence of emotional problems. . . ," why must the woman again be made to bear the brunt of the burden? In tone as well as in deed, there seems to be a general lack of concern for the special needs of women students. As a result of such attitudes, many Yale and Dartmouth women felt surrounded, as they were, by a sea of men. Always on stage, never able to have any relationships with other women, they had severe identity problems.[170]

As we alluded to previously, at the coeducational school both women and men pay equal tuition to help defray the costs of their education. Yet women are discouraged from participating in the more expensive laboratory courses. It would seem that the woman is made to play the role of camp follower, attempting to lure her male; only in this instance she pays for the privilege of being abused. Even the extracurricular activities, subsidized by everyone, are more heavily utilized by the males. A woman "seeking a mate either actually or prospectively" is not going to endanger her prospects through vigorous competition but rather will work toward a long-term sexual relationship.[171] President Simpson has argued that Vassar "is not going to have male dominated coeducation." Reflecting on the effects of Vassar's decision to go coeducational, he observed,

> If you look at the thing systematically, what would you find? Here I'll try to be very honest: I don't think you'd find there's been any takeover in these offices. You'll certainly find men represented in the offices, but the president of student government is a woman, and I'm sure a man could not have got himself elected to that position: the editor-in-chief of the *Misc.*, the student newspaper, is a woman, and you could go down the board.[172]

In the Spring of 1973 the Vassar student body, which was then only 27 percent male, ". . . elected a male student-body president. Twice as many males had run for student offices as females."[173]

Interestingly, while President Simpson believes in an equal sharing of coeducational activities, he nonetheless reflected that the new male coeds have

> male energy which is rather more energetic looking and sounding than is female energy. And I suppose you might have the experience, from time to time, when the men seem to have an influence out of proportion to their numbers.[174]

Expectations help to create "realities." If this "female energy" of Simpson's is defined as less energetic, then it will be treated differently. Also, since "male energy" seems to be more strenuous, it might require the construction of additional athletic facilities, placing a burden on all students equally but with the males as chief beneficiaries.

The remaining chapters of the book will focus on the probable changes envisioned by the onslaught of the women's revolution. We will consider the ramifications of the infusion of women studies and its effect on the organization and substance of knowledge. We will delve into counseling, teaching techniques, role-model theory, and finally affirmative action policies along with the structural accommodations that will have to be realized if the manifest function of the academy—that of equal educational opportunity for all—is finally to be fulfilled.

FOOTNOTES FOR CHAPTER IV

[1]Frederick Rudolph, *The American College and University—A History* (New York: Vintage Books, 1962), pp. 307-308.

[2]Ann Trabue Bass, "The Development of Higher Education for Women in This Country," *Contemporary Education* 41 (May 1970): 288.

[3]Thomas Woody, *A History of Women's Education in the United States,* Vol. 2 (New York: Octagon Books, 1974), p. 137.

[4]Bass, "The Development of Higher Education for Women in This Country," p. 286.

[5]Feldman, *Escape from the Doll's House—Women in Graduate and Professional Education,* pp. 23-24.

[6]Jill K. Conway, "Coeducation and Women's Studies: Two Approaches to the Question of Woman's Place in the Contemporary University," *Daedalus* 103 (Fall 1974): 241.

[7]The Carnegie Commission on Higher Education, *Opportunities for Women in Higher Education,* p. 15.

[8]Ibid.

[9]Feldman, *Escape from the Doll's House—Women in Graduate and Professional Education,* p. 28.

[10]Conway, "Coeducation and Women's Studies: Two Approaches to the Question of Woman's Place in the Contemporary University," p. 242.

[11]Caroline Bird. "Women's Colleges and Women's Lib," *Change* 4 (April 1972): 60-61.

[12]Feldman, *Escape from the Doll's House—Women in Graduate and Professional Education,* p. 26.

[13]Ibid.

[14]*Report of the Commission on the Future of Wellesley College* (Wellesley, Mass.: ERIC Document Reproduction Service, March 1971), p. 14.

[15]Liz Schneider, "Our Failures Only Marry: Bryn Mawr and the Failure of Feminism." eds. Vivian Gornick and Barbara K. Moran (New York: Basic Books, 1971).

[16]M. Cary Thomas, "Present Tendencies in Women's University Education," In *And Jill Came Tumbling Down,* eds. Susan Bereaud, Joan Daniels, and Judith Stacey (New York: Dell Publishing Co., 1974), pp. 277-278.

[17]*Graduate Education for Women: The Radcliffe Ph.D.,* p. 8.

[18]Feldman, *Escape from the Doll's House—Women in Graduate and Professional Education,* p. 27.

[19]Ruth M. Oltman, *The Evolving Role of the Women's Liberation Movement in Higher Education* (Washington, D.C.: ERIC Document Reproduction Service, ED 049 489, 15 March 1971), p. 1.

[20]Christopher Jencks and David Riesman, *The Academic Revolution* (Garden City, N.Y.: Anchor Books, Doubleday and Company, Inc., 1969), p. 304.

[21]Bird, "Women's Colleges and Women's Lib," p. 62.

[22]Ibid.

[23]Bernice Sandler, *A Feminist Approach to the Women's College* (Washington, D.C.: ERIC Document Reproduction Service, ED 071 561, November 1971), p. 8.

[24]Bird, "Women's Colleges and Women's Lib," p. 63.

[25]Liz Schneider, "Our Failures Only Marry: Bryn Mawr and the Failure of Feminism." eds. Vivian Gornick and Barbara K. Moran (New York: Basic Books, 1971), p. 434.

[26]Ibid., p. 432.

[27]Norma Rosen, "Mount Holyoke Forever Will Be Mount Holyoke Forever Will Be for Women Only," *New York Times,* 9 April 1972, sec. 6, p. 65.

[28]Betty Littleton, "The Special Validity of Women's Colleges," *Chronicle of Higher Education,* 24 November 1975, p. 24.

[29]Pauline Tompkins, "What Future for the Women's College?" *Liberal Education* 58 (May 1972): 298.

[30]Beverly Jensen, "Single-Sex Education: The Case for Women's Colleges," *College and University Business* 56 (February 1974): 16.

[31]Robert L. Jacobson, "Coeducation's Siren Song Lures Colleges," *Chronicle of Higher Education,* 31 May 1967, p. 6.

[32]Charles C. Cole, Jr., "A Case for the Women's College," *College Board Review*, no. 83 (Spring 1972): 20.

[33]Tompkins, "What Future for the Women's Colleges?" p. 302.

[34]Husbands, "Women's Place in Higher Education?" p. 270.

[35]Conway, "Coeducation and Women's Studies: Two Approaches to the Question of Woman's Place in the Contemporary University," p. 244.

[36]Lynn White, Jr., *Educating Our Daughters,* p. 38.

[37]Jencks and Riesman, *The Academic Revolution,* p. 305.

[38]Ibid., pp. 305-306.

[39]Harris, "The Second Sex in Academe," p. 293.

[40]Rosen, "Mount Holyoke Forever Will Be Mount Holyoke Forever Will Be for Women Only," p. 56.

[41]Ibid., p. 58.

[42]"Number of Women's Colleges, 300 in 1960, Down to 146," *Chronicle of Higher Education* 7 (3 May 1973): 3.

[43]Jencks and Riesman, *The Academic Revolution,* p. 310.

[44]Elga R. Wasserman, "Coeducation Comes to Yale College," *Educational Record* 51 (Spring ⅃970): 143.

[45]Alan Simpson, "Coeducation," *College Board Review,* Winter 1971-1972, p. 17.

[46]Kate H. Mueller, "Sex Differences in Campus Regulations," *Personnel and Guidance Journal* 32 (May 1954): 530-531.

[47]Freeman, "Women's Liberation and Its Impact on the Campus," p. 470.

[48]Mary Breasted, "Yale Shuts Gates to Curb Assaults," *New York Times,* 5 February 1976, p. 60.

[49]Ronald Thomas, "Coed Housing in One Fell Swoop," *College and University* 49 (Spring 1974): 276-277.

[50]John H. Bushnell, "Student Culture at Vassar," in *The American College: A Psychological and Social Interpretation of the Higher Learning,* ed. Nevitt Sanford (New York: John Wiley and Sons, 1962), p. 489.

[51]Ibid., p. 490.

[52]Ibid., pp. 495-496.

[53]Ibid., pp. 497-499.

[54]Ibid., pp. 499-500.

[55]Ibid., p. 503.

[56]Ibid., pp. 506-507.

[57]Ibid.

[58]Ibid., p. 509.

[59]Ibid.

[60]Ibid., p. 510.

[61]Elizabeth Tidball, "Perspective on Academic Women and Affirmative Action," *Educational Record* 54 (Spring 1973): 132.

[62]Ibid., pp. 132-133.

[63]Ibid.

[64]Ibid.

[65]*Report of Conference on the Undergraduate Education of Women,* p. 4.

[66]The Carnegie Commission on Higher Education, *Opportunities for Women in Higher Education,* pp. 71-72.

[67]Simpson, "Coeducation," p. 17.

[68]Bill Kovach, "Wellesley Says It Won't Go Coed," *New York Times,* 9 March 1973, p. 43.

[69]Cole, "A Case for the Women's College," p. 21.

[70]Ibid., p. 20.

[21]Ibid.

[72]Tompkins, "What Future for the Women's College?" p. 299.

[73]Lynn White, Jr., *Educating Our Daughters,* p. 54.

[74]Howe and Ahlum, "Women Studies and Social Change," p. 401.

[75]Mary Lefkowitz, *Final Report on the Education and Needs of Women* (Wellesley, Mass.: ERIC Document Reproduction Service, ED 081 329, September 1970), p. 9.

[76]David B. Truman, *The Single Sex College—In Transition?* (South Hadley, Mass.: ERIC Document Reproduction Serivce, ED 065 031, 1971), pp. 7-8.

[77]Rosen, "Mount Holyoke Forever Will Be Mount Holyoke Forever Will Be for Women Only," p. 56.

[78]Sandler, *A Feminist Approach to the Women's College,* p. 2.

[79]Truman, *The Single Sex College–In Transition?* pp. 3-5.

[80]Jencks and Riesman, *The Academic Revolution,* p. 306.

[81]Jensen, "Single-Sex Education: The Case for Women's Colleges," pp. 16-17.

[82]"The Case for Women's Colleges," *Intellect* 102 (March 1974): 345.

[83]Husbands, "Women's Place in Higher Education?" pp. 268-269.

[84]Florence Howe, "Introduction," in *Women and the Power to Change,* ed. Florence Howe (New York: McGraw-Hill, 1975), p. 8.

[85]Conway, "Coeducation and Women's Studies: Two Approaches to the Question of Woman's Place in the Contemporary University," p. 244.

[86]Sandler, *A Feminist Approach to the Women's College,* p. 4.

[87]Bird, "Women's Colleges and Women's Lib," p. 65.

[88]Truman, *The Single Sex College–In Transition?* p. 5.

131

[89]Cole, "A Case for the Women's College," p. 17.

[90]Jensen, "Single-sex Education: The Case for Women's Colleges," p. 16.

[91]"The Case for Women's Colleges," p. 344.

[92]Jensen, "Single-sex Education: The Case for Women's Colleges," p. 16.

[93]"The Case for Women's Colleges," p. 344.

[94]Dexter M. Keezer, "Watch Out Girls!" *The New Republic*, 6-13 September 1969, p. 31.

[95]"The Case for Women's Colleges," p. 345.

[96]"Smith College and the Question of Coeducation—A Report with Recommendations Submitted to the Faculty and the Board of Trustees by the Augmented College Planning Committee," Northampton, Mass., April 1971, p. 1.

[97]Ibid., pp. 2-3.

[98]Ibid., pp. 8-9.

[99]Ibid., pp. 9-10.

[100]Ibid.

[101]Ibid., p. 11.

[102]Ibid.

[103]Ibid., p. 12.

[104]Ibid., p. 14.

[105]Ibid., pp. 16-17.

[106]George Langdon and Clyde Griffen, "Report on Men's Education," Poughkeepsie, N.Y., 1968, preface.

[107]Ibid.

[108]Ibid., pp. 3-4.

[109]Ibid., p. 5.

[110]Ibid., pp. 7-8.

[111]Ibid., p. 9.

[112]Ibid., pp. 9-10.

[113]Ibid., pp. 10-11.

[114]Ibid., p. 16.

[115]Ibid., p. 19.

[116]Ibid., p. 23.

[117]Ibid., p. 24.

[118]Ibid., p. 35.

[119]David Riesman and Verne Stadtman, eds., "Academic Transformation," in *The Carnegie Commission on Higher Education,* ed. Lewis B. Mayhew (San Francisco: Jossey-Bass, 1973), pp. 188-190.

[120]Langdon and Griffen, "Report on Men's Education," p. 41.

[121]Ibid.

[122]Ibid., pp. 47-48.

[123]Ibid., preface.

[124]Ibid., p. 53.

[125]Ibid., p. 60.

[126]Ibid.

[127]Ibid., pp. 37-38.

[128]Ibid., p. 89.

[129]Ibid., p. 119.

[130]North Burn, *Cooperative and/or Coeducation* (Hartford, Conn.: ERIC Document Reproduction Serivce, ED 065 078, May 1970), p. 4.

[131]Ibid., abstract.

[132]Ibid., pp. 5-6.

[133]Ibid., p. 3.

[134]"Coed Status Pleases Vassar Despite Problems," *New York Times,* 19 November 1974, p. 45.

[135]Ibid., p. 86.

[136]Ibid.

[137]Langdon and Griffen, "Report on Men's Education," p. 29.

[138]Rosen, "Mount Holyoke Forever Will Be Mount Holyoke Forever Will Be For Women Only," p. 67.

[139]Cole, "A Case for the Women's College," pp. 19-20.

[140]Truman, *The Single Sex College—In Transition?,* p. 2.

[141]"Wellesley President Says School Can Do Without Men," *New York Times,* 23 April 1973, p. 22.

[142]Pepper Schwartz and Janet Lever," "Women in the Male World of Higher Education," in *Academic Women on the Move,* eds. Alice S. Rossi and Ann Calderwood (New York: Russell Sage Foundation, 1973), p. 74.

[143]Richard Crockford, "The Forgotten Sex in Education," *Junior College Journal* 42 (October 1971): 18.

[144]Keezer, "Watch Out Girls!" p. 30.

[145]Schwartz and Lever, "Women in the Male World of Higher Education," p. 57.

[146]Wasserman, "Coeducation Comes to Yale College," p. 145.

[147]Ibid., p. 146.

[148]Jencks and Riesman, *The Academic Revolution,* p. 301.

[149]Ibid.

[150]Lillian Radlo, "Boys and Girls Together(?)" *The Independent School Bulletin* 29 (December 1969): 12.

[151]Schwartz and Lever, "Women in the Male World of Higher Education," p. 76.

[152]Joanna Henderson Sternick, "'But I Love It Here'—Coeducation Comes to Dartmouth," *The Journal of the National Association for Women Deans, Administrators, and Counselors* 37 (Spring 1974): 142.

[153]"Amherst College to Admit Women in '75," *New York Times,* 3 November 1974, p. 58.

[154]Lynn White, Jr., *Educating Our Daughters,* p. 35.

[155]Oltman, *The Evolving Role of the Women's Liberation Movement in Higher Education,* p. 1.

[156]Schwartz and Lever, "Women in the Male World of Higher Education," p. 64.

[157]Michael Knight, "Yale's First Full Class of Women, About to Graduate, Looks Back with Pride and Hope," *New York Times,* 3 June 1973, p. 39.

[158]Schwartz and Lever, "Women in the Male World of Higher Education," p. 67.

[159]Ibid., p. 69.

[160]Lisa Getman, "From Conestoga to Career," in *Women in Higher Education,* eds. Todd Furniss and Patricia Albjerg Graham (Washington, D.C.: American Council on Education, 1974), p. 64.

[161]Sternick, "'But I Love It Here'—Coeducation Comes to Dartmouth," p. 142.

[162]Schwartz and Lever, "Women in the Male World of Higher Education," p. 60.

[163]Robert G. Cope, "Sex-Related Factors and Attrition Among College

Women," *Journal of the National Association of Women Deans, Administrators, and Counselors* 33 (Spring 1970): 121.

[164]Vivian Gornick, "Why Radcliffe Women Are Afraid of Success," *New York Times,* 14 January 1973, sec. 6, p. 56.

[165]Ibid.

[166]"New College Trend: Women Studies," *New York Times,* 7 January 1971, pp. 37, 70.

[167]Sheila Tobias, "Teaching Female Studies: Looking Back Over Three Years," *Liberal Education* 58 (May 1972): 262-263.

[168]"Women Make Strides: On Bases and into Mory's," *New York Times,* 30 March 1974, pp. 1, 25.

[169]Paul Goldberger, "Girls at Yale," *Today's Education* 59 (October 1970): 51.

[170]Sternick, "'But I Love It Here'—Coeducation Comes to Dartmouth," p. 143.

[171]Keezer, "Watch Out Girls!" p. 30.

[172]Simpson, "Coeducation," p. 19.

[173]"The Case for Women's Colleges," p. 344.

[174]Cole, "A Case for the Women's College," p. 18.

Chapter V

WOMEN STUDIES:
HOPES AND PROSPECTS

WOMEN STUDENTS, WOMEN STUDIES, AND THE WOMEN'S MOVEMENT

Perhaps more than any other development, the introduction of women studies on campus is potentially revolutionary in its impact on the standard curriculum as well as on the prevailing life-style of academe.

Women studies were born out of the student activism of the 1960s, the result of women students who, becoming embroiled in wider social movements, came to realize the dismal state of their own human condition. As the women's movement spread on campuses such as Yale, Cornell, and Northwestern, reaction was immediate but not uniformly friendly. It is ironic that where women's ideas would be expected to make their greatest inroads, among the elitist students on the elitist campuses, it is also where they frequently have met their stanchest resistance—among those highly specialized, research-oriented university professors who have neither the time nor the inclination to be sympathetic to such incursions into their scholarly domain.

Of course, women students, as a product of the women's movement, were not only interested in reexamining the status of women in the textbook but also on campus.[1] In questioning the hiring and promotion practices of academe, for instance, they challenged the fundamental way in which the power structure perpetuates itself.[2] Thus the intention of women activists was not to ameliorate their condition by joining the power structure but to change it entirely. Only through a radical departure from old ways and the adoption of new procedures could women be truly equal.

Other campus practices formerly taken for granted were

quickly challenged. A drive toward a new and more equitable housing arrangement was one of the earlier demands quickly conceded.[3] Health services were modified in recognition of the fact that the male body is not the norm for all of humankind but only for mankind.[4] Intercollegiate competitions were revised to take into account that they are subsidized by all and should be participated in by all.[5] An awareness of the function of sports in character building as described two decades earlier by Simone de Beauvoir finally gained acceptance.[6] It was now seen as a tool needed for the healthy development of everybody, and not as a women's spectator sport for the glorification of men.

That the general women's movement helped in laying the groundwork for reform on campus is undebatable. As an illustration, Alexander observed that freshmen women, who carried the seeds of reform from the external world into the campus, are more liberally inclined than their predecessors. He found that, since 1966, there was a threefold increase in the number of women who said they would enter masculine fields.[7] While Astin does not "know if these careers are opening up or women are just moving in," he stresses that "the influx of women into traditionally masculine careers is going to have an impact on the careers themselves."[8] Yet the impact is not limited to careers, for as women increase their enrollment in the masculine fields they automatically decrease their numbers in the humanities. Since the humanities program remains generally "cheaper" for the college to maintain, women were, in the past, effectively subsidizing the male students in that everyone paid equal tuition but not everyone had an equal amount of the resources expended on them. The impact of a humanities decline, if realized, could not merely mean a cut in humanities offerings but a rise in tuition as well.

Other findings in the Astin survey reveal that whereas 9.1 percent of the freshman women interviewed in 1971 believed that they would like to pursue advanced degrees, this increased to 16.6 percent by 1975.[9] In addition, there has been a rise of over 10 percent (to 92.2 percent) since 1970 in "freshwomen's" assertions of the desirability of equal pay for equal work.[10] Perhaps most dramatic is the change in the way women view their societal role. Only 28.3 percent of those women surveyed in 1975 believed women should conform to the sexual stereotype that limited their activities to the home and the family, while 47.8 percent of those interviewed in 1970 were willing to acquiesce to that role.[11] In conclusion, Mr. Astin forewarns that these statistics "reflect a profound social change that has been regular, predictable, and consistent."[12]

It would be dangerously erroneous to assume that reform is largely confined to the coming generation of "freshwomen," lest we prepare only for the future while tacitly ignoring the present. Thus

> Women, graduate students, who once had a dropout rate
> twice that of their male counterparts at the University
> of California at Berkeley, now complete their doctorates
> as often as men.[13]

The message for graduate schools and the disciplines is loud: more women are planning to enter graduate school than ever before and are determined to stay as never before. While the remarkable statistics may be attributed to a pilot project designed to encourage women, they nevertheless demonstrate impressively the results of such assistance. Certainly, it seems probable that the mutual reinforcement created by this program may also be conducive to reducing the male drop-out rate, thereby eliminating most of the current waste in higher education.

Simply stated, as we shall see throughout this discussion, women studies endeavor to alter the status of women by changing the way women are perceived in the curriculum. The prevailing assumptions are that women are portrayed in an unflatteringly biased way in academe, and by revising this presentation women will be able to gain more self-respect as well as respect from the male world. Once men and women become conscious of the arbitrary sex roles perpetrated by the curriculum, change will follow.[14] Hence, the objectives are multifaceted: to assist women in having a higher opinion of their sex; to encourage men to view women as partners; and to restructure societal institutions to take into account the new attitudes. How women attempt to accomplish these objectives is the focal point of the forthcoming sections.

As in any movement, once people start to implement their objectives, disagreement over the direction it should take usually emerges. For the very manner chosen to proceed will determine who holds sway. Women, like men, are human, and the struggle for power is inevitable. This is not to maintain that the women's dialogue is controlled by power considerations, but only to recognize that new power structures must automatically emerge in any changed relationship.

Clearly, the interdisciplinary or multidisciplinary orientation of women if realized could be tantamount to the "breakdown of the traditional departments."[15] Since higher educational institutions are organized under the premise that the department is the basic unit on campus and is responsible for the hiring, firing, salary schedules and curricular content, the ramifications are considerable. As an illustration, many feminist advocates stress that

> Instead of cutting knowledge into disciplines called economics or psychology or English literature, women's studies cuts through all the disciplines to study a particular group of people, their history, economics, psychology, politics. and so forth.[16]

This procedure for effecting change is necessarily subversive. Professors would be required to be reeducated not only to understand the role of women but in order to comprehend the new organization of knowledge. Tobias highlights the dimensions of the problem in demonstrating the reluctance of even sympathetic professional women to change their frame of reference:

138

> It was in every case disturbing to realize how separate
> we are in our professions. The sociologist doubted that a
> character's need in a novel are relevant to cultural his-
> tory. The literature professor had a hard time staying
> awake when the sociologist described "studies."[17]

Recognizing the difficulties of feminist-oriented scholars in the cause of women studies, it is problematical whether the male world would enthusiastically undertake a diversion from their stated priorities of publishing, in order to pursue the arduous task of reeducation that would in turn eventually terminate their superior status.

At this juncture, the interdisciplinary advocates seem to have alternative formulas: either to embrace a new and separate women studies department existing alongside the traditional departments, or to effect a total change in the organization of knowledge running through all departments. The disadvantage of the first option is that women may become isolated and subsequently ignored; that of the second proposal is one of procedure—how to arrive at a formula that would substantively change the ordering and pursuit of knowledge. To merely add women to the departments risks having them "coopted" into the respective disciplines. Certainly, given the continued maintenance of the department structure, an interdisciplinary professor could not hope for speedy advancement and might therefore reassess her/his orientation and commitment to women studies. In any event, by attaching women to the various departments, the fragmentation of knowledge is perpetuated. In order to make the study of women meaningful, therefore, some feminists suggest that control must "be kept in the hands of women."[18]

WOMEN STUDIES WITHIN EXISTING DISCIPLINES

Recognizing the very real danger that the threat of women studies poses to traditional academe, destroying them through a self-imposed isolation must appear attractive to the academic establishment. Clearly the spectre of the somewhat discredited Home Economics Movement looms over the heads of many women. It is only through integration, some maintain, with the women's discipline being absorbed into all aspects of the curriculum, that a new and better curriculum can emerge. While involving themselves throughout the entire curriculum structure makes women more vulnerable to cooptation and subordination, this still may be preferable to the alternative of separate but meaningless sovereignty over an isolated women studies department. In isolation women can be ignored and eventually forgotten.

Many authorities, including the Carnegie Commission, suggest the importance of making women studies an intricate part of the various disciplines. The Harvard Report referred to earlier concurs:

> We have also not seen fit to recommend the creation of a new department devoted to "women's studies" and predisposed, most likely to fill its ranks with women. There are many subjects of special interest to women or focused in some special way on the history or the psychology or on the factional representation of women which surely ought to be studied at the university level, but none of these seem to us likely to prosper in isolation from the study of humankind. . . . We suggest, instead, that courses dealing with these and similar subjects ought to be initiated in departments where they are relevant.[19]

In sum, we seem to be facing the dilemma of either the isolation of the department from the mainstream of the university, or the isolation of the particular women who are scattered and diluted in that mainstream.

Of course, it would be easier to establish a women studies program alongside the established curriculum than to institute an alternative plan for the reordering of knowledge. Yet what might be easy to accomplish may not be worth realizing. Ida Cannon reflected in the 1940s that one of the reasons she could not gain acceptance of a health-care delivery system was that her reforms were discussed within the confines of what was regarded as the women's domain and were summarily dismissed by the wider world.[20] Tobias is also mindful of Cannon's fate.[21] Yet if Cannon were not in a separate, albeit isolated department, would she have had the full freedom to pursue her theories and espouse her doctrines?

Another argument enlisted by Jill Conway against the exclusiveness of a women studies department is that it would train women with questionable credentials.[22] One might also ponder, as an offshoot of this concern, whether the most talented women would be reluctant to enter such a program, especially when they are attracted by the standard curriculum of the established departments.[23]

A compromise solution seems to rest in the construction of a women studies program housed under a single roof but with attachments, perhaps through joint appointments, to the regular departments. Under such an arrangement it would seem that the integrity of the women studies offerings could go on unimpaired while the assault against the traditional department structure could be pursued. From the students' vantage point, too, being keen on maintaining the integrity of their credentials, some concentration in women studies while keeping their allegiance to the traditional fare seems ideal. Even the most skeptical students would be less fearful of being exposed to courses knowing that they were sanctioned by the academic establishment. Their training might not be as intensive or thorough as some would like, but it would nonetheless acquaint the brightest students with an area they might ordinarily shun. Finally, it should be remembered that although women studies would be diluted by blending with the common whole, in the dilution process the established male curriculum would be diluted as well.

THE DANGERS TO WOMEN STUDIES

Women, while they are not subject to masculine frailties, are nevertheless subject to human temptations. Thus, since the women's movement envisages a dramatic alteration in the power arrangement, it sows the seeds of human rivalry.[24] One must always remember that the world is political. Actions are not neutral in their consequences; neither are people. In the act of promoting new academic priorities, old disciplinary masters who are usually male will be displaced. Benson sums up the problem:

> Women's studies, too is not considered by some academicians to be quite "legitimate" as part of a college curriculum. In response to this, one might say simpy that the definition of "legitimacy" is itself political, that the notion of legitimacy is a strategy to keep the in-people in, and the out-people out.[25]

Conway presents the logistical implications of what is entailed in women studies when she states:

> It will take more than hundreds of hastily assembled courses to reorient disciplines whose entire range of methodological assumptions is based upon norms derived from male experience.[26]

In the marketplace of courses there is a finite number that may be offered at any one time. The battleline may represent not only the seeds of intellectual supremacy, but much more importantly, of job security.

Finally a danger for women studies exists in their massive appeal—the greatest strength is also the greatest weakness; for if with this universal attraction they become in danger of being vulgarized by amateur practitioners and fleeting students, then the subsequent impact on the male world will be correspondingly diminished.[27] Thus there is the ever-present prospect of "charlatans" within the movement—of women who regard themselves as experts by virtue of the fact that they are women. Truly the person who defends her expertise on the basis of "experiencing child birth" or a "woman's disease" is on as faulty ground as the woman who stresses that men cannot understand the woman's plight because they cannot undergo these experiences. "Many people want in on the benefits," says Catharine Stimpson speaking in a related context. "If honey has flies, we have them."[28]

FOOTNOTES FOR CHAPTER V

[1]Ronald W. Thomas, "Coed Housing in One Fell Swoop," pp. 278-279.

[2]Howe and Ahlum, "Women's Studies and Social Change," p. 400.

[3]Ronald W. Thomas, "Coed Housing in One Fell Swoop," p. 275.

[4]Jean Leppaluoto, *Attitude Change and Sex Discrimination: The Crunch Hypothesis* (Bethesda, Md.: ERIC Document Reproduction Service, ED 071 548, 1972), p. 7.

[5]"College Sports Sanction Plan Set for Women," *Chronicle of Higher Education*, 12 January 1976, p. 6.

[6]Simone de Beauvoir, *The Second Sex* (New York: Alfred A. Knopf, 1953), p. 330.

[7]Beverly T. Watkins, "This Year's Freshmen Reflect New Views of Women's Role," *Chronicle of Higher Education*, 12 January 1976, p. 3.

[8]Ibid.

[9]Ibid.

[10]Ibid.

[11]Ibid.

[12]Ibid.

[13]"Graduate-Level Women Reduce Dropout Rate," *Chronicle of Higher Education*, 21 January 1974, p. 7.

[14]Catharine Stimpson, "The New Feminism and Women's Studies," *Change* 5 (September 1973): 43-48.

[15]Adrienne Rich, "Toward a Woman-Centered University," in *Women and the Power to Change*, ed. Florence Howe (New York: McGraw-Hill, 1975), pp. 32-33.

[16]Jennie Farley, *Women's Studies: Where to Now?* (Ithaca, N.Y.: ERIC Document Reproduction Service, ED 086 078, 1973), p. 32.

[17]Tobias, "Teaching Female Studies: Looking Back Over Three Years," pp. 260-262.

[19]Janice Law Trecker, "Woman's Place Is in the Curriculum," *Saturday Review*, 16 October 1971, p. 92.

[19]*Report of the Committee on the Status of Women in the Faculty of Arts and Sciences, Harvard University*, p. 44.

[20]Conway, "Coeducation and Women's Studies: Two Approaches to the Question of Woman's Place in the Contemporary University," p. 246.

[21]Tobias, "Teaching Female Studies: Looking Back Over Three Years," p. 263.

[22]Conway, "Coeducation and Women's Studies: Two Approaches to the Question of Woman's Place in the Contemporary University," p. 245.

[23]Cheryl Fields, "Women's Studies Gain; 2,000 Courses Offered This Year," *Chronicle of Higher Education*, 17 December 1973, p. 6.

[24]Robinson, *Women's Studies: Courses and Programs for Higher Education*, p. 9.

[25]Ruth Crego Benson, "Women's Studies: Theory and Practice," *AAUP Bulletin* 58 (September 1972): 283.

[26]Conway, "Coeducation and Women's Studies: Two Approaches to the Question of Woman's Place in the Contemporary University," p. 246.

[27]Sicherman, "The Invisible Woman: The Case for Women's Studies," p. 156.

[28]Kenneth L. Woodward, with Elaine Sciolino, "Clio Tells Herstory," *Newsweek*, 8 December 1975, p. 51.

Chapter VI

WOMEN AND THE CURRICULAR DEBATE

Women studies envision a change in the curriculum. Yet regardless of the dialogue as to whether these studies should exist within existing departments or apart from them, the debate will be meaningless unless women themselves adopt new curricular preferences. Women studies are a means to an end. Whether women should be treated as separate but equal with men, or whether the sexual designations should be finally dissolved, is the scope of the present discussion. Should women be given a coordinate but equal curriculum? Are their preferences truly innate? And, finally, should and can we resolve instead to build a new common academic curriculum applicable to all?

WOMEN AND THEIR DISCIPLINARY PREFERENCES

Many fundamental questions must be answered before we can gauge the scope and intensity of the women's movement on campus. For example, will the ultimate direction of the new movment be concerned with altering women's traditional disciplinary preferences or will the energy of the movement be directed toward making certain that the current academic curriculum is appropriately modified to take into account woman's present role in contemporary society? In other words, will it confirm the present by making a woman's education more compatible with her traditional life-style, or will it embark instead on a new roleless society?

The problem posed in encouraging women to enter masculine disciplines is considerable. Perhaps the chief objection against such an undertaking is that the women will be trained in a curriculum that is irrelevant to their present needs. Accordingly, so the argument goes, if society does encourage women to enter masculine professions, then the time spent in educating women in those areas would be ill spent. However, this objection is fallacious in that the standard humanities fare typically offered to the traditional female undergraduate has been nearly as irrelevant to her future requirements of wife and mother without evincing much lamentation from academicians.

The arguments for encouraging women to enter masculine fields of study are strong. Women have been indoctrinated from birth with the idea that masculine pursuits are distasteful. The perpetuation of this myth is in fact the perpetuation of an injustice. Only through the woman's assumption of masculine roles on a truly random basis will the artificial demarcation between different disciplines be finally and irrevocably eliminated. In addition, since male occupations are, by definition of being male, viewed as more prestigious, they attract men of lesser caliber while simultaneously discouraging women of impressive ability, to the detriment of the individuals concerned and ultimately of society.

Helen Astin writes that even those few women who opt for more masculine fields as freshmen would eventually change their course preferences to conform to a future career more compatible with their perceived sexual role.[1] It seems disheartening that when, despite the massive conditioning against pursuing masculine offerings, some women enter college with the expectation of pursuing the nontraditional courses, they are discouraged by the academy. This is added indication that higher education acts to confirm the devastating prior socialization process rather than to restore a woman's confidence.

It is not strange to find women coalescing around the disciplines that they find most acceptable.[2] Even among those subjects characterized as sexually integrated, e.g., psychology, women have preferred subspecialities within the larger discipline—in this instance usually centering on the study of children.

This tendency to ghettoize women into certain specialities has meant a correspondingly lower status and pay scale for those areas defined as the feminine domain.[3] Thus, it may be that the best thing that could happen to such fields and to women is for them to part company temporarily; for once fields are known as not predominantly for women and all are mixed equally, the salary and prestige scale of the "lower" disciplines may rise accordingly. In the past people were awarded recognition not necessarily according to their contribution to society or the state of their acquired expertise but less relevantly on the basis of sex.[4] With sex eliminated as a criterion, the over-inflated, formerly masculine professions will be deflated to their true worth. The implication for academe is clear. If publishing, no matter how irrelevant or worthless, attracts men because men have more frequently published in the past, thereby differentiating them from women, then the creation of a climate whereby women will publish could mean an upgrading in the value of teaching. Perhaps, then, the way to finally put to rest the sanctity of the publishing ideal is for women to publish!

Other reasons compel women to reassess their professional preferences. Today, the more women remain steadfastly committed to their traditional disciplines, the more the position of their sex will deteriorate. A new trend must be encouraged to have women enter men's fields as fast as men are displacing women in such feminine citadels as library science and elementary school teaching.[5] These professions allowed women a meaningful if underrated outlet for their intellectual energies. Previously, regardless of the husband's place of employment and no matter how often he moved, a woman could always be assured of the availability of a new teaching position with its reasonable hours and convenient locations. Now a husband's moving could be tantamount to a professional death sentence for his working wife. Openings in teaching, the main employment staple of the American woman, are far fewer today. In 1972, for example, 337,619 people graduated from teaching programs and applied for 179,000 positions. Moreover, while there is an ever-diminishing number of vacancies due to a lowered birth rate, there remains a steadily increasing number of both men and women applying for openings formerly regarded as the female

146

preserve. While in 1930, 65 percent of all secondary school teaching positions were occupied by women, by 1971 this figure fell to 46 percent.[6] Certainly men were displacing women in the feminine fields while remaining sexually restrictive in their own. If the aforementioned trends were to continue, women would eventually become professionless.

Teaching in the past performed perhaps as important a functional role for the education of children as it did, albeit unknowingly, for the sanity of their educated mothers. The modern family had an "affinity" to women's teaching. Even though the husband's mobility was fluid, a woman could always find a job in any geographical location. She could even "drop out" for a few years during the child-rearing stage with complete confidence that a similar position awaited her upon her return. Indeed, the position was agreeably feminine—that of providing services for children. Finally it provided a public rationale for a woman to receive a college education in the first place.[7]

The primary-secondary school option which became synonymous with job opportunity represented an "attractive nuisance" to the cause of women's liberation. However, change seems to be in the offing. By the mid-1970s, with "men's careers" providing less job security, and with the marital institution in an increasing state of disarray, women in greater numbers may flock to the sciences for the same reason that they earlier flocked to teaching—for some semblance of job security. The curricular prescription is apparent. Women are entering and must continue to enter the scientific disciplines in ever-increasing numbers and be expected to take on the burdens as well as the privileges of their newly acquired role. The statistics betray the trend. While in 1967 only 9.3 percent of the medical students were women, this contrasted with 16.8 percent five years later.[8]

Of course, if these statistics are to be encouraged, the educational establishment must alter those "innate" preferences of females by purging itself of its own biases. For instance, in the past, young girls were socialized to find science "innately" distasteful. Margaret Mead, in a study of high school students, asked them "to write a brief essay on a topic set by an incomplete sentence which was printed at the top of the page...."[9] Mead's intent was to see what high school students of various ages thought of scientists and the scientific career, not to determine how many potential scientists there might be.[10] To the female, a commitment to science would conceivably eliminate the possibility for them of enjoying the traditional life of wife and mother.[11] Importantly, even when both sexes viewed science positively there remained sexual differences—the boys delighting in the possibility of adventure that science portends while the girls found the favorable attributes of the scientists to be in their common concern for humanity—a helping function. Indeed

> the girls reject science both as a possible form of work for themselves, concerned with things rather than with people...and for their husbands, because it will separate them, give their husbands absorbing interests which they do not share, and involve them in various kinds of danger.[12]

The overall image of the scientist is appalling to young women. To them, scientists will either travel to far away places or limit themselves to the confines of their laboratories, talk incessantly or remain mute, and display other aberrations not appealing to the "feminine" nature.[13] To make matters worse, the scientist was often depicted as working on dead or nonliving objects or fragmented human organs, rarely as dealing with the active present.[14]

In sum, Mead suggests that science is possessed of a generally unwholesome image among the nation's youth. She stresses the importance of conducting a media campaign to show that the contemporary scientist enjoys working with people and is neither alone nor isolated. Anticipating the importance of role models for all, she recognizes that

> Pictures of scientific activities of groups, working together, drawing in people of different nations, of both sexes and all ages, people who take delight in their work could do a great deal of good.[15]

Without question, the scientific image as portrayed was completely incompatible with the life-style and ambition of the American girl. What is needed then is a broad advertising campaign to illustrate how the images of the various scientific practitioners do not square with reality, e.g., how the physician is no longer on the twenty-four hour vigil but rather is more likely to be found as a member of a team with fixed hours and a fixed salary who can easily be substituted for by other members of the medical group. Professions change but images cling, reflecting bygone realities. Unfortunately, however, images have a way of becoming self-fulfilling. Accordingly, if scientists are viewed as dull, then impressionable youth who happen to like science may adopt those characteristics as integral parts of their personality. Moreover, dull people may, by virtue of their disinterest in people, be attracted to the scientific sector although they may not have any special scientific talents.

Given the notion that science is a masculine preserve, many women are psychologically inhibited from entering the scientific theatre. Women who found the lore of science irresistible may have felt it necessary to adopt masculine attributes on the assumption that this was the only way they would be acceptable. Thus, inadvertently they provided added reinforcement to the notion of science as essentially incompatible with feminine traits.[16]

Alice Dement studied over one hundred undergraduate women majoring in one of the scientific disciplines.[17] The findings are intriguing. For example, the educational backgrounds of the women's fathers indicated that they were "unusually high or quite low." It was theorized that the educationally higher background woman feels secure while the low background individual is motivated out of rejection of her current condition rather than stimulated by the inevitable rise in status accruing to her as a future scientist. In addition, of course, the "lower" individual may be more concerned with scholarship aid and the prospects of eventual employment and may see a scientific major as more conducive to both.[18]

Other findings disclose that a woman's fortitude in maintaining her scientific propensities is attributable to early childhood upbringing. If she evinced a long, enthusiastic interest in science rather than an ephemeral concern triggered by some high school course, there would be a greater probability of her remaining attached to her scientific leanings.[19] Of those women who elected to discontinue their scientific pursuits, one of the deciding factors was their concern that they would be unable to use their training fully.[20] Taking all this into account, it is not surprising to find Lucy Sells writing that

> A study of admissions applications of Berkeley freshmen shows that while 57% of the boys had taken four years of high school math only 8% of the girls had done so. The Four Year Math Sequence is required for admission to the first year calculus sequence, Math 1A-B-C. This sequence is a prerequisite for the undergraduate majors in every field at the U of California except the "traditionally female"....[21]

These statistics are commonplace. Nancy Schlossberg reported that as of 1973 the then entering "freshwomen" in the sample consistently and dramatically veered away from certain male-stereotyped disciplines.[22]

If women are successfully to enter the sciences, they must be encouraged to review their family obligations. Science changes at a rapid rate and the woman who stays at home—no matter how briefly—is quickly made obsolete. We cannot expect science to slow down to accommodate the woman's traditional life cycle. The only solution seems to lie in modifying her extra-professional obligations. As Virginia Woolf reflected, while an artist can create in "a room of one's own" it is impractical to provide a homemaker-scientist with "a lab of one's own."[23] Equality can only come about if everyone truly has an equal opportunity. Making a virtue out of necessity, such as extolling the new status of homemaking, is not the same as equality of opportunity.

Alice Rossi suggests that many college women are hesitant to choose a scientific career because of the lack of available part-time opportunities, and cautions that

> there is an unfortunate tendency in the past few years to overstress part-time work as "the" solution to the con-

temporary woman's needs for both personal fulfillment and societal contribution.[24]

The important point to make is that women should not lose sight of their ultimate goal of breaking all shackles to full opportunity. In the long run, they should not seek accommodation to a biased system; for as long as they have an opportunity to work part-time and take care of their families, while the husbands work full-time with no other obligations, men will necessarily be more professionally advanced than women.

Finally, to Stimpson and others, the importance of attracting women to the sciences is fundamental. For science represents the very citadel of power in American academe and society at large. The alternative, to attempt to upgrade the feminine fields alongside the masculine, is the work of charity, and what can be given can be taken away.

> Unless women enter fully into science and technology, they will remain outside a source of power in modern society. They will also perpetuate the ugly myth that women are too weak for the rigors of scientific thought and unfit for the management of its apparatus.[25]

WOMEN ENTERING THE MASCULINE PROFESSIONS
A CASE STUDY: MEDICINE AND THE LAW

Medicine. Medical practice today, popularly regarded as a masculine profession as in days of old, is a life ideally suited for a woman. Like her teacher-mother, she can take her craft anywhere with the assurance of being able to practice. Moreover, she can join a medical firm, thereby regularizing her hours while permitting her vacations. Finally, the prevailing occupational mode of the physician is that of applied practitioner, and is not research oriented. Therefore the physician need not have her "own lab" or be required to read the "latest" journals to practice her craft. Indeed, judging from the self-attested case loads of many physicians, few if any have the time or the energy to pursue the latest developments after hours. Yet despite the fact that medicine

151

appears to be uniquely suited for the woman's traditional role, many high school counselors, imbued with the myth of the lone medical physician working odd hours and traversing an extended terrain, will act to dissuade their charges from seeking careers as physicians.[26]

The struggle by women to achieve parity with men in the medical field has an extended history and provides a revealing case story. The record dates back to the middle part of the last century when an aspiring medical student, Elizabeth Blackwell, met repeated frustration in her bid to secure admission to a medical school. Finally, perhaps by happenstance, she applied to the Geneva Medical School:

> the faculty, not wanting to take responsibility for her rejection, had turned the matter over to the students, who—in an uproarious general assembly—voted a unanimous "yes" as a joke.[27]

Given the historical legacy, the problems confronting a woman medical student are unrelenting. She is in a male's domain not as a participant or even as a guest but more as a transgressor. Her prior socialization and conditioning, which stress the unfemininity of competition (especially with males) work against her being a successful student.[28] She not only faces the typical problems of the fledgling medical student, but because of her situation must be provided with counseling, an abundance of peer reinforcement, and the necessary faculty role models if she is to succeed and prosper.[29] Her environment, being artificially hostile, must be made less so through affirmative means. More women should be admitted, not merely because it is equitable to have a sexual balance but because this is the only way the few can survive.

Professional women students in the medical field have been defined as "occupational role innovators" because they are essentially pioneering in what is generally regarded as an all-male field. To survive, many of these "role innovators" have taken on the "majoritarian" negativistic views of women and accordingly tended to disassociate themselves from their sex.[30] This self-denial is as destructive as it is inevitable. Yet it will pervade for as long as women categorize themselves as an identifiable minority. However, once "role innovators" are made to feel solidarity with instead of antagonism toward the other women, they then may be an even greater asset in the furtherance of women in the profession.[31]

The contemporary woman medical student seems to have an evolving view of her role. For example, in the R. H. Hudson Rosen study, it was found that "only 8 percent of female medical students believe that childrearing is necessary to the average woman's fulfillment."[32] While most of these students were not against the maternal role, they no longer seemed to believe in the primacy of their maternal obligations. Reflecting upon the changing attitudes, the Rosen findings suggest that women medical faculty members are more traditional in their role outlook than their women students. This is attributed to "the impact of societal change with regard to female role images. . ."—further indication that the entire women's movement is intricately involved in many facets of the educational world.[33]

Various theories have emerged in an effort to explain the disciplinary preferences of women in medicine as elsewhere. According to such studies, women may be categorized into the "pressure" or "preference" school. Briefly, as its name indicates, the "pressure" advocates believe that women are not free agents, that they are forced by external circumstances to enter the specified feminine fields without regard to their own true interests. Correspondingly the "preference" theorists hold that women select their fields entirely of their own volition, without regard to outside influences.[34]

Reviewing the evidence, women do appear to be herded into specialties they might not otherwise have preferred if they were truly free agents. Society seems determined first, to keep women within feminine-designated occupations and, failing that, to create separate professions within the masculine ones. As it has evolved in medicine as everywhere else, women appear to have been made separate and unequal.

Medical schools exacerbate this tendency by orchestrating a curriculum predicated entirely on the single male model. In addition, various subspecialties demand different internship requirements that also may be incompatible with the present and future life-styles of budding women professionals. As a result, women have tended to coalesce around certain fields. Whether we maintain that women innately prefer these subspecialties or are forced to enter them, all must agree that the so-called women's fields are more convenient for the women to enter. Hence women are seen congregating in pediatrics, psychiatry and internal medicine— fields which incidentally carry lower status within the medical profession. Patterson sums up the feminine specializing propensities:

> More women—one fifth of all women physicians— specialize in pediatrics than any other area. These figures seem to imply that women's choice of specialty is determined, in part, by a desire to minimize role conflict. By practicing pediatrics women conform to the feminine role stereotype of caring for children. Psychiatry, another "caring" specialty, also draws large numbers of women. Perhaps not coincidentally, psychiatry ranked lowest when medical students of both sexes were asked to evaluate the relative standing of specialities within the profession.[35]

The hostility of the medical environment takes its toll of feminine students: "The attrition rate in medical school is twice as great among the women medical students as it is among the men."[36] These figures are cause for added suspicion when it is recalled that under the equal rejection theory—evaluating students separately by sex—women were generally required to have higher averages in order to secure admission into a medical school. Also, remembering that their undergraduate work, upon which they were evaluated for medical school admission, was usually taken in areas similar if not identical to what they would find in medical schools, their subsequent lack of motivation is intriguing. Nadelson, for example, observes that 8 percent of women students but only 3 percent of their male counterparts drop out for nonacademic reasons.[37] The medical school seems remiss in not understanding the importance of adjusting their institutions to accommodate the needs of women. The male world, then, which provides the male student with all the reinforcement he requires, makes it easy for the medical school to view the introduction of extra-supporting services for women as unnecessary.

The Law. The predicament of women law students closely parallels their medical school sisters.[38] While in 1961 only 3.6 percent of those enrolled in American law schools were women, this figure jumped to 12 percent in 1972. In addition, like their medical school counterparts, there is a dearth of role models on the faculty, and as late as 1968 only 1.6 percent of the faculty of the nation's major law schools were women.[39] Also, of that number there were few full professors, and it was not until 1972 that Ruth Ginsburg was to emerge as Columbia Law School's first woman professor.

The oppression meted out to women students by officialdom was harsh. Law school is known for its excessive attrition rate even among men. Students, especially women, are in need of a reinforcing structure. Indeed, even though women are often most in need of encouragement, they are typically confronted with discouragingly negative utterances. The dual function of the law school, it would appear, is to graduate men lawyers while "cooling out" as many women as possible:

> Professor Ginsburg personally experienced a case of law school sexism in her first weeks as a student at Harvard. (She later transferred to Columbia.) She and the other women in her class were invited to dinner at the home of Dean Erwin Griswold. "I thought: 'How nice,' she recalls, 'the dean wants to make us feel welcome.'" After dinner, however, Griswold asked each woman to justify why she was occupying a place that could be held by a man. Apparently he assumed that women would not put their education to use.[40]

Once graduated, women lawyers were encouraged to enter "women specialties" within the law. Matrimonial law and trusts seemed to attract many new women recruits. As one contemporary observer noted: "Basically, you are not going to have a lot of client contact unless the clients were women or dead."[41]

A particular handicap to women in their pursuit of an academic legal career lies in the necessity of acquiring a fed-

155

eral court clerkship upon graduation. Unfortunately, prior to 1972, only four women in American history were able to secure such positions. Judges have stated their reluctance to recruit women: "I use very coarse language and I just wouldn't feel comfortable with a woman" has been a frequent explanation.[42] Yet how inverted it is and how illogical it must appear to the female to have to "pay" for the biases of the male judge.

A danger perhaps peculiar to the woman attorney is falling easily into complacency.[43] As Rossi seemed to indicate earlier, part-time employment is really not the solution to the woman's problem. Yet the law seems to provide this seductive opportunity. Indeed, a law career may offer the contemporary woman a convenient compromise between her fear of success and fear of failure. She may, after all, enter law school, opt for one of the female specialties and eventually practice part-time.[44] For women to succeed in law, as everywhere else, they must get out of the "backroom" and into the spotlight, practicing their craft on a totally equal basis with men.[45] Women should not accommodate themselves to the circumstances of society. To reiterate, once their career pattern can be differentiated from that of men, they will be discriminated against. Only in a genuine fusion of roles can there be equality.

In conclusion, women in the law, unlike the other professions, have a special obligation to their sex. For law not only reflects society's mores but also provides a spearhead for changing them. In the past, law merely confirmed what already existed. It was not an innovator. Nevertheless there is now movement—perhaps without parallel—of a massive number of legally discriminated against people who are entering the gates of the legal profession. Attorneys, acting in the past as retardants to change, can in the future be the pioneers of a new tomorrow.

A SPECIAL CURRICULUM FOR THE WOMAN'S ROLE?

An alternative to encouraging women to enter the male curriculum is to design a new curriculum in recognition of the "woman's role" in contemporary society. Not surprisingly, there are defects in this orientation. For one thing, it will be constructed on what has been the woman's traditional role and not what could be her future projected role. For another, it seeks to codify the position of women by making their subordinate role more bearable. The adoption of such a curriculum could serve as a tranquilizing agent, subduing the awareness of many women regarding their inferior station in life. Yet when all is said and done, those women who eagerly anticipate the homemaker role might well be benefited by the inclusion of such a curriculum. Certainly the prevailing male mode of learning is dysfunctional to the future life expectations of the homemaker. The statement that women are not men needs no explanation. Nevertheless women are trained in the colleges and universities to be surrogate men, their future destiny being totally ignored. It is natural then that many women are quick to argue that they should chart a curriculum best suited to their own needs as defined by society.[46] This idea would carry considerable weight if "different" were not also equated with "inferior." Nevertheless, to make no curricular modifications for those career homemakers is to perpetuate another generation of unhappy people. We all know the plight of the man who faces imminent retirement. However the retirement of women from their familial obligations takes place at an increasingly earlier age and is virtually ignored. Thus, whereas a man increases in importance as his life progresses, the exact opposite happens in the case of a woman. She is most needed when her child is first born but her role steadily diminishes as her child matures. Indeed, the very success of the mother may perhaps best be measured by how quickly her role is made obsolete. Lynn White summarizes the problem:

> What is she to do with her released energies and intelligence during the next three decades? For the second time in her life she must choose as a man never chooses; for even to do nothing is to choose.[47]

The notion that women should receive a special curriculum that best reflects their future role is quite old. In 1900 Edward Bok observed:

> There is no doubt that the average girls' college would
> be more useful to girls themselves and to American
> domestic life in general, if the practical components of a
> woman's life entered a little more into its cur-
> riculum. . . .[48]

The question now is whether women can achieve their rightful status through a rejection of the male curriculum altogether or by forcing it to conform to totally different requirements.

The supporters of the special women's curriculum seem
to assume that the problems facing women can be ameliorated through a modification of their course of study, the assumption being implicit that the curriculum is largely responsible for the woman's predicament. Accordingly Harold
Taylor suggested that a woman should "be allowed to develop. . . without inhibiting relationships with other groups,
in this case pressures of male society."[49] However, the male
curriculum gives expression to certain "preferred" roles that
women are not encouraged to pursue. The conclusion might
thus follow to create "preferred" social roles uniquely designed for women. Yet the problem remains; women will not
be equal unless they are socialized as people, and not cast
aside because of their sexual identity.

Whatever the merits of the special curriculum for women, its advocates have difficulty in discerning which
women would be the most appropriate candidates for their
curricular option. Lenore Harmon attempted to discover the
differing characteristics of those young women who would
eventually seek outside career fulfillment and those who
would not. Unfortunately it is not easy to predict which
women would eventually embark on a particular career.

> One solution would be to educate all women as
> though they will be career women. Another would be to
> educate all women as though they will be housewives
> exclusively.[50]

Without doubt, either solution is unacceptable; for how do
those women who have been "indoctrinated" into thinking
that they prefer the "housewife career" have an opportunity

to know otherwise? Are we encouraging a budding Einstein or Pasteur, or someone who could probe and settle the mysteries of cancer or the intricacies of the universe, into premature acceptance of the homemaker life-style?

Harmon believes that young girls should be informed of the choices available to them before they begin their college education.[51] In accordance with our thesis of the need to abolish sex roles, this would be fine, providing young boys were also granted the identical choice. In fact, though, given the massive indoctrination encouraging females to be homemakers, what may be required is not a balanced approach but an affirmative action bias toward showing young girls the advantages of the career alternative.

There is no question that women are different from men. The basic question is whether they should be treated differently from men. In one very real sense a woman must have a special curriculum because she is entering college with a bruised ego in need of remedial assistance.[52] But the point of the assistance is that she should eventually take her place in the world as an equal. The aims of a remedial curriculum should be to make everyone the same—not to accentuate the woman's disparate role, but rather to correct past abuses inflicted upon her.

It is important to reaffirm that after being exposed to alternative curricula, the women might nonetheless opt for the traditional one. Hence the woman who prefers the domestic lifestyle should be educated in such a way as to reflect her inevitable period of sustained inactivity.[53] Independent study, for example, should be considered as an integral part of the woman's curriculum in that hopefully it will train her in the art of studying by herself.[54] Jacques Barzun, however, reflects upon the monumental problem for the married woman who desires to retain her college skills:

> Whereas the very essence of thought is continuity, the very essence of domestic life is interruption. If a young woman dared disconnect the doorbell, smash the phone, and gag the baby, she might be able to read a book or think a thought; but with a duty towards everybody but herself, her mind necessarily reverts to the feral state. It is not a matter of intelligence or good will or even energy,

159

but of hourly preoccupation. Robinson Crusoe would have a better chance of remaining cultivated.[55]

The arguments of Lynn White and others that "women should be told of the importance of maintaining their skills" is incontrovertible.[56] But given Barzun's characterization of the contemporary woman's role, the validity of White's remarks palls in practicality as we grope for a way to give them modern-day meaning.

The suggested curriculum for women, that of emphasizing independent study and principles over facts, may take on greater relevance if we view it as applicable for men as well. Naturally, men must cope with a society that will provide more leisure time for all.[57] Recognizing the finite number of jobs and the increasing number of women and minorities who are now clamoring for the diminishing number of positions, it seems probable that people will have to accept periods of sustained inactivity either in the form of a shortened work week or earlier retirement or both. Coupled with this is the fact that the world is changing at such an incredibly rapid rate that it may very well be impossible to specialize excessively without simultaneously planting the seeds of personal "obsolescence." Coincidentally, the theoretical education for women may well be becoming the practical education for men.

THE FINAL SOLUTION: A NEW CURRICULUM FOR ALL

With the old curriculum never having been valid for women and fast becoming outmoded for men as well, a new common arrangement is necessary to take into account evolving unisex patterns and extended leisure activities. Such a new curriculum, designed for equals, would be revolutionary in scope, affecting both the ordering and content of knowledge.[58] The former curriculum, after all, merely rationalized the prevailing inequities in society. With men as the sole breadwinners, the academic world lent justification to this scheme of things by asserting that a change in roles

160

would imperil not only women but her children as well. History, psychology, sociology and all the disciplines were mobilized in common purpose to prove that this order of things was truly natural.

Feminists have long contended that while there may be differences between the sexes, these have never been examined with sexual detachment. Psychologists, they say, have prejudiced women by studying female behavior without taking into account their social environment. Weisstein states the ignored obvious:

> In some extremely important ways, people are what you expect them to be, or at least they behave as you expect them to behave. Thus, if women, according to Bruno Bettelheim, want first and foremost to be good wives and mothers, it is extremely likely that that is what Bruno Bettelheim (and the rest of society) want them to be.[59]

For a woman to be other than what she is, she would have to deny her very upbringing. In religion and literature, for example:

> "God's plan" for women was revealed through St. Paul. . . . For a man ought not to cover his head, since he is the image and glory of God; but woman is the glory of man. . . . Wives, be subject to your husbands, as to the Lord.[60]

To John Milton in *Paradise Lost:*

> O why did god
> Creator wise, that people'd highest Heav'n
> With Spirits Masculine, create at last
> This noveltie on Earth, this fair defect
> Of Nature, and not fill the World at once
> With Men as Angels without Feminine,
> Or find some other way to generate
> Mankind?[61]

Regardless of the field, historical figure, or the epoch, the utterances share a common theme of women's subordination. To Napoleon Bonaparte:

Nature intended women to be our slaves.... They are our property.... They belong to us, just as a tree that bears fruit belongs to a gardner.[62]

The sage Aristotle agrees:

We may thus conclude that there is a general law that there should be naturally ruling elements and elements naturally ruled... the rule of the freeman over the slave is one kind of rule; that of the male over the female is another....[63]

And the great radical, reform educator-philosopher, Jean Jacques Rousseau reaffirms:

The whole education of women ought to be relative to men. To please them, to be useful to them, to make themselves loved and honored by them, to educate them when young, to care for them when grown, to counsel them, to console them, and to make life sweet and agreeable to them—These are the duties of women at all times and what should be taught them from their infancy.[64]

From whatever corner, regardless of their own bitter intellectual disagreements with each other, many men seem to find a common ground with respect to their opinion of women. The agreement being so complete, it is no wonder that women and men think the way they do. They could think no other way. Clearly, if the slaveholder is as much a prisoner of his dogma as is the slave of the slaveholder, then a radical expunging of the biased curriculum is in order.

The academic revolution that women propose is not only in acquiring new knowledge but also in pursuing the search for knowledge differently. To feminists, the contributions of women cannot be gauged by reviewing the ancient press or the distribution of medals of honor. The substitution of old methods for new ones will unearth different heroes, both female and male; old categories symbolizing the traditional research such as "class rivalry" and "war" will have to take their place alongside the sexual classifications.

The bias of the contemporary disciplines has been appalling. To psychologists a healthy adult was defined in terms of a healthy man and, in history, those institutions that included women through the ages—such as the primary and secondary schools—were virtually ignored by the male historian as unimportant.[65] The function of the new curriculum therefore must be not only to explain things as they really are but to analyze why they were transmitted incorrectly in the first place.[66]

The Psychological Example:
A Case Study in Bias

To Naomi Weisstein, the basic premise of psychology is faulty in laying excessive stress on the individual.[67] Accordingly, a woman is told in various ways that men have made all the significant contributions and then when she acts as if men should make all contributions, psychologists seize upon this as prima facie proof of women's innate deference to men. The psychoanalytic technique clearly assists the "individual. . . to adjust to a 'sick society.'"[68] In addition, the Freudian psychologist's method of inquiry is blatantly discriminatory: ". . . maleness is the norm and femaleness an incomplete or, even worse deficient aspect of it."[69] Bruno Bettelheim adds to the official chorus:

> We must start with the realization that, as much as women want to be good scientists or engineers, they want first and foremost to be womanly companions of men and to be mothers.

And Erik Erikson reaffirms:

> Much of a young woman's identity is already defined in her kind of attractiveness and in the selectivity of her search for the man (or men) by whom she wishes to be sought.[70]

Without question, many psychologists base their theories on the fundamental importance of sexuality. Yet Evelyn Hooker recently presented some interesting findings. She administered the Thematic Apperception Test (TAT), the Make-A-Picture Story Test (MAPS) and the Rorschach Test to a group of homosexual and heterosexual males. A predetermined, distinguished panel of judges was asked to isolate one group from the other using the tests as their guide. In all cases, their results were "no better than chance."[71] What this study clearly suggests is that the members of the psychological fraternity are espousing ideas on the basis of ill-conceived speculations. Given the fact that they appear to be so wrong, how can we trust them ever to be even half right? In this situation we are talking not about a revision of a discipline but a total dismemberment of many of its theories and conceptualizations. Thus

> On the basis of Freud's half a dozen experiences with hysterical women a construct about the female personality has been developed which is now taught in psychology classes as if it were a tested theory.[72]

Perhaps in frustration Weisstein asks: "How, in all good conscience, can clinicians and psychiatrists continue to practice?"[73] Moreover, can we generalize the psychologist's propensities concerning women to other disciplines? The elements that make psychological practitioners and theorists willing recipients of their "established facts" may be less blatantly apparent in other fields but are nonetheless as real and as pitifully damaging.

FOOTNOTES FOR CHAPTER VI

[1]Astin, *The Woman Doctorate in America,* p. 39.
[2]Patterson and Sells, "Women Dropouts from Higher Education," pp. 322-323.
[3]Juanita Kreps, *Sex in the Marketplace: American Women at Work* (Baltimore: The Johns Hopkins University Press, 1973), p. 60.
[4]Harris, "The Second Sex in Academe," p. 288.
[5]Howe, "Women and the Power to Change," p. 165.
[6]John B. Parrish, "Women, Careers and Counseling: The New Era," *Journal of the National Association for Women Deans, Administrators and Counselors* 38 (Fall 1974): 12.
[7]Ibid., pp. 12-13.
[8]The Carnegie Commission on Higher Education, *Opportunities for Women in Higher Education*, pp. 102-103.
[9]Margaret Mead and Rhoda Metraux, "Image of the Scientist Among High School Students," *Science,* 30 August 1957, p. 385.
[10]Ibid., p. 384.
[11]Ibid., p. 387.
[12]Ibid.

¹³Ibid., p. 388.

¹⁴Ibid.

¹⁵Ibid., pp. 388-389.

¹⁶Bruno Bettelheim, "The Commitment Required of a Woman Entering a Scientific Profession in Present-Day American Society," in *Women and the Scientific Professions,* eds. Jacquelyn A. Mattfeld and Carol G. Van Aken (Cambridge, Mass.: The M.I.T. Press, 1965), p. 5.

¹⁷Alice L. Dement, "What Brings and Holds Women Science Majors?" *College and University* 39 (Fall 1963): 44.

¹⁸Ibid., pp. 44-45.

¹⁹Ibid., p. 46.

²⁰Ibid., pp. 49-50.

²¹Sells, *Availability (sic) Pools as the Basis for Affirmative Action,* p. 6.

²²Nancy K. Schlossberg, "The Right to Be Wrong Is Gone: Women in Academe," *Educational Record* 55 (Fall 1974): 258.

²³Vivianne Nachmias, "Panelist," in *Women and the Scientific Professions,* eds. Jacquelyn A. Mattfeld and Carol G. Van Aken (Cambridge, Mass.: The M.I.T. Press, 1965), p. 29.

²⁴Rossi, "Barriers to the Career Choice of Engineering, Medicine, or Science Among American Women," p. 100.

²⁵Stimpson, "What Matter Mind: A Theory About the Practice of Women's Studies," p. 7.

²⁶Nadelson and Natman, "The Woman Physician," pp. 177-178.

²⁷Feldman, *Escape from the Doll's House—Women in Graduate and Professional Education,* pp. 34-35.

²⁸Nadelson and Natman, "The Woman Physician," p. 179.

²⁹Ibid., p. 182.

³⁰R. A. Hudson Rosen, "Occupational Role Innovators and Sex Role Attitudes," *Journal of Medical Education* 49 (June 1974): 554-555.

³¹Ibid.

³²Ibid., pp. 555-557.

³³Ibid., p. 560.

³⁴Patterson and Sells, "Women Dropouts from Higher Education," pp. 329-330.

³⁵Ibid., pp. 316-317.

³⁶Astin, *The Woman Doctorate in America,* p. 104.

³⁷Nadelson and Natman, "The Woman Physician," p. 180.

³⁸Susan Edmiston, "Portia Faces Life: The Trials of Law School," *Ms.* 2 (April 1974): 74.

³⁹The Carnegie Commission on Higher Education, *Opportunities for Women in Higher Education,* pp. 100-101.

⁴⁰Edmiston, "Portia Faces Life: The Trials of Law School," p. 76.

⁴¹Ibid., p. 78.

⁴²Ibid., p. 93.

⁴³Thelma Z. Lavine, "The Motive to Achieve Limited Success: The New Woman Law School Applicant," in *Women in Higher Education,* eds. Todd Furniss and Patricia Albjerg Graham (Washington, D.C.: American Council on Education, 1974), p. 189.

⁴⁴Ibid., p. 190.

⁴⁵Patterson and Sells, "Women Dropouts from Higher Education," p. 320.

⁴⁶Littleton, "The Special Validity of Women's Colleges," p. 24.

[47]Lynn White, Jr., *Educating Our Daughters*, p. 20.

[48]Bass, "The Development of Higher Education for Women in This Country," p. 287.

[49]Crockford, "The Forgotten Sex in Education," pp. 17-18.

[50]Lenore W. Harmon, "Anatomy of Career Commitment in Women," *Journal of Counseling Psychology* 17 (January 1970): 79-80.

[51]Ibid.

[52]*Report of Conference on the Undergraduate Education of Women,* pp. 7-8.

[53]Harbeson, "The New Feminism," p. 55.

[54]Cross, *College Women: A Research Description,* p. 16.

[55]Jacques Barzun, *Teacher in America* (Boston: Little, Brown and Company, 1945), p. 243.

[56]Lynn White, Jr., *Educating Our Daughters*, pp. 118-119.

[57]Jo Anne J. Trow, "Higher Education for Women," *Improving College and University Teaching* 20 (Winter 1972): 19.

[58]Conway, "Coeducation and Women's Studies: Two Approaches to the Question of Woman's Place in the Contemporary University," p. 239.

[59]Hole and Levine, *Rebirth of Feminism,* p. 181.

[60]Ibid., p. 382.

[61]Ashley Montagu, *The Natural Superiority of Women* (New York: Collier Books, 1974), p. 22.

[62]Joanne B. Lantz, *On the Position of Women in Society,* Report of the American Personnel and Guidance Association (Bethesda, Md.: ERIC Document Reproduction Service, ED 049 486, 1971), p. 2.

[63]Ibid.

[64]Eleanor Flexner, *Century of Struggle: The Woman's Rights Movement in the United States* (New York: Atheneum, 1974), pp. 23-24.

[65]Tobias, "Teaching Female Studies: Looking Back Over Three Years," pp. 258-260.

[66]Sheila Tobias and Ella Kusnetz, "For College Students: A Study of Women, Their Role and Stereotypes," *Journal of Home Economics* 64 (April 1972): 17.

[67]Weisstein, "Woman as Nigger," p. 20.

[68]Hole and Levine, *Rebirth of Feminism,* p. 182.

[69]Robinson, *Women's Studies: Courses and Programs for Higher Education,* p. 5.

[70]Weisstein, "Woman as Nigger," p. 20.

[71]Ibid., p. 22.

[72]Sheila Tobias, *New Feminism on a University Campus: From Job Equality to Female Studies* (Pittsburgh: ERIC Document Reproduction Service, ED 065 073, 1970), ҧ 5.

[73]Weisstein, "Woman as Nigger," p. 22.

Chapter VII

STRATEGIES FOR CHANGE

Whatever the curricular reforms decided upon, and whatever new curricular hybrids might ultimately emerge, it seems evident that certain innovations are inevitable. While there may be indecision as to the most appropriate curriculum, there is sufficient unanimity as to the need to approach pedagogy from a new, more humane perspective. The importance of role modeling for the young woman has only recently come to light. The need for improved counseling as an adjunct to learning will receive renewed emphasis. Finally, the need to retrain discipline-oriented faculty so that they will have a greater receptivity to the proposed innovations will become commonplace. In this chapter, greater attention will be directed to these concerns.

THE COUNSELING FUNCTION

Altering the curriculum and changing the teaching techniques will be inadequate without comcomitant supporting services. Granted that the subject content may be expunged of bias and the teaching atmosphere may be made more receptive for learning, the problems and consequences of social abuse still remain. For example, the attrition rate caused by marital and familial situations still takes its toll and will continue to do so unless the priorities of the young woman are modified so that she may be receptive to the advantages accorded her with the advent of the new modified curriculum. In other words, there must be an extensive counseling network.

The counseling function preferably should begin well before the young girl enters college. Recognizing the social abuses she is exposed to, a whole generation may be lost if counseling commences only with freshman matriculation. Many talented females who, if IQ were the sole criterion, would certainly be professional material, may drop out prematurely. Many others may be actively dissuaded from college attendance altogether as a result of negative counseling.[1] Perhaps no one stated the dangers implicit in counseling better than Margaret Mead: "Counseling based on obsolete assumptions is routine at best; at worst it is dangerous."[2] Many counselors have been educated according to the traditional beliefs; others may be uninformed regarding the new avenues available to young women. Clearly, bad counselors may be worse than no counselors at all in that the impressionable youth may be more vulnerable to their faulty and ill-considered advice given in the name and under the pretense of expertise.

The Carnegie Commission recently reported a ratio of one high school counselor for 621 students.[3] Certainly this lack of institutional demand for counselors means that the "best" people who might otherwise go into counseling may opt for the more open professions leaving the counseling services critically understaffed. For a variety of reasons, then, counseling is deficient. While we know that some counselors, especially in high schools, are uniformed concerning the opportunities opening up for women, we are also reminded that very few counselors at the college level, through perhaps no fault of their own, may have only a negligible impact on their client wards.[4] Whether this is because the college counselors are perceived of as inadequate or whether they are in fact inadequate, the results are the same. Elizabeth Friskey observed in a poll concerning the career goals of women that "only one person, a senior, mentioned she had been affected by career services."[5] Other authorities support Friskey's findings.[6]

The entire concept of counseling may have to be revised. For instance, Susan Mitchell noted that about 75 percent of academically inclined women received positive reinforcement from their mothers.[7] It follows from this that for counseling to have its intended effects on the daughters, their mothers may have to be embraced by the counseling family.[8]

Professors, given a change in their orientation, can be

168

invaluable career counselors, certainly in an ancillary capacity.[9] Because of the respect that many students have for their teachers, and the regular contact students have with them over a sustained period of time, professors are in an advantageous position to provide needed encouragement. Yet counseling is generally viewed apathetically if at all by the professoriate. Unfortunately the problem is compounded not only by the professors' inability to extend their role function but also by the students' reluctance to seek professorial advice. Arlie Hochschild sums up the problem:

> Professors are the last people most students come to with an intellectual problem, and the first people they come to when they have solved it. To expose their vulnerability or confusion is to risk being marked "mediocre" on the confidential form.[10]

Regretfully, the students' perception of the situation is frequently correct. For them to seek out a professor, trusting that their stature would not be imperiled, would be a truly dangerous assumption indeed.

At many institutions such as Princeton and Stanford there have been various petitions by women for an invigorated counseling system. Indeed, some Stanford women have suggested that there is a need for counseling within the department and that this function should be institutionalized, perhaps being assigned to a particular faculty member.[11] The defect of this solution is that there may be a personality conflict between a student and the assigned faculty counselor, or the faculty member may be out of the student's particular field of interest or unfamiliar with the student's work. Also, the faculty member thus assigned, barring a change in academic values, might be the "lowest" status member and consequently have neither the requisite knowledge nor the incentive to devote to the counseling position. Nevertheless, acknowledging all these drawbacks, recognition at least of the fact that counseling is a function that should be performed within the department is a good beginning.[12] What may be emerging is a consensus that there should be many different counselors for a student to seek out and tap. A departmental counselor may be quite effective in advising on the professional prospects of the student but may be ignorant of the extraneous factors impeding the student's academic development.[13] The nondepartmental counselor, on the other hand, while he or she may be knowledgeable concerning social problems that constitute bottlenecks to full academic maturation, may be unable to judge whether the student's difficulties are caused by a lack of innate ability. Either counselor, of course, might be prone to emphasize his or her respective background thereby getting a undimensional view of the student. Perhaps the ideal arrangement might be to have individuals in the various disciplines also trained in counseling as a part of their overall professional education.

That women need positive reinforcement is self-evident. Bernard, for example, reports that many women become academicians "by having a college-level job offered to them."[14] In other words, women seem to be particularly vulnerable to academic "drift."[15] Finding direction only through accidental association is leaving to chance the prospect of good talent going to waste. Exacerbating the problem, many women are convinced that they cannot make it professionally but if through fortuitous circumstances they do succeed, they will have strong forebodings over the life they will be obliged to lead as a result.

Finally, for the counseling function to succeed for women it must embrace men.[16] If men fail to alter their attitudes concerning a woman's fundamental right to fulfilling her own destiny, then many budding scholars will be thwarted in their attempt to realize their abilities, while those who do achieve professional status may be prevented from practicing their professions because of the harassment and hostility engendered by their male peers and mates. In either case there is unhappiness, and where one half the nation is unhappy, the other half cannot be of sound mind. Women's need of men is not based on exclusive dependence but mutual survival.

ROLE MODELS FOR WOMEN?

The role-model concept in higher education is naturally controversial. At stake is the integrity of the idea that recruitment should be based solely on faculty expertise. Yet a prior question must be pondered before the concept of role models can be fully explored: mainly, what was the rationale for giving favored treatment to those with the most expertise? If they were recruited as teachers, the presumption would be that they are the ones who are effective with students. Since few faculty members actually publish or do significant research, the teaching criterion must loom large. What then, is the measure of a good teacher? Perhaps one of the most objective standards is the end product of the professor's teaching. Specifically, where do the students go and what do they do after they leave the class? Is the professor's own established expertise necessarily the best instrument to assist these students in gaining confidence in themselves, in learning, and ultimately leading a self-fulfilling life, or must other variables be included? More germane to the present discussion, if the woman student sees a young professional woman at the head of the class, will this stimulate her to greater learning and achievement? If the answer is yes, then the criterion for basing one's utility exclusively on individual merit is necessarily faulty. For if faculty members, even those having greater demonstrated knowledge to relate, cannot excite or invigorate their students, then their knowledge has no meaning except to themselves.

If we assume that the question of how well faculty members can beneficially instruct their students is the foremost consideration, and if we see the role model as a significant factor in learning, will this not automatically and rightfully diminish the rationale behind the purely "expertise" approach to recruitment?

The role model may be defined as:

> Usually an individual rather than a group... the role model demonstrates for the individual how something is done in the technical sense.... The essential quality of the role model is that he possesses skills and displays techniques which the actor lacks (or thinks he lacks) and from whom, by observation and comparison with his own performance, the actor can learn.[17]

Accordingly, professors are positive role models to the degree

171

that they are effective with students. Yet in the case of a woman, would not common sense seem to dictate that a man professor may actually serve as a negative role model? If a woman seees a preponderance of males in engineering or medicine she may be discouraged from entering these endeavors. Similarly, when an impressionable young female sees the academic world exclusively dominated by a male professoriate, would she be incorrect to infer that she would be unwelcome as a professional within this academic circle? Moreover, the imbalance of females in college positions is taken as added confirmation of what the young woman already knows and has always seen throughout her life. Even in elementary school, while most of the teachers were female, women occupied a miniscule number of administrator-principal positions. This trend is further aggravated in high school where the young girl witnesses an ever-growing proportion of male teachers, with men occupying about 97 percent of the supervisory high school principal posts.[18]

Remembering that women in each generation seem to be as unachieving as the generation before, the question remains whether there is in fact something wrong with women or with the teacher and society at large?

Certainly if the purpose of education is meritocratic, to encourage each student to achieve to maximum potential, then it might have antimeritocratic effects if recruiting is based only on the educational credentials of the teacher. One may counter that this perpetuates an injustice on the professor—and it does. One may exclaim that to base recruiting solely on academic credentials may perpetuate an injustice on the student—and it does. The point is that the function of the teacher is to maximize student learning, rather than to have the most knowledgeable individual in the classroom as the end in itself.

People learn by being shown. Ethnic groups take pride when they see others of their kinspeople succeeding in the new society. Irishmen take pride in JFK, Jews in Einstein. They are more than points of pride; they provide convincing evidence of an open society. In this vein, Shirley Angrist stresses that:

172

> Women can more readily perceive themselves in careers
> when those around them demonstrate that having an
> occupation is an important personal commitment.
> Others serve as reference groups by showing how to
> perform in a specific occupation.[19]

The evidence in favor of role models is strong. Children who come from professional homes are more likely to be professionals themselves. While this may be partially due to the economic opportunity afforded them, the incentive model cannot be dismissed. Furthermore, various authorities concur that professional women, more often than homemakers, have come from homes where the mothers were employed.[20]

Not only was career realization greater among those women who had seen their mothers engaged in outside enterprises but, as a bonus, their own career commitment appears to have been heightened.[21] Again this adds weight to the argument that working mothers, in serving their own fulfillment needs, are simultaneously helping their children. Also, as we noted earlier, upper- and lower-class college women seem to be relatively more adventuresome in experimenting with the masculine curriculum than their middle-class sisters[22] Although we considered the negative role model for the lower-class girl regarding the inadequacy of her father as a breadwinner and the unhappiness of the mother over her situation, the lower-class environment may constitute other negative role models which may stimulate the young woman's incentive positively. For example, unlike the upper- and middle-class family which can usually afford to send all their children to college, the lower the socioeconomic background, the more likely the parents are to opt for the son's education, thus ensuring him a better future life-style than could be expected for the daughter. Recognizing the unavoidability of sibling rivalry that enjoys no class distinction, this may well spur filial resentment. Consequently the presence of sons in a lower-class family where the family is forced to choose may inadvertently act to promote awareness in the daughter.

In sum, the evidence regarding the effect of role models, both in a positive and negative capacity, is strong. Au-

thorities like Helen Astin relate that among women doctorates she surveyed:

> One-fourth of all the women reported that their mothers
> were working while they were growing up. Moreover,
> 70 percent of these working mothers were engaged in
> either professional or managerial occupations.[23]

Almguist likewise confirms in a survey that women students
who had a low career salience generally had mothers who
were engaged in nonprofit activities as opposed to the
career-salient women who were more likely to have had
career-professional mothers. Also, Theodora Patrick reaffirms that the fathers of professional daughters were perceived as encouraging them to entertain career ambitions.[24]
Understandably the perception of a beloved father who is
hostile to feminine career objectives must have a deleterious
effect despite the presence of more positive role models. The
authors of role-model behavior may indeed be underrating
the importance of the father-daughter relationship. If the
father is seen as approving of feminine professional aspirations and this perception is given practical expression in the
mother's assuming meaningful external employment, then
the female child is awarded double reinforcement in seeking
a career.

Finally, Lewis Mayhew, long before the full blossoming
of the current women's movement on campus, gave tacit recognition to the importance of role models, especially for wom-
en. He not only reaffirms the importance of sexual identification but suggests the need for the designated role model to
be positive in nature. In a somewhat different context, he
writes:

> An institution that faces young women with a faculty of
> older and somewhat disillusioned female teachers at-
> tuned to standards prevailing at the turn of the century
> denies itself the patent educational tool of possible stu-
> dent identification with faculty.[25]

The "Deviance"—"Enrichment" Hypotheses
One theory concerning the role-model concept is whether

174

women choose masculine professions out of "deviance" or "enrichment." The "deviance" hypothesis stresses that the young woman who chooses the masculine field is rejecting her traditional environment while the "enrichment" advocates retort that the young woman has received some "additional enriching experiences" from her environment that stimulated her new awareness.[26] In one interpretation the woman is acting out a form of rebellion; in the other she has been positively stimulated by additional features in her environment. Both theories are applicable and no doubt different career women are affected by their surroundings in different ways. For instance, Rossi indicates that many women who have become career-oriented have done so precisely because they find the alternative of domestic life so unappealing.[27] Almguist, in reflecting upon the "deviance" hypothesis, writes:

> Such girls are supposedly the product of negative, strained and faulty relationships in the nuclear family. For them, motherhood, marriage and family have become reference groups from which they turn away. Altogether, the results do not confirm the deviance hypothesis strongly, but neither is it totally disconfirmed.[28]

On the other hand, the "enrichment" hypothesis suggests that those young women who do not have their environment enriched through seeing their mothers engaged in meaningful professional activity are more likely to be noncareer salient.[29] The "enrichment" hypothesis not only stresses the importance of a professor working with a student, thereby adding to her environment, but also that the school should perhaps provide its young charges with meaningful work experiences since it has been found that "women who have had work experience are more likely to be interested in the serious pursuit of a career."[30]

Naturally, both theories are applicable to the career development of different women. Yet the college cannot institute the "deviance" hypothesis in the curriculum while it could do much to articulate the "enrichment" hypothesis. Thus, it may very well be the function of the college to confirm the negative judgment of the "deviant" through enriching the environment and thereby encouraging the contented young woman to question her former happiness.

The Queen Bee

There are, of course, problems with the role-model theory as there are with all conceptual frameworks. One major difficulty is the assumption that for women to succeed, they require the presence of female role models. As we know, many women have been highly successful under the traditional formula. Is such success to be equated with their having "sold out" to the male world? Are they to be vigorously incorporated within or denied membership in the feminist circle? Whatever the answer, role-model theory cannot be modified to suit the convenience of its advocates. No matter how reciprocal the hatred between the academically traditional female scholar and the new feminist, it cannot be denied that the lone woman professor, in succeeding, laid the groundwork for the success of others.[31]

In much of the professional literature, this "super nigger" has been dubbed the "Queen Bee."[32] The super nigger or Queen Bee is depicted as a success by establishment standards. With reference to women, the Queen Bee often had to succeed by occupying two full-time jobs which were contradictory: that of wife and professional. The Queen Bee's life is exemplary but it is a life of hardship wrought by the injustices of a woman's presumed and nontransferable roles. The new feminists, of course, are demanding changes in the roles that the Queen Bee has long been accustomed to accept.[33] Furthermore, it is natural to defend the system through which one succeeded.[34] In sociological terms, the Queen Bee has become coopted by the male establishment.[35] She has been sufficiently compensated so that she has become attitudinally indistinguishable from her male colleagues. Indeed, the very temperament of the Queen Bee is that of an independent loner. She truly made it against all odds with little encouragement and small initial prospects for success.

The contemporary feminist is different. Arguing from the premise that society is prejudiced, she states that the

176

prescription for change lies in collective action—a formula incomprehensible to the established life-style of the Queen Bee.[36] Hence while the Queen Bee is presumably concerned only with her own personal success, many of the contemporary feminists maintain the need for group cohesiveness.[37] Yet despite the bitter rhetoric that might ensue between the two groups, perhaps exacerbated by different generational orientations, the Queen Bee does in fact remain a role model for many women. She may not be a role model that young women would desire to emulate, but she is a model nevertheless in that she proves the feminist thesis: she is living testimony that women are men's equal and her usually lower status adds fuel to the feminist argument concerning academic discrimination. Because of the example of the Queen Bee, young women know that they have the ability to be scholars, and given the promise and hope of the modern feminists, they have good reason to believe that the academic road will not be as rough and unrewarding for them as it was for their predecessors. Each needs the other if the success of womanhood is to be assured.

Concluding Remarks on the Queen Bee

While the blanket condemnation of the Queen Bee as a negative role model is not valid, this is not to suggest that there are not professional academic women who, perhaps inadvertently, contributed to the "lowering" of a woman's self-image. Accordingly, the woman who resigns as president of a prestigious woman's college to take a vice presidency at a prestigious coeducational institution may, by the inference that people seek better posts than the ones they hold, be suggesting that it is preferable to work at the coeducational institution in a lower capacity than at the helm of a great female institution.[38] Naturally such a woman might constitute a negative role model to women at the female institution she was leaving while providing a positive role model, in her post as vice president, at her new institution. In this context, like the Queen Bee example, women may be positive role models to some and negative models to others. Likewise, the husband-wife faculty combination, the reform advocated by many feminist groups, can, from afar, provide a positive role model to the aspiring young woman. However, the young female who happens to know the couple well may observe "that the wives fulfilled the traditional role of homemaker whether or not they also had a professional job to perform."[39] Perhaps the point is not that a woman must provide a positive role model for all women but that there should be enough role models available so that any young woman can find someone to relate to positively.

RETRAINING THE MALE: FACULTY AND STUDENT

As we can now see, the problems of reeducating women are considerable. Yet any program aimed exclusively at women will be for naught if similar effort is not expended in modifying masculine attitudes as well.[40] For example, in a 1972 poll of Princeton freshmen a whopping 75 percent of those surveyed, presumably from favored backgrounds, agreed that "a woman's place is in the home."[41]

Obviously, basic attitudes about women will have to change. Otherwise, men might identify the entrance of women as symbolizing the feminization of hitherto masculine occupations. Given the connotations of entering a "feminine field," many of the best young men who otherwise might have been inclined to study a particular subject may look elsewhere. Under these circumstances, the women role models might be a positive influence for women but a negative one for men[42]. In their rush to integrate a specific field, they might find an outward exodus of males bringing about a new segregation.

For women's emancipation to be effectuated, men must be emancipated as well. Only in this way, some reflect, will men be mentally equipped to deal with women in all walks of life.[43] Similarly, Bernice Sandler reiterates that "men should realize that women are as capable as they."[44] Clearly, it is to the advantage of both sexes that this truism should be finally acknowledged. Men should realize that with the advent of a changing life-style they will have considerably

178

more time to spend with their wives. Recognizing the inevitability of earlier retirement, shorter working hours, and smaller families, it should be far more amenable for the man as well as his mate for the couple to have common interests so that their added hours together are spent in stimulating pursuits rather than outright boredom.[45]

In the following chapter we will explore the educational alternative to the rocking chair existence—lifelong learning. After an introductory section outlining the basic tenets and roots of the nontraditional philosophy, special attention will be devoted to the specific problems of the older woman, the changing structure of academe to accommodate her needs, and the overall impact that this movement must have on the regular, internal degree environment.

FOOTNOTES FOR CHAPTER VII

[1]The Carnegie Commission on Higher Education, *Opportunities for Women in Higher Education*, pp. 44-45.

[2]Elizabeth Duncan Koontz, "Counseling Women for Responsibilities," *Journal of the National Association for Women Deans, Administrators and Counselors* 34 (Fall 1970): 13.

[3]The Carnegie Commission on Higher Education, *Opportunities for Women in Higher Education*, pp. 46-47.

[4]Elizabeth A. Friskey, "College Women and Careers," *AAUP Bulletin* 60 (September 1974): 318.

[5]Ibid.

[6]Eckert, "Academic Woman Revisited," p. 481.

[7]Susan B. Mitchell and Robert T. Alciatore, "Women Doctoral Recipients Evaluate Their Training," *Educational Forum* 34 (May 1970): 534-535.

[8]Michele H. Herman and William E. Sedlacek, *Career Orientation of University and High School Women* (College Park, Md.: ERIC Document Reproduction Service, ED 074 950, 1972), p. 4.

[9]Friskey, "College Women and Careers," p. 318.

[10]Hochschild, "Inside the Clockwork of Male Careers," p. 64.

[11]Friskey, "College Women and Careers," p. 318.

[12]Evelyn A. Mayer, "Women at the University of Virginia," *Journal of the National Association for Women Deans, Administrators and Counselors* 35 (Summer 1972): 161.

[13]Lefkowitz, *Final Report on the Education and Needs of Women*, p. 6.

[14]Bernard, *Academic Women*, pp. 64-65.

[15]Friskey, "College Women and Careers," p. 319.

[16]Steinmann, Levi, and Fox, "Self-Concept of College Women Compared with Their Concept of Ideal Woman and Men's Ideal Woman," pp. 373-374.

[17]Almguist and Angrist, "Role Model Influences on College Women's Career Aspirations," pp. 264-265.

[18]McLure et al., "Sex Discrimination in School," p. 35.

[19]Angrist, "Counseling College Women About Careers," p. 495.

[20]Theodora Anne Patrick, "Personality and Family Background Characteristics of Women Who Entered Male-Dominated Professions" (Ed.D. dissertation, Teachers College, Columbia University, 1973), pp. 110-111.

[21]Kinnard White, "Social Background Variables Related to Career Commitment of Women Teachers," *Personnel and Guidance Journal* 45 (March 1967): 650-651.

[22]Dement, "What Brings and Holds Women Science Majors?" pp. 44-45.

[23]Astin, *The Woman Doctorate in America*, p. 25.

[24]Patrick, "Personality and Family Background Characteristics of Women Who Entered Male-Dominated Professions," pp. 114-114.

[25]Lewis B. Mayhew, *Colleges Today and Tomorrow* (San Francisco: Jossey-Bass, 1971), p. 137.

[26]Elizabeth M. Almguist and Shirley S. Angrist, "Career Salience and Atypicality of Occupational Choice Among College Women," *Journal of Marriage and the Family* 32 (May 1970): 242-243.

[27]Ibid.

[28]Ibid., p. 245.

[29]Ibid., pp. 246-247.

[30]Ibid. pp. 243-244.

[31]Stimpson, "What Matter Mind: A Theory About the Practice of Women's Studies," pp. 2-3.

[32]Graham Staines, Carol Tavris, and Toby Epstein Jayaratne, "The Queen Bee Syndrome," *Psychology Today* 7 (January 1974): 55.

[33]Ibid., p. 57.

[34]Ibid.

[35]Ibid., p. 55.

[36]Ibid., p. 57.

[37]Ibid., p. 58.

[38]"Ruth Adams, Head of Wellesley, Named an Officer of Dartmouth," *New York Times*, 21 January 1972, p. 24.

[39]Abby Gouldner, ed., *At Kirkland* (Clinton, N.Y.: ERIC Document Reproduction Service, ED 063 912, 1972), abstract.

[40]Lynn White, Jr., *Educating Our Daughters*, pp. 52-53.

[41]Friskey, "College Women and Careers," p. 319.

[42]Bernard, *Academic Women*, pp. 137-138.

[43]Trecker, "Woman's Place Is in the Curriculum," p. 86.

[44]Sandler, *A Feminist Approach to the Women's College*, p. 3.

[45]Calderone, "New Rules for Women," p. 279.

Chapter VIII

THE EXTERNAL DEGREE
AND THE TRADITIONAL CAMPUS

SETTING THE STAGE:
THE EMERGENCE OF THE EXTERNAL DEGREE

Spurred on by the women's movement there has been an acceleration in educational innovation most particularly in the expansion of lifelong learning and nontraditional programs. Unfortunately, many of those assorted programs listed under the external degree label have been isolated from the regular educational environment. As it has evolved, then, lifelong learning usually formed a parallel structure taking the "leftovers" of what academe had to offer.

Higher education in the magnificent splendor of the 1960s easily ignored the new nontraditional happenings burgeoning on the academic horizon. Certainly the doors to the regular academic institutions were filled to overflowing and beyond. A regular academic degree constituted the best guarantee of the good life and women were told to accommodate themselves to the traditional system or do without. Then, almost overnight, events occurred which questioned the integrity of the internal degree philosophy while providing the nontraditional movement with a new impetus. Perhaps starting with the end of the draft and the deteriorating condition of the job market, coupled with an overexpansion of facilities brought about by the zealous construction boom of the 1960s, the internal degree academies found themselves with increasing numbers of empty seats. This condition was further exacerbated by an unprecedented tuition inflation which, when combined with the shrinking job market, made the college degree singularly unattractive. Simultaneous to this new state of affairs, women as never before began to demand changes in the standard academic format.

Given the apparent vulnerability of academe plus the new muscle of the nontraditional adherents in the form of an aroused womanhood, accommodation seemed inevitable.

In order to better understand the ramifications for the internal degree structure, a glimpse into the various tenets of the nontraditional approach might be illuminating. Unhesitatingly, one of the basic underlying themes of the new learning is that "... education should be measured by what the student knows rather than how or where he learns it. ..."[1] In accordance with this notion, women suggest that they have many life experiences which should be given academic recognition, and furthermore, that they should be given formal credit if they can demonstrate that they have learned the traditional curriculum, albeit through nontraditional ways.

In the past, the traditional academic institutions have had a near monopoly on one's educational development. They governed admissions, instruction, and evaluation, and awarded the degree.[2] Thus the woman who thoroughly mastered the material on her own could not be considered professionally responsible to practice unless she undertook the specified internal degree program with its bothersome residence requirements, its daytime instruction, its high tuition costs, and a host of other encumbrances suitable for the hasty dispatch of the single young male undergraduate but constituting an all too certain veto on the career ambitions of married women.

Moreover, its advocates maintain, the nontraditional formula is more meritocratic and equal than the regular program. For under the traditional degree,

> satisfactory completion of a course results in the award of a fixed number of credits regardless of the student's level of performance. Grades vary with performance; credits do not.[3]

To the nontraditionalists, recognition of achievement should reflect that which has actually been achieved. The traditional procedures, therefore, have become thoroughly preoccupied with educational method to the virtual abandonment of educational purpose. In addition, the nontraditionalists argue that by allowing individuals to pursue knowledge in their own way and at their own speed, we are actually extending the competition to its outer limits by eliminating the financial and other extraneous considerations that have been so effectively detrimental in retarding the intellectual development of womankind.

The internal degree structure of the 1960s approached the depression precipice of the 1970s as if that system would last forever. There was no awareness of impending disaster. Accommodation was to the present, and future planning was based on current needs. Yet unplanned change, which is perhaps the most dynamic because it is uncontrollable, was imminent. Thus in the early part of the 1960s, when individuals entered the ivied towers they knew that:

> American degree patterns. . . were to be secured only by full-time study by young people (mostly men) in residence on the campus of a college or university. . . . The student must march along in step with his contemporaries through the same curriculum. . . . And, since each college had its own program, transfer between institutions was almost impossible.[4]

However by the mid-1970s, even in the absence of the nontraditional student in academe, the situation had dramatically changed. The terms "drop out" and "stop out" became part of a new educational lexicon. Without the enticement of good future jobs or the negative incentive to stay in school to avoid the draft, the young man, for whom academe was so meticulously designed, became disenchanted. Students would now leave their institutions either temporarily or permanently. They would travel endlessly and change addresses. If academic institutions did not want to lose large segments of the undergraduate male population, they would have to construct a system based on the transferability of credits. Specific requirements that discouraged transfer students from applying had to be minimized. The academic institution, although still unprepared to open its doors to older women en masse, nevertheless opened its doors slightly to new ideas. For the traditional constituency of academe started to lead nontraditional lives and did not wish to be governed by specific time requirements or arbitrary course designations. Furthermore, many youth who would have been regarded as prime internal degree material now opted for the flexibility of the external degree program.[5]

The American student clearly rebelled against the earlier straightjacket, time-confining educational system imposed by academe. Attrition rates were reaching alarming proportions.[6] The academy now had to worry not only over losing students to other institutions but losing them to the outside world.

Coupled with this change in mood was a change in technology. New audiovisual techniques added to the versatility of teaching, encouraging the encroachment of nontraditional methods upon the traditional framework. With the instructor now visible on the screen, with the availability of cassette tapes allowing the student to go over the same material repeatedly, one could well ponder the methodological integrity of the traditional approach.

Other advances in knowledge gave the continuing education movement added credibility. For the notion was commonplace until recently that adults, and hence returning women could not compete because their age made it impossible for them to learn as effectively as their children. However, by 1959 various studies started to gain the attention of the academic world. Old myths were cast away; older minds were officially reinstated. Roger DeCrow, among others, recited that:

> There is considerable evidence that adult students are equal or perhaps slightly superior to undergraduate students in learning performance.[7]

The true significance of such studies for women as well as for men was unforeseeable. It was an idea that was to lie dormant pending the outbreak of the depression in higher education and the advent of the women's movement.

The impact on women was, of course, especially important. They could raise a family under modified conditions and still entertain the prospect of a meaningful career. Also, the technological advances in life-style and the ensuing breakthroughs in medicine meant that women would be free from their household tasks and, because of the ever-increasing longevity of women, free from their husbands as well.[8] Clearly, the woman's function was fast becoming obsolete and she faced increasing years alone, and increasing hours even during her "productive" years with the spectre of little to do.

Through a combination of factors, then—the decline in regular students, the new theories on education and the availability of consciously aroused women—the stage was set for a reordering of academe.[9]

The Convergence of the Old and New

It appears inevitable that adult education and consequently adult women's education will remain subordinate to traditional undergraduate programs until conditions are finally ripe for a coalescence between the internal and external academic degree structures.[10] This convergence seems to be occurring. We saw how the traditional establishment incorporated many nontraditional approaches in a bid to retain the traditional student. The consequences of such a trend are far-reaching. Women, who were formerly denied the opportunity to pursue a degree because of their preordained life-style, will have their lives resurrected and will be judged by their biological abilities not by their socially contrived disabilities. As John Gardner so ruefully commented: "Most human societies have been beautifully organized to keep good men down."[11] He was not yet concerned about women!

While the nontraditional approach may be the salvation of the adult woman, she, in turn, may be the salvation of the adult man. For as many more men are forced to go back to school, they face conditions and injustices similar to those their womenfolk had long experienced at the hands of academe. After all, the woman was victimized by the internal degree structure not only because she was a woman but because she was an adult woman. Diane Margolis reports that, upon entering the academy, the aspiring female finds: "Professors are her own age, or worse yet, not much older than her children. She doesn't know how to deal with them, nor they her."[12] Not only have adult women pioneered change in academe that will now benefit their mates, they will also perform the function as role models for their husbands.[13] It is, for instance, certain that many men who will be forced to go back to school will be mentally unprepared for the arduous adjustment to academic life. The example of their women must provide new hope to despairing men in an ever-changing professional world.

As more and more adults enter the "traditional campus" there will emerge both a general blurring of sex distinctions and an overall abandonment of the generational divide. This will be especially true as fewer young people plan on automatic matriculation from high school to college while grown women and men opt for more and more learning.

An ominous note must be sounded and resolved if women and their adult men are to pursue their educational birthright. If the various schools are allowed to segregate the respective programs, there may emerge a caste system whereby adults are routed one way and the regular students go forward under another formula—with the consequence that the degrees earned by adults will be made separate and unequal to those of their children.[14] While this is a legitimate fear, many authorities concur in the view that the internal degree cannot maintain its current form, confronted as it is with the nontraditional onslaught. "Many educators believe, in fact, that the greatest effect of the external degree will be its influence upon the internal degree."[15] Convergence theory appears in the process of being confirmed.

THE WOMEN'S MOVEMENT AND CONTINUING EDUCATION

The debt that the academic nontraditionalists owe to the women's movement can never be underestimated. It was they who provided the constituency-muscle, with the external degree advocates providing the formula. It was the perfect marriage of two philosophies which, had they remained separated, might have floundered. The full blossoming of the external degree movement most assuredly had to await the rising consciousness of women. This was soon in coming. Susan Jacoby describes the burgeoning feelings of some East Flatbush women who, while they do not appear to sympathize with "Gloria Steinem with her streaked hair and slinky figure" nevertheless had to face "the realization that they were 'out of a job' in the same sense as a middle-aged man who is fired by his employer of 20 years."[16] Many of these women realized that they had been "negative role models" for their daughters. This is significant, for if the mothers of the girls understand that their daughters will emulate them, they may seek ways to provide the positive example so necessary for a young girl if she is to break away from her seemingly predetermined course.

Obviously, as women's liberation talks to all women, it affects each generation differently. The older may seek to instill in the younger a sense of mission and purpose that they were deprived of, while the younger generation (especially those in college) may offer renewed hope to their mothers to start life anew. The process is mutually reinforcing. Jacoby related that the mothers indicated:

> We had to fight our girls, too, until they were old enough to have some sense. They used to remind me that I got married when I was 19 and their dad and I were happy. I just told them their grandparents never finished high school and they were happy too, but it's not progress if the next generation lives in the same way. To me, that's what women's lib is all about—progress.[17]

These women have lost hope for themselves but not for their daughters. Yet in time, it remains for their educated daughters to instill in their mothers a new identity and purpose. Once these older women come to college they will in turn provide a positive role model for the college daughters of others. For they may tend to espouse the cause of the egalitarian marriage and stress the right of a woman to a career as an inalienable birthright.[18]

Clearly, the women's movement has assured the adult woman a permanent place in academe. In the forthcoming sections we will explore the options open to her as well as the recommendations that must be implemented if her academic association is to be as mutually beneficial in fact as it appears to be in theory.

One attractive alternative for women who seek renewed education but for various reasons cannot or prefer not to go to a four-year senior institution is the community college. Aside from the obvious advantages of geographical proximity and the tendency to offer courses with a greater vocational emphasis, the community college is usually appreciably less expensive than the senior college or university.[19]

Of course, the community college may cater to a different group of emerging women from the senior colleges and universities. For while many community colleges welcome and receive women who have some college background, many others attract women with "less than a high school education."[20] Moreover, many of the women students, perhaps coming from blue-collar backgrounds, have less confidence and social awareness than their sisters who return to the four-year campuses. Also, since some community colleges do considerable advertising and have special "re-entry" programs especially designed for the "hesitant" returning woman, the community college will attract those who have to be "converted" while the adult who prefers the senior college may come to the campus more often of her own volition. Certainly, since the community college provides easily available facilities at low cost, it requires less of a commitment on the part of its clients than it would of a college-bound woman who may have to travel a great distance while sustaining considerable tuition expense in a frequently hostile environment. Indeed, the fact that a college will generally be more expensive and will lack many of the supporting inducements found in the community college will mean that a college-bound woman must be prepared for greater sacrifice.

188

The point is that it is not the function of women to help the educational system but of the system to help women. Women, regardless of whether they are middle class with some college background or lower class with only a high school education, are naturally apprehensive about returning to school during their middle years. Whatever institution offers them the most comfort, no matter how ill-conceived the motive, ought to be utilized. A woman with a one-year Smith education, having a husband, son, and daughter with Ph.Ds, may be as uncomfortable and ill-suited for a local community college program as a high school drop-out would be at a major university. Once and for all the world should stop generalizing about women; programs ideal for some women may be abhorrent to others. The administration that organizes a program for returning women and believes that it will be applicable to all is guilty of the same stereotyping about women that caused their original agony.

ENTERING ACADEME—BRINGING HER PROBLEMS WITH HER

The problems for this new woman, regardless of the nature of her background, are considerable and will require sophisticated supporting services if the mental injury inflicted upon her by a prejudiced society is to be ameliorated. The kind of assistance envisaged should take into account all aspects of the woman's prior experience. Certainly any woman, or man for that matter, who has spent years in a nonstimulating environment and is suddenly catapulated into the academic world of the student will require special assistance. In a sense, she will not be suffering from an inferiority complex, for she is in fact inferior. Her lifestyle, barren of intellectual stimulation, is not conducive to the work skills required of a budding professional.[21] It is thus natural that a woman suffers a double burden: as a woman she is violating her emotional conditioning by seeking fulfillment outside the family; and as a person she is unfit in preparation to take her place among other professionals.[22] Understandably, while she wants desperately to succeed, she is wary about her ability to overcome these obstacles.[23]

189

Learning even under the best of circumstances is an arduous undertaking as documented by the massive attrition rate among traditional males. For women, then, their failure should not be measured in attrition statistics; rather, their strength is demonstrated not only by their success or return to school but in their contemplation of returning to academe. The physical burdens they must transcend before they can hope to reestablish the academic connection are formidable—financial, transportation, babysitting and other related considerations may make their academic attempts appear futile at the start. Taking cognizance of their overwhelming problems, the actual waves of women descending onto the campuses might be testimony not only to their search for a better life but also to their flight from the desperation of their present existence.

To a woman student, unlike her husband, a return to school can detonate a severe identity crisis.[24] In the past her identity had always been defined by her relationship to others; now, for perhaps the first time, she is seeking to develop a meaning for her own existence apart from her familial obligations.[25] When a man returns to school he has to master new skills; when a woman returns to school, she has to do that as well as learn to master herself.[26] This problem is manifested in many ways. Women's orientation is made difficult by the lack of specifity as to what constitutes the female role. Women, for example, have usually tended "to perceive their career in terms of what men will do, whereas men perceive their career in terms of their own needs."[27]

Various studies depict what the adult woman regards as her chief obstacles to educational advancement. Characteristically it has been found that the pressure of her familial commitments, which both she and her family regard as primary and unalterable, constitutes a very real hindrance to the furtherance of her educational objectives.[28] Following from this, she often thinks she is selfish in allotting time for herself instead of dispensing all her available energies on the family. The additional concern involving the deflection of the family's financial resources to her own needs only serves to escalate this feeling.[29] For her, education is of secondary

190

importance, to be considered only when all other family priorities have been properly resolved.[30]

A woman, regardless of her station in life, and totally unlike a man, does not resign her former obligations when she undertakes new academic commitments. At a Berkeley Women's Caucus, surveys revealed that a married woman graduate student spends approximately fifty hours a week on household obligations, and if she has children she may expect to add another ten hours to her domestic chores. Alternatively, men graduate students even with children, diverted less than ten hours a week to family assignments.[31] The important thing to note is that presumably many of these couples are newly married. The young woman may have enjoyed continuous and uninterrupted enrollment from childhood; yet she was automatically assigned the responsibility of assuming the domestic burden upon taking her marriage vows. What the reaction would be of the older and generally less liberal man, whose wife had long ago established an extensive domestic routine before wishing to embark on a new course of studies, is sadly predictable.

In her study of Lansing Community College, Hunt concurs with the findings of the Berkeley Caucus and the observations of Patricia Graham that marriage is a serious, perhaps fatal impediment to the career fulfillment of women.[32] Her study strongly supports the Berkeley thesis, especially focusing on children as an added load on the already heavily ladened shoulders of the married woman. Beverly Hunt asks:

> How much does having children affect the presence of women in college? As would be expected, women without children were more often full-time students than women with children. Forty percent of the full-time married women students did not have children, while twenty-four percent of the part-time married women students were childless.[33]

The Husband or the Child, Who Is Worse?

Like the younger woman, to the adult returnee there is no one more crucial to her future academic success than her husband.[34] Indeed, it might be better for a woman to have the enthusiastic endorsement of a husband who nevertheless expects her to also fulfill all her regular household obligations than to have a mate who begrudgingly acquiesces but then actively assists in the chores.

Unfortunately not even the most sympathetic husband may fully realize the ramifications of his wife's new academic ventures; for while the wife is away at school and the husband is performing her "natural" tasks, there will be an inevitable alteration in the husband-wife relationship.[35] Accordingly, it might be advisable for the husband to undergo counseling along with his wife, not only to ensure her academic success but in order to better safeguard their mutual happiness. Various studies repeatedly emphasize the importance of the husband for the success of the program, yet only a few seem to make allowances for involving the husband and the family in the wife's endeavors.[36]

Finally an important problem frequently unrecognized by the woman is the effect which her newly acquired education will have on her outlook and temperament. While it is important to give her emotional and intellectual encouragement as well as involve her family where necessary, she must be cautioned that she can truly be her own worst enemy. In breaking loose from the domestic shackles for the first time, she may rebound as a social isolate within her own home. Margolis relates:

> We overwork, overworry, and overbear to the annoyance of our husbands and younger fellow students. One woman I know went so far as to take her textbooks to bed with her; feeling crowded, her husband soon left.[37]

THE IMPORTANCE OF COUNSELING

By now the importance of counseling should be taken as an incontrovertible fact. Certainly, as we alluded to earlier, the deplorable lack of adequate counseling in academe may account for the excessive attrition casualties even among the traditional students. In the past, counseling was largely regarded as an incidental, ancillary activity but currently it seems to be making effective inroads particularly as a result of the female influx into academe. For the resolution of such problems as the lack of incentive or the inability to believe in one's own native ability to succeed, awaits the construction of a sophisticated counseling network if the adult is to perform up to his or her capacity or is to perform at all.

Various avenues have been explored in the recognition that nonacademic impediments are detrimental to student scholastic performance. In some cases, special academic counseling classes have been organized.[38] Essentially, while there might be variations in emphasis and design, these tend to take the form of a relaxed, orientation type of seminar where students of similar bent can meet together, and in so doing understand the universality of their seemingly unique predicament.

One of the more important attributes intrinsic to the campus counseling programs lies in their emphasis on collective therapy: the woman comes away with the realization that her problems are socially conceived and do not emanate from individual inadequacy. When a woman previously sought medical assistance in the private sector for her emotional problems, she contacted a medical practitioner on the assumption that there was something wrong with her. In the act of accepting her as a patient, the physician confirmed her judgment regarding her inadequacies. Yet the practitioner has neither the knowledge nor the inclination to correct societal abuse. Hence, only in the academic setting, where there is a strong sociological presence and women's problems are viewed in a global societal context rather than limited to the confines of the physician's offices, can she be made to understand the nature of her dilemma.

THE IMPORTANCE OF PART-TIME STUDY

Akin to the need for counseling is the importance of facilitating a part-time study arrangement; for most adults neither have the time, nor the financial resources, or perhaps the emotional resolve, to abruptly commit themselves in a full-time capacity.

To Mary Bunting, the importance of part-time study is that it not only allows the adult woman to allocate her time among conflicting demands, but also that it permits an educated woman to sustain an interest in her premarital career while simultaneously raising a family.[39] Unfortunately, few traditional disciplines recognize the importance of part-time study as a suitable vehicle for achieving a professional license.[40] Without question, the nontraditional part-time study option for all is perhaps one of the most important innovations that remains to be permanently affixed onto the reluctant academic mind.

Fortunately, the part-time debate may ultimately be decided by external exigencies; for we appear to be evolving toward a part-time learning and part-time working society. Accordingly, as we all have to share the diminishing amount of available work and suffer the dislocations wrought by new technologies, we will have to seek continued education as a means of gaining new job skills, and as an alternative to the job-oriented existence. In addition, there does not seem to be the same need or incentive for the youth of today to expedite their education as was the case in an unlimited job market. Moreover, with rapidly changing knowledge it may be inefficient for a student to spend a concentrated period of time in the classroom. Since one cannot learn what is not yet known, it may be best to spread one's educational career in juxtaposition to one's career employment pattern. Thus in medicine, physicians who train exclusively full time at the beginning of their careers soon become outmoded as changes develop. In days gone by, the information available at professional schools was sufficient for one to understand the developments in a particular area without significant reeducation. Those days seem to be over. Looked at in this light, part-time study should not be viewed as a luxury granted to women but as a future necessity for all. Indeed, if it is difficult for women to take up the books after years of family life, is it any easier for practitioners in mid-years to humble themselves to student status and learn from younger but better informed professors? In the past, full-time study was functional in that new knowledge came about slowly.[41] Today, with the rapidity of new developments, the assumption implied in full-time study—that one's life calling can be learned during one's early years—is patently false. Part-time study must begrudgingly but inevitably become the norm.

As we have seen, the women's platform subscribes to a host of educational innovations. Suggestions calling for greater attention to counseling programs and the importance of part-time study have been considered. Other frequently mentioned modifications include the need for greater weekend and evening study, block class scheduling, transferability of credits, expansion of parking facilities and the creation of an academic club for adult women. But perhaps the most frequently expressed need is for child-care accommodations.[42]

It should be emphasized that any child-care complex must be designed to take into account the multiple life-styles and cycles of the modern American woman. Hence the young female graduate student whose husband is also a budding scholar may require different hours from the older woman whose husband works full-time. Especially for the young woman, child-care facilities are important because they allow her time to engage in study alongside her graduate husband.[43] With the inclusion of this service a young woman would be spared the later expenses (such as commuting) incurred by the older homemaker while simultaneously she would be maintaining continuity in the learning process. In addition, the argument that the mind is at its greatest potential precisely when half of humanity is obliged to drop out lends further support to the cause of child care.

To institutionalize child-care service on campus it should be given the status of a fringe benefit with the same participatory rules as retirement funds for professors or medical plans for students.[44] The argument of single people, both male and female, who might maintain that they are being discriminated against in "subsidizing" a service which they may never use, may be answered by awarding a cash allowance to each faculty member in addition to regular salary, which then must be used for fringe benefits selected from a preoffered college list. Thus the single woman or man may opt to put more into the retirement program or the medical plan. The important point to emphasize is that regardless of how the equity is established, it should be taken for granted that child care is as much a basic fringe right to be subsidized by the university as any of the other more traditional but perhaps less important services.

THE WOMEN'S CENTERS: A SURVEY

In the foregoing sections we have seen that special arrangements and various supporting services are vital if the success of adult women in academe is to be assured. Now we shall illustrate the operationalization of many of these concepts in a review of the workings of the women's centers.

Certainly the potential for change that these structures portend is far-reaching, for the requirements of returning women anticipate in large measure the problems of their husbands. And as services become more available, a steadily increasing number of people of both sexes will be attracted to them. The process is cyclical and escalating.

In order to understand the importance and attraction of these centers it would be useful to understand the function they perform. In the past, when an adult woman returned to college she received considerably fewer services than her son or daughter. The center became the popular answer for redressing this imbalance and at the same time it added a new dimension, not only for the adult learner but to the campus environment. The early plight of the adult female on the college campus was captured by a visiting parent:

Last May, on parents' day, my husband and I visited our son at college. We. . . toured the library and the student union. . . . As we were leaving, I had a thought. "Harry," I asked, "You haven't shown us any classrooms—this is a school, isn't it?" "Oh, ... They're not really that important; I only spend 12 hours a week in class." I knew then that I had never really returned to college: I only napped off a small portion of that experience.[45]

Thus, what was considered "everything" to the returning adult was not even considered worth mentioning by the traditional student. The adult presence clamors for equivalent or alternative facilities to meet special requirements. The colleges and universities are beginning to comply in the form of the center. Yet these centers are needed precisely because the academic environment is so oblivious to the needs of adults. They are manifestations of an environmental deficiency: the services accorded women are miniscule not only in substance but also in size as compared to what the undergraduate has long grown accustomed to receiving.

Certainly, as presently constituted, the women's center caters to women. They are its constituency. However, women's coming of age will not automatically assume its eventual abandonment. For once any organization is established, it will seek ways to ensure its survival by branching out and creating new constituencies.[46] Since the services it performs are reasonably attractive as well as necessary for much of the population, its rapid expansion and solid future seem assured—first for women, then for adults in general, and finally for the traditional student. It is, of course, in the interest of women that the women's center becomes universal in scope, for if it is concerned exclusively with the women's role, not only will it become extinct as the aspirations of women are realized, but its clientele will be unnecessarily isolated from the mainstream of academe. Rossi sounds the warning:

> During the last 5 years there has been a mushrooming of centers for counseling and retraining older women who wish to return to professional employment. I think there is a danger that by thus institutionalizing the withdrawal-and-return pattern of college-educated women, we may reduce ever further the likelihood that women will enter the top professions.[47]

That the center's clientele is expanding is apparent. Initially the services were geared to the needs of the disenchanted middle-class housewife. Soon more and more women from different walks of life were attracted back to school because of the center. The escalating divorce rate, once the near exclusive province of the upper and upper middle classes, is now associated with all elements of the population; and the trauma of breaking with old routines and customs provides women with the added incentive to experiment with the previously unexperimentable.

The early pioneering services for women existed before the full blossoming of the women's movement. The University of Minnesota, for example, developed a plan calling for "individual counseling and information services."[48] The Minnesota program was a unique undertaking for a large university in that it sought not only to assist women in adjusting to academic life, but was an harbinger of what was to follow.

Another Center for returning women was developed at the University of Michigan. Given added impetus from alumnae financial support, it was designed to assist women who were matriculating as regular students both at the graduate and undergraduate levels.[49] As it has evolved, the Center's program on the University of Michigan campus is intricately involved in the academic life of the institution. Attached to the Office of Academic Affairs, it seeks to change university policy by making it more responsive to the particular exigencies of the woman's role. In addition to providing information and counseling, it is an "advocacy" institution attempting to champion the legitimate grievances of all women on campus.[50] As we might have anticipated, the Michigan Center's appeal has broadened. Interestingly, it has expanded not only in clientele but also in services to include scholarships, publications, research on women's education, the sponsorship of various affirmative action complaints, and the development of evening programs along with a host of other activities.[51] Jean Campbell interestingly reflects: "The Center designs its program with the changing needs of women in mind, and presumably this will determine to some extent who utilizes the Center."[52]

The aforementioned trend toward universality is incontestable.[53] Hence, at its inception, the Michigan Center was concerned primarily with the needs of middle-class adult women, but subsequently expanded to engulf many of the needs of middle-class college women as well; and today, it is moving toward an all-inclusive concern for women in general. In the future, it appears, the Center will be an umbrella institution looking after the needs of all people, regardless of age, class or sex. Reforms granted to some, if they are to have legitimacy, must eventually be shared by all.

The Center for Continuing Education of Women at the University of California at Berkeley is similar to its sister counterpart at the University of Michigan. It was organized by concerned women who recognized that the academic rules and regulations constituted a barrier to the fulfillment of women's rightful ambitions. At its conception, it was developed with the idea of assisting women from all walks of life.[54]

Still another Center devoted to the development of women was created at the New School for Social Research. A faculty was recruited on a part-time basis. Once enrolled at the Center, the student has many discretionary alternatives. She may decide, with the approval of the school, whether to go into the certificate or AB Program.[55] The certificate program is geared to the homemaker and designed to give her time to reexplore academe, and in the process to reexamine her own strengths and weaknesses. As it has evolved, the Human Relations Certificate of the New School can be transferred into 30 credits applicable toward the baccalaureate degree at the New School. Recognizing that this "competence-oriented" certificate program is expensive, it seems designed for the middle-class woman.[56]

Perhaps one of the more publicized women's Centers was developed at Radcliffe. The Radcliffe Institute was founded in 1960 under Radcliffe's president, Mary Bunting. In design and purpose, it remains different from many of the other female centers in that its overriding concern is in developing the talents of especially gifted women. Stress was placed on providing women an opportunity to expand their horizons through a carefully orchestrated guidance and fellowship program.[57] At the outset, it allocated fellowships to be awarded to gifted women whose ambitions had been blunted. Also, the Institute provided a place for the woman to work without the distractions of hubby and children. In the late 1960s the Institute expanded its activities by providing financial assistance to enable part-time women students to receive the coveted Harvard doctorate.[58] Perhaps as a way to encourage camaraderie, the women were expected to live within the Boston area so as to ensure close attachment to the Program.[59]

The Sarah Lawrence Center: A Study in Depth

The Sarah Lawrence Center offers an exemplary program for those women who desire to complete their education. Initiated in 1962, it stresses counseling and orientation courses as a prerequisite for admission into the regular degree program. At first, the students assume a part-time course load.[60] To ensure maximum success, Sarah Lawrence encourages only those faculty who have a demonstrated interest in the older woman to become instructors. In addition, to assist the student in adjusting to her new life, there is considerable use of peer counseling.[61] The results are impressive. As we shall see, women returning to college via the Sarah Lawrence route generally achieve higher averages than their traditional undergraduate counterparts.[62]

Unfortunately, the reasons for the Sarah Lawrence program's success are unique. For one thing, Sarah Lawrence has always had an institutional commitment to female education. But just as significant, the very philosophy of Sarah Lawrence, emphasizing small classes, discussion groups, and individualized work for its traditional students, is the optimum formula for the mature woman. The Sarah Lawrence community in general had every reason to want the Center to succeed since it blended so harmoniously into the existing Sarah Lawrence environment.

The mechanics of the program were designed to protect the woman from being prematurely exposed to the Sarah Lawrence community—to the detriment of all. "The Center is both a place and a program."[63] Physically it is housed in its own building where there is an informal common lounge area as well as the more standard classrooms. Upon acceptance, the women is required to complete four Center offerings. If her work is deemed satisfactory, she may then matriculate within the regular community and her Center work is credited toward her Bachelor's degree.

The typical Center student is a woman who is married to a professional or executive, has children of school age, is in her thirties, and is interested in community activities. Not surprisingly, from a financial point of view, only 15 percent of the women had to borrow in order to support their education. About half were supported by their husbands while 25 percent got assistance either from their parents or from an inheritance.[64] Given such a background, these women seem to take special pride in the prospect of being acknowledged not merely as "college material" but as "Sarah Lawrence material."[65] Characteristic of women in general, they have suffered a loss in confidence; yet their exceptional opportunity provides them with considerable incentive. The almost instant renewed pride in themselves at being associated with a quality institution is an undoubtedly important ingredient to them as well as a source of pride for their families. Women attracted to Sarah Lawrence despite the arduous nature of the program seek the challenge of the Center curriculum, whereas they may find the community college alternative not worthy of the struggle. This is another affirmation of the importance of providing diversity of programming for different women.

Women from the surrounding community who desire to apply to the Center must do so by way of the counseling service. Before coming to the interview, a woman is requested to furnish a letter describing her interests along with a transcript detailing her prior academic work. Generally about 25 percent of those who are counseled eventually seek admission to the program.[66] The requirements for admission are unusual. Prior academic performance is not necessarily a determining factor as these women have been out of school for some time and consequently their past grades may inaccurately reflect their present potential. While there is no age limit, a woman is expected to have at least the equivalent of a high school diploma and must not have been in full time attendance at another college for at least four years. Interestingly, men may also apply and are subject to the same conditions, giving added credence to the argument that programs initiated for women may include men as well.[67]

Upon acceptance, the woman is assigned a "don" who helps to plan her courses and whose relationship is considered to be that of "a faculty advisor and friend." The Center Director is the "don" for all the students but once they matriculate within the college they are assigned regular Sarah Lawrence faculty.[68]

Center classes are tailored to give the student an opportunity to acclimate herself to academic life in order to ensure the greatest possibility of success upon matriculation. Accordingly, these students are not permitted to enroll in regular college classes although regular students may take a course at the Center "if space is available."[69] Upon completion of their Center courses, students are not encouraged to return to the Center as this will tax its resources and facilities in fulfilling the primary objective of helping to acquaint a new class of incoming women with academic life.[70]

Academically, the Center students seem to do better as they progress. Approximately twice as many adult women, 44 percent, received the "A" grade in the regular curriculum as contrasted with their Center grades. Indeed, it may very well be that the adult woman is undergraded in relation to the traditional student. The regular Sarah Lawrence undergraduate is expected to do well and might in part be evaluated and behave according to that expectation, whereas the burden of proof is on the adult woman to show that she can do well both for herself and her professor.

> This study indicates that those faculty who teach at the Center do not have a double standard favoring the performance of these women. If anything, the teachers expect more of the newly returned students perhaps because they are aware of their probationary status and are assessing their ability to sustain high level work throughout their career at Sarah Lawrence.[71]

Furthermore, the attrition rate of the adult women is 22 percent as contrasted to 36 percent for the typical Sarah Lawrence student.[72]

Not unexpectedly, as these women progress their attitudes change both toward themselves, as they gain new self-respect and awareness, and toward their families. Thus while the education may make a woman happier in marriage, it may also bring her to the realization that her marriage is no longer viable. Various women have indicated the effects of their Sarah Lawrence education:

> My continued education meant continued growth which enabled me to leave a marital situation that denied my basic needs. . . . It gave me the courage for a separation which was long overdue. . . . It is ironic that the education which has so enriched my life, both my inner life and my life as a teacher, was also a factor in my marriage upheaval.[73]

In conclusion, the Sarah Lawrence program is certainly worth watching not only for what it is doing but also for its evolutionary potential. Given a sympathetic environment it is perhaps a generation ahead of most other institutions. While the present Center is still a "stepdaughter" of the institution, whose main commitment is to its undergraduates, this may change.[74] In the future the Center and adult women and men might become an intrinsic and indivisible part of the institution.

CONCLUDING REMARKS: THE NECESSITY FOR CONTINUING EDUCATION

Educational reform can help dramatically in salvaging the lives of adult women and simultaneously the aspirations of younger women. Lynn White points up the living agony for women in contempoary America:

> The chief reason for wishing to change the condition of the grandmother, however, is ethical. To be useless is not good for the soul. Many a woman in her forties turns

to bridge, chatter, shopping expeditions, aimless clubs and, in extreme cases, to alcohol to gain an illusory sense of activity. She often becomes fatuous, because life, in the form of her children, has walked out on her, leaving only a husband who is mostly at the office. At times she becomes bulbous from overeating induced by a sense of insecurity and uncertainty. She becomes timorous of all change, since change has wronged her.[75]

Women, then, need a new life if they are to have any life at all. In the past, woman's role was valued because it was important. Now, with the twentieth-century conveniences, a woman is needed primarily during the early years of her children's lives. She no longer makes the clothes or necessarily prepares the food. Cleaning the house has been made simple as a result of the latest technological devices. Educated to be equal, women are not "being treated as equals."[76] Not surprisingly, women of the upper and middle class began to trickle back to school. Initially, of course, they may not have been motivated out of a desire to increase their education but rather to escape boredom.[77] They were escaping from an unbearable existence to the only apparent alternative. The connection between women and higher education was assured. Younger college women, seeing the plight of their "mothers," slowly began to identify their future with the adult woman's present.

Women are educated to be men until they marry into womanhood whereupon, in the consummation of their vows, they assume the lower position of wife. "In the United States, social and occupational identities are closely related; a person is what he or she does."[78] Since Americans equate social standing with professional position and financial compensation, the married woman's fate appears to be predetermined downward.[79]

For too long, work in America has been viewed almost exclusively in terms of financial reward. Yet as our work week shortens and jobs become fewer, men will be faced with the sudden "re-realization" that people also work to work as well as work for money. Marnie Clarke observes:

Work allows us to meet people and make friends, and is a major determinant of our social status. Moreover, work contributes to our self esteem, and by providing us with socially useful and challenging tasks, it fosters a sense of self-fulfillment.[80]

In various studies, adult women have confirmed the non-monetary satisfaction in acquiring an education: "They were interested in goals like finding stimulation, enlarging their own interests and pleasures. . . ."[81] This is not meant to detract from the fact that as of the early 1970s "nearly half were working because of pressing economic need," but to emphasize that dignity is as important as financial remuneration although it has too often been relegated to a lower status as an intangible.[82] In America, it seems, that which is not quantifiable is ignored, no matter how relevant it might otherwise be.

The problem faced by a woman in her role as mother is partially that she is not rewarded financially and thus is degraded socially. Accordingly, Joan Huber writes that "volunteer work may be loosely defined as white collar busy work that no one cares enough to pay for."[83] As we face the spectre of fewer productive jobs in the future, and since prestige is accorded through monetary recognition, it might be wise to pay adults to attend college. In this way society, through its individual members, will enhance itself intellectually. Money will be tied to intellectual accomplishment, and the status of the individual adult woman and man will rise along with the status of academe in general.

FOOTNOTES FOR CHAPTER VIII

[1]Patricia K. Cross and John R. Valley, "Introduction," in *Planning Non-Traditional Programs,* eds. Patricia K. Cross and John R. Valley (San Francisco: Jossey-Bass, 1974), p. 1.
[2]Cyril O. Houle, *The External Degree* (San Francisco: Jossey-Bass, 1973), p. 19.
[3]Jonathan Warren, "Awarding Credit," in *Planning Non-Traditional Programs,* eds. Patricia K. Cross and John R. Valley (San Francisco: Jossey-Bass, 1974), p. 126.

[4]Houle, *The External Degree*, p. 5.

[5]Ibid., p. 60.

[6]Ibid., p. 63.

[7]Ibid., p. 159.

[8]Hazel Markus, *Continuing Education for Women: Factors Influencing a Return to School and the School Experience* (Bethesda, Md.: ERIC Document Reproduction Service, ED 078 296, April 1973), p. 2.

[9]Elizabeth Stone, "Women's Programs Grow Up," *Change* 7 (November 1975): 17.

[10]*American Women, Report of the President's Commission on the Status of Women* (Washington, D.C.: Government Printing Office, 1963), p. 13.

[11]Gardner, *Excellence—Can We Be Equal and Excellent Too?* p. 3.

[12]Diane Rothbard Margolis, "A Fair Return? Back to College at Middle Age?" *Change* 6 (October 1974): 35.

[13]Susan Jacoby, "What Do I Do for the Next 20 Years?" *New York Times*, 17 June 1973, sec. 6, pp. 42-43.

[14]Houle, *The External Degree*, p. 130.

[15]Ibid., p. 17.

[16]Jacoby, "What Do I Do for the Next 20 Years?" p. 11.

[17]Ibid., p. 49.

[18]Markus, *Continuing Education for Women: Factors Influencing a Return to School and the School Experience*, p. 27.

[19]Beverly English Hunt, "Characteristics, Perceptions and Experiences of Married Women Students at Lansing Community College" (Ed.D. dissertation, Michigan State University, 1966), p. 3.

[20]Beatrice Taines, "Older Women, Newer Students," *Community and Junior College Journal* 44 (August/September 1973): 17.

[21]Carole LeFevere, "The Mature Woman as Graduate Student," *School Review* 80 (February 1972): 281.

[22]Elizabeth Hansot, "A 'Second-Chance' Program for Women," *Change* 5 (February 1973): 49-51.

[23]*Graduate Education for Women: The Radcliffe Ph.D.*, p. 67.

[24]George E. Letchworth, "Women Who Return to College: An Identity-Integrity Approach," *Journal of College Student Personnel* 2 (March 1970): 103.

[25]Elizabeth Douvan, "Internal Barriers to Achievement in Woman—An Introduction," in *Women on Campus: 1970 a Symposium,* ed. Louise G. Cain, Symposium Chairman (Ann Arbor, Mich.: The University of Michigan Center for the Continuing Education for Women, 14 October 1970), p. 2.

[26]Ibid.

[27]Walter R. Gove and Jeanette F. Tudor, "Adult Sex Roles and Mental Illness," *American Journ·l of Sociology* 78 (January 1975): 815-816.

[28]Letchworth, "Women Who Return to College: An Identity-Integrity Approach," p. 105.

[29]Ruth Helm Osborn, "Developing New Horizons for Women," *Adult Leadership* 19 (April 1971): 351.

[30]Patricia Thom, Anne Ironside, and Eileen Hendry, "The Women's Resources Centre—An Educational Model for Counselling Women," *Adult Leadership* 24 (December 1975): 129.

[31]Patterson and Sells, "Women Dropouts from Higher Education," p. 87.

[32]Patricia Albjerg Graham, "Women in Academe," in *The Professional*

Woman, ed. Athena Theodore (Cambridge, Mass.: Schenkman Publishing Company, 1971), p. 729; Hunt, "Characteristics, Perceptions and Experiences of Married Women Students at Lansing Community College," pp. 50-51.

[33]Hunt, "Characteristics, Perceptions and Experiences of Married Women Students at Lansing Community College," pp. 50-51.

[34]Markus, *Continuing Education for Women: Factors Influencing a Return to School and the School Experience,* p. 5.

[35]Marnie A. Clarke, "Transitional Women: Implications for Adult Educators," *Adult Leadership* 24 (December 1975): 126.

[36]H. Greenberg et al., "Personality and Attitudinal Differences Between Employed and Unemployed Married Women," *Journal of Social Psychology* 53 (February 1961): 91-92.

[37]Margolis, "A Fair Return? Back to College at Middle Age?" p. 36.

[38]Britt Sandlund, "Adult Education of Women in Sweden," *Improving College and University Teaching* 20 (Winter 1972): 64.

[39]Jean W. Campbell, "Women Drop Back In: Educational Innovation in the Sixties," in *Academic Women on the Move,* eds. Alice Rossi and Ann Calderwood (New York: Russell Sage Foundation, 1973), p. 94.

[40]The Carnegie Commission on Higher Education, *Opportunities for Women in Higher Education,* p. 158.

[41]Mary Bunting, "A Huge Waste: Educated Womenpower," *New York Times,* 7 May 1961, sec. 6, p. 23.

[42]Kathryn L. Mulligan, *A Question of Opportunity: Women and Continuing Education* (Washington, D.C.: ERIC Document Reproduction Service, ED 081 323, March 1973), p. 6.

[43]Kathryn F. Clarenbach, "Can Continuing Education Adapt," *AAUW Journal* 63 (January 1970): 63-64.

[44]Beverly Schmalzried, "Day Care Service for Children of Campus Employees," in *Women in Higher Education,* eds. Todd Furniss and Patricia Albjerg Graham (Washington, D.C.: American Council on Education, 1974), p. 140.

[45]Margolis, "A Fair Return? Back to School at Middle Age?" p. 37.

[46]Philip Selznick, *TVA and the Grass Roots: A Study in the Sociology of Formal Organization* (New York: Harper Torchbooks, 1966), pp. 230-238, 259-264.

[47]Rossi, "Women in Science: Why So Few?" p. 1199.

[48]Jean A. Wells and Harriet C. Magruder, "Education Programs for Mature Women," *Education Digest* 37 (January 1972): 43.

[49]Campbell, "Women Drop Back In: Educational Innovation in the Sixties," p. 98.

[50]Ibid., p. 104.

[51]Jean W. Campbell, "The Nontraditional Student in Academe," in *Women in Higher Education,* eds. Todd Furniss and Patricia Albjerg Graham (Washington, D.C.: American Council on Education, 1974), pp. 194-195.

[52]Campbell, "Women Drop Back In: Educational Innovation in the Sixties," p. 105.

[53]Campbell, "The Nontraditional Student in Academe," pp. 196, 198.

[54]Barbara Wilms, "Getting at the Women's Market in Higher Ed," *College Management* 8 (August/September 1973): 32-33.

[55]Hansot, "A 'Second-Chance' Program for Women," pp. 49-51.

[56]Ibid.

[57]Constance Smith, "The Radcliffe Institute," *Improving College and University Teaching* 20 (Winter 1972): 42-43.

[58]Angela Stent, "The Radcliffe Institute: Is There Life After Birth?" *Change* 7 (September 1975): 13.

[59]Ibid., pp. 14-15.

[60]Wells and Magruder, "Education Programs for Mature Women," p. 44.

[61]Mulligan, *A Question of Opportunity: Women and Continuing Education*, p. 16.

[62]Ibid., p. 17.

[63]Melissa Lewis Richter and Jane Banks Whipple, *A Revolution in the Education of Women—Ten Years of Continuing Education at Sarah Lawrence College* Bronxville, N.Y.: Sarah Lawrence College, Center for Continuing Education and Community Studies, 1972), p. 12.

[64]Ibid., pp. 32-33.

[65]Ibid., p. 13.

[66]Ibid., pp. 18-20.

[67]Ibid., pp. 20-21.

[68]Ibid., p. 24.

[69]Ibid., pp. 26-27.

[70]Ibid., p. 28.

[71]Ibid., p. 36.

[72]Ibid., p. 39.

[73]Ibid., p. 49.

[74]Ibid., pp. 51-52.

[75]Lynn White, Jr., *Educating Our Daughters*, pp. 113-114.

[76]Gove and Tudor, "Adult Sex Roles and Mental Illness," p. 816.

[77]Letchworth, "Women Who Return to College: An Identity-Integrity Approach," p. 104.

[78]Joan Huber, "From Sugar and Spice to Professor," in *Academic Women on the Move*, eds. Alice S. Rossi and Ann Calderwood (New York: Russell Sage Foundation, 1973), p. 125.

[79]Ibid.

[80]Clarke, "Transitional Women: Implications for Adult Educators," p. 125.

[81]Markus, *Continuing Education for Women: Factors Influencing a Return to School and the School Experience*, p. 10.

[82]Mulligan, *A Question of Opportunity: Women and Continuing Education*, p. 4.

[83]Huber, "From Sugar and Spice to Professor," pp. 131-132.

PART THREE

THE IMMINENCE OF CHANGE

Chapter IX

AFFIRMATIVE ACTION AND THE ACADEMIC POWER STRUCTURE

We have repeatedly seen throughout this discussion the rampant discrimination inflicted on women by academe. Recognizing the intensity and universality of such abuse, it is dubious whether the various institutions can or will reform themselves without the external imposition of a remedy. President Martha Peterson, formerly of Barnard college, emphasized that the

> higher education community seemed unable to recognize and to take action in correcting injustices until forced to do so.... The disgrace of "affirmative action" is that HEW had to get into it at all.[2]

While Peterson as an academician may not relish the prospect of the government superimposing its will on the university campus, as a woman she sees little alternative if the grievances perpetrated against her sex are to be finally resolved.[3] Certainly the various agencies of academe that might have worked to eliminate sex discrimination are in fact part of the problem. The grievance procedures as constituted have been organized to air the complaints of males within the establishment; women, as second class citizens, have no internal appellate court sympathetic to their cause.

Another problem indicating the need for external restraints is that it is an extremely arduous task for the lone woman either to claim or to prove that she has been the victim of discriminatory policy.[4] In addition, those women who "made it" or regard themselves as "making it" may view their own positions as imperiled by the person who raises

211

her sex as an issue of contention.[5] To make matters still worse, if the faculty woman is married to a faculty member, he, too, may be ostracized for the actions of his wife.[6] For all of these reasons it is clear that a woman neither has the means to prove discrimination nor should she be expected singly to endure the emotional upheaval that such a charge would inevitably entail. Rather, only an outside agency related to the government has both the ability to investigate and the power to sanction. To the feminist complainants, only by placing governmentally inspired guidelines on the university and by actively appraising university behavior in light of particular circumstances can the wrongs previously committed be finally redressed.

THE IDEA OF MERIT

So much controversy centers around the notion that the new affirmative action guidelines constitute a frontal assault on the sanctity of the merit standard that it might be useful in this section to consider the affirmative action dialogue within the context of the meritocratic system.

Nepotism and Merit

We know that rules and regulations once promulgated may perpetuate themselves out of inertia. A carefully conceived regulation may become an impediment over time if it is not modified to reflect changing conditions. Accordingly, anti-nepotism rules at the turn of the century were considered necessary to prevent the public state universities from becoming repositories for patronage positions.[7] Yet although public officialdom did not see fit to use the university as its own private employment preserve, regulations with no redeeming social value remained, thereby frustrating feminine ambitions and talents. It is at least suspicious that despite the obvious inconsistency between intent and deed of nepotism regulations, it took the women's movement to reform what should have atrophied years before. Perhaps Lilli Hornig hints at the possible explanation:

212

> The reason why affirmative action programs are so bitterly criticized is precisely that when equal opportunity is granted to all, those who have hitherto been privileged will have to give up some of what they regard as their natural prerogatives.[8]

Viewed in this manner, it is not surprising that the academic establishment was seemingly so negligent and unresponsive in changing such outworn procedures. For although these rules were dysfunctional with respect to seeking the best available talent, they were functional in the enhancement and perpetuation of the male's career prospects. The university could get women to work as faculty members at an exceedingly low rate, and perform tasks that the male world would find onerous. Moreover, since the woman may be deprived of a meaningful outlet for her energies, she might devote her excess energy to the success of her professor-husband who becomes in fact an "overachiever"—at the cost of her own under-fulfillment.

Upon reflection, it appears that despite affirmative action's popularization as anti-meritocratic, the reverse may actually be the case. Sandler relates:

> Academic standards, contrary to myth, are likely to increase as a result of affirmative action. Despite claims of a glorious objective merit system, academic judgments have too often been intuitive and subjective. Now, instead of being able to justify a candidate merely by saying "He's a well known and respected scholar," department heads will now have to develop specific objective criteria and be able to demonstrate that the candidate is indeed the very best person recruited from the largest pool possible.[9]

Publishing and Merit

It is self-evident that the system whereby we evaluate the publishing history of an individual to assess merit and future potential is blatantly discriminatory against women. Recognizing women's unique life cycle, where they must devote an excessive amount of time to childrearing, which will not be repeated later, their future accomplishments cannot be measured by their past inactivity. Therefore while a man's publishing record may be consistent, reflecting the relative harmony between his work and family activities, to measure a woman by a man's life-style is as irrelevant as it is unfair. In addition, as a result of having arrived on the academic scene later, and because of her poorer bargaining position (especially caused by her lack of geographical mobility if she is married), she must endure an excessive teaching load which further handicaps her in the research competition.[10]

It is beyond question that the publishing index is generally biased. Yet perhaps one of the greatest contributions of the women's movement on campus is that it will oblige academe to reexamine the very tenets of the publishing mystique. For example, how many men actually publish? Of those who do, how many make a meaningful or even minor contribution in the search for knowledge? Given the fact that the art of research and writing a manuscript is time consuming, time which could be better spent teaching and counseling, we may speculate whether the publishing idol is dysfunctional to the cause of learning. How many young men and women of considerable talent were lost because of uninspiring and unconcerned teachers who were busy writing manuscripts to enhance their curriculum vitae?

The argument can at least be toyed with that if men have been socialized to pursue solitary scholarship, remembering however that few people have the innate ability to make a meaningful contribution to their field, then men may be dysfunctional to academic life altogether. Temperament may be a question of socialization; genius is not. Alternatively, women, we will recall, have been conditioned to be people-oriented.[11] In other words, they have been temperamentally conditioned to be superior teachers. Since the function of most academic men cannot be scholarship, as few men actually produce, then by default they should be teaching—if they are to perform any role at all.

That publishing as it is now practiced has little to do with good teaching, or with extending the realm of knowledge, or as a uniform measure of promotion, is obvious. Abramson reflects:

> If good teaching and good research went hand in hand, one would expect good research to be rewarded by both more research opportunity and more teaching opportunity. Instead, assignment to teaching is treated as a form of punishment. . . .
>
> The second crack in the rationale is in the nature of publication itself. Ideally, publication means publication of research of good quality. "Deans can't read, . . . they can only count."
>
> A third crack is the failure of institutions to apply the publication yardstick uniformly. . . . .Why is it that there are so many men who have not published and who are enjoying these rewards.[12]

The prevalence of the publishing mystique has in effect preempted academe from searching for a more meaningful measure by which to evaluate performance. This luxury will soon pass as women, with governmental license, demand that the university become accountable for its actions.[13] Tenure can no longer be based on the fiction of publishing or publishing potential without showing why publishing is valuable and before assuring that the publishing formula is universally applied. Tenure, as presently conceived, is not meritocratic because it is not arrived at through an objectively proven merit procedure.

Recognizing the determination of women's groups, and the vulnerability of institutions to governmental pressure, dramatic innovation appears imminent. Cheit reflected: "What is surprising is how quickly things changed, and with what inevitability the new order of change has been accepted."[14] Clearly, through an accident of favorable circumstances, the women's movement has peaked precisely at the lowest ebb of university resistance.

THE PHILOSOPHY OF AFFIRMATIVE ACTION:
AN OVERVIEW

Affirmative action is a philosophy conceived in desperation and promulgated in hope. It is a response to the ceaselessly failing commitment of academe to seek any

215

meaningful changes in the deeply entrenched pattern of discrimination, and a recognition that only through some external regulatory authority can this condition be rectified.

Perhaps no other concept has caused such heated controversy and lingering bitterness as these new government-inspired policies. The ensuing polarization that developed was neither accidental nor avoidable. For affirmative action principles, if carried to the fullest extent, could radically alter the world of academe as it has come to be known. Thus, the bitterness stems from a recognition that this is a policy with the requisite muscle to implement its stated aims. The hostility it has engendered is not symbolic, but real and formidable.

Affirmative action is no one program but rather a series of policies designed to eradicate the discriminatory tendencies in the academy.[15] If a core affirmative action policy could be identified it might embrace the following guidelines: (a) that every department and division of the academy should establish goals in the recruitment of women; (b) that all possible sources should be explored to contact all eligible women who might be interested in recruitment; (c) that a general timetable for the realization of aspired goals should be proposed allowing for modest deviations caused by unforeseen circumstances; (d) that eligibility be redefined to take into account the function to be performed. Accordingly, if the assignment is primarily a teaching position, then scholarship should be deemphasized and (e) that people should be judged on the basis of future potential, not only on past performance. This is essential because the rationale for judging people on the basis of past performance is not to reward past performance so much as it is to anticipate future productivity. However, as we saw, because of their obligations during the child-rearing years, women necessarily have a poor scholarly record when compared to male professionals. Yet the assumption in hiring the man over the woman is that the woman will continue to be childbearing—which is clearly erroneous. If the academy is truly sincere in its meritocratic pretensions, in seeking to hire the best available candidates it may have to discard aspects of one's prior record as misleading as it relates to future promise.

The mainstay of affirmative action policy rests on the notion of "goals." To Stanley Pottinger, one of the architects of the present policy, goals should not be construed as quotas.[16] To him, goals are something positive—an ideal to be strived for, while quotas are negative—an objective which must be attained. In the search for greater equity, affirmative action does not require or suggest that women be arbitrarily selected in preference to their male competitors:

> Affirmative action does require, however, that any standards or criteria which have had the effect of excluding women and minorities be eliminated unless such criteria are conditions of successful performance in the particular position involved.[17]

This then, might very well be the heart and muscle of the affirmative action policy: to make academe redefine job recruitment to better reflect the nature of the job to be performed. If the position calls for teaching, the question is what constitutes a good teacher and whose background is truly superior in the context of that reexamination? Academe will no longer be able to espouse one goal (teaching) but practice another (research) to the detriment of both. If they hire for research they must hire the best researcher based both on past performance and future promise. Therefore, if a male and female are competing for the same research assignment and the male has two books to the female's one, the female might still be the superior intellectual candidate when it is considered that the woman had to endure many extra hardships such as childbearing which she will not have to undergo in the future.

In sum, affirmative action has at least two simultaneous jobs: to end discrimination and to redress the wrongs academic policies have fostered. To effect its goals it is not enough to show good faith in allowing all groups to compete equally for all positions. Institutions must evince a policy that demonstrates that they are actively engaged in seeking to correct the biased imbalance through actively seeking out women who are equal and qualified to fill a particular vacancy.[18] In this context, affirmative action can be construed as meritocratic in (a) making employers widen their scope of

217

candidates to include all truly qualified people; (b) making the employers define precisely what the job entails and basing "qualifiability" on that standard only.

There are, naturally, many other dimensions to the affirmative action policy. For example, by suggesting goals and requiring good faith performance, the government is forcing the institution to terminate its decentralized, often covert operations in favor of public scrutiny.[19] People who know that the manner in which they reach their decision will become part of the public record may, under that public eye, reach different decisions than if they believed that their actions could be shrouded in the cloak of professional secrecy. Moreover, excessive decentralization must inevitably cause duplication of services which could be avoided if there were greater publicity and definition of responsibility.

One problem with the critics of affirmative action is that while they recognize the deficiency in the academic hiring and promotion process, they can come up with no meaningful alternative. Instead of complaining what is wrong with the policy, it might be more advantageous to see what is right with it:

> Several years ago the postmaster of a Southern city said he just didn't know how he could possibly comply with the equal opportunities requirements without "discrimination in reverse." The equal opportunity officer, who was black, simply said: "Try, Mr. Postmaster, to use as much ingenuity in getting us in as you have used in keeping us out."[20]

And not to be overlooked is that colleges and universities are not isolated from society. They derive overwhelming support from governmental assistance which emanates from the tax monies of working women. Should these women be required to subsidize a system that discriminates against them?[21]

Alternatively, the arguments against affirmative action are also based on meritocratic principles; chief among them is that recruitment and promotion will be carried out on the vagaries of group membership, not individual accomplishment.[22] The detractors of affirmative action maintain that it is in fact a thinly veiled quota system:

> HEW knows that morally its case is lost if it involves a quota system on the barbaric notion that we can atone for past injustices toward innocent victims by present injustices to innocent victims.[23]

Sidney Hook derides the government's contention that goals are different from quotas because the figures strived for need not be met as long as a good faith effort is made. Yet, "How does this differ from saying, 'We don't demand that the quotas actually be filled or reached, only that you honestly try.'"[24] Moreover, from a practical perspective there is probably a dearth of qualified women.[25] Certainly, due to this lack of definitiveness as to what constitutes good faith, would not the practical consequence be the hiring of some incompetent women? In addition, Hook cites a government edict as saying:

> Make certain worker specifications have been validated on job-performance related criteria. Neither their minority or female employees should be required to possess higher qualifications than those of the lowest qualified incumbent.[26]

Consequently as hiring standards have progressively risen especially in the buyer's market of the 1970s, colleges are obliged to recruit individuals who compare favorably with faculty members who were hired when standards were considerably lower. Is our definition of "qualified" to be broadened to include the lowest performer? Hook retorts that: "What the guidelines should have stressed is that current standards of qualification and promotion, whatever they are, should be applied without any discrimination."[27]

Unfortunately, in academe a person's qualifications may not be entirely relevant to the functions to be performed. Thus, in reassessing the recruitment standard, our goal should be based on how well faculty members perform their assigned functions. If women can help students by virtue of the fact that they are women, and if excessive numbers of men do serve as negative role models, should this not be taken into consideration? Some women, who by all "objective" criteria are not equal to some of their male counterparts, may still be superior in the performance of their task—in salvaging highly talented women students who might otherwise be lost to the outside world. Indeed, the whole purpose of looking at qualifications is not as an end in itself, although it often is confused with the end. Qualified people are supposed to perform better. Individuals who have more native intelligence should not be hired for that innate ability, for if they cannot transfer knowledge their ability is meaningless to others and has relevance only for themselves. The question remains, should individuals be hired for what they have or for what they can do with what they have? Viewed in this way, the meritocratic formula may be enhanced even by hiring women who may actually have less intrinsic ability because they may nevertheless make a greater contribution to the coming generation of students.

In any new program there are defects. Can we balance the rights of one innocent male generation against the rights of endless generations of still unborn women? The problem with affirmative action is that it involves the rights of innocent parties. In some feminist writings there is talk of retribution against the male world. Unfortunately, the male establishment, which helped to perpetuate the abuses, will go unpunished, and it is the sons of the feminists who will bear the brunt of prior discrimination. All of male society should pay the price through higher taxes and other sacrifices, and certainly the blow should not fall on the innocent albeit powerless group who happen to be young males. When we balance the rights of one generation against many generations it is clear that the male's rights are dwarfed in comparison. But righting a wrong through a smaller wrong is not the answer. We should do what is right in a manner that is right. It is right that women should receive parity and it is right that the whole of society should bear the cost. Women today are receiving their just due not because they have justice on their side (their cause was always just), but because they have acquired power. Justice should not be based on power but reason. Power is ephemeral; those who have it today will lose it tomorrow and their reforms as well. Wrongs righted in wrong ways rest on an unstable foundation. The ends, no matter how noble, should not be used to justify any means if better, more equitable means are available.

The probable changes envisioned amount to nothing less than a revolution. Recruitment efforts will be public; a central office will dispense all information concerning the pool of candidates and the availability of positions. The department, because it will no longer hold exclusive sway over the employment-promotion process, will diminish in importance with the demise of its powers. Centralized recruitment will become the norm, taking into account the true needs of the school rather than the contrived whims of a particular department. There will be more faculty sought on an interdisciplinary basis, as those who do the hiring will have a campus-wide, not departmentally confined, perspective. Since it is one of the common axioms that those who hire can also fire, the accountability process will become more public and more centralized. Faculty members, too, realizing that their future livelihoods and careers will be evaluated by "nonspecialists," will become more interdisciplinary. No longer will departmental members be able to hide behind the cloak of expertise as a cover for their own ignorance.

The affirmative action movement is in large measure an accountability movement. People will be held responsible for what they do by objective, predetermined measures of performance. Inevitably the values and prestige of teaching will rise as the myth of the scholarship standard is laid bare. The institution of tenure does not appear to be imperiled by the women's movement except in the way it is practiced.

In conclusion, women have most to gain in the construction of a truly meritocratic order, for in the final analysis, it is not compensatory measures that will guarantee them a permanent place under the academic sun but a change in procedures that solidifies equality of opportunity as the immutable standard. The common phrase "let the best man

221

win" has been taken to literally mean just that. While the "best man" has not always won, women will change the system to "let the best person win," and in changing it will ensure that the best person does in fact win. In opening up the system they will guarantee favors for none. The only males who have anything to fear are those who have reason to fear.

FOOTNOTES FOR CHAPTER IX

[1]This section is intended as an overview of some of the more pronounced issues evolving around the affirmative action dialogue. Affirmative action was selected for scrutiny because it, perhaps more than any other formula on the contemporary horizon, represents the force for greatest academic change.

[2]The Carnegie Commission on Higher Education, *Opportunities for Women in Higher Education*, pp. 135-136.

[3]Martha E. Peterson, "Women, Autonomy, and Accountability in Higher Education," in *Women in Higher Education,* eds. Todd Furniss and Patricia Albjerg Graham (Washington, D.C.: American Council on Education, 1974), p. 9.

[4]Abramson, *The Invisible Woman: Discrimination in the Academic Profession,* p. 208.

[5]Ibid., pp. 111-112.

[6]Ibid., pp. 106-107.

[7]Malcolm Moos and Francis E. Rourke, *The Campus and the State* (Baltimore: The Johns Hopkins University Press, 1959), p. 149.

[8]Lilli S. Hornig, *Affirmative Action Through Affirmative Attitudes* (Albany, N.Y.: ERIC Document Reproduction Service, ED 076 091, November 1972), p. 3.

[9]Bernice Sandler, "Discrimination Is Immoral, Illegal and, Offenders Find, Costly," *College and University Business* 56 (February 1974): 29.

[10]Hornig, *Affirmative Action Through Affirmative Attitudes,* pp. 8-9.

[11]Jencks and Riesman, *The Academic Revolution,* pp. 299-300.

[12]Abramson, *The Invisible Woman: Discrimination in the Academic Profession,* pp. 71-72.

[13]Sylvia Roberts, *Equality of Opportunity in Higher Education—The Impact of Contract Compliance and the Equal Rights Amendment* (Washington, D.C.: ERIC Document Reproduction Service, ED 074 920, 15 January 1973), pp. 28-29.

[14]Earl F. Cheit, "What Price Accountability?" *Change* 7 (November 1975): 30.

[15]The Carnegie Commission on Higher Education, *Opportunities for Women in Higher Education,* pp. 148-149.

[16]Stanley J. Pottinger, *Statement on Guidelines for Application of Executive Order 11246 to Higher Education Institutions Receiving Federal Funds* (Washington, D.C.: ERIC Document Reproduction Serivce, ED 069 225, 4 October 1972), p. 1.

[17]Ibid., p. 3.

222

[18]Stanley J. Pottinger, *Affirmative Action and Faculty Policy* (New Orleans: ERIC Document Reproduction Service, ED 062 929, 5 May 1972), pp. 9-10.

[19]Ibid., pp. 18-19.

[20]Ibid., p. 23.

[21]Ibid., p. 8.

[22]Paul Seabury, "The Idea of Merit," *Commentary* 54 (December 1972): 44.

[23]Sydney Hook, "Semantic Evasions," *College and University Journal* 2 (September 1972): 16.

[24]Ibid., p. 17.

[25]Ibid., pp. 17-18.

[26]Ibid.

[27]Ibid.

Chapter X

CONCLUSION:
WOMEN IN A CHANGING AMERICA

Until the last decade, it was largely assumed by the dominant culture that all of womankind, regardless of educational background, could be happy performing the same role—that of housewife. More specifically, a middle-class woman would typically spend four years in college, preferably majoring in education, get married and teach at the local secondary school whenever family conditions permitted. Yet changing times were fast diminishing even this life-style, thereby contributing to the radicalization of women. For as men began encroaching upon the secondary school teaching profession, and with the concomitant decline in the need for teachers caused by planned parenthood, it became apparent that women were losing their tenuous hold on their last remaining vocational opportunities. Women, then, merely to retain some semblance of the status quo, had to acquire a new militancy. The figures bear grim testimony to the trends. In 1950, 57 percent of the nation's secondary school teachers were women. Fifteen years later the percentage of women teachers plummeted to 46 percent. Masculine infiltration was equally dramatic in secondary school administration. For example, in 1928, women were 55 percent of the nation's principals but by 1968 it was estimated that they occupied only 22 percent of the principal positions.[1] Concurrently, the schools of education were producing teachers at a rate well in excess of projected needs. These developments would not be so appalling if women were able to find alternative outlets for their energies. However, for the middle-class woman the educational profession represented the ultimate rationale through which she could justify her college education in intellectual and financial terms as well being able to look forward to a career after her family had grown. Now, it appeared, the newly educated woman, the most

224

sophisticated in history, was faced with the prospect of being limited to the home and any voluntary activities that she might beg to undertake. It might be a modest understatement to assert that if there were no secondary education profession, it would have had to have been invented. For too long the role of secondary education was viewed exclusively as that of socializing a new generation of youngsters to take their part in the American mainstream. All too often it was forgotten that the same profession was simultaneously performing a vital "tranquilizing" (latent) function for adult females. It gave meaning to what otherwise would have been an unacceptable existence—thereby exercising a stabilizing effect upon society. For regardless of the mobility of their husbands, there was always a local secondary school in the new area with predictable vacancies. Husbands did not have to take offense or feel threatened by their wife's employment—the low status and salary presenting no threat to the husband's overriding hegemony. In other words, this latent function of the educational system served to solidify the American family in the 1940s and 1950s as perhaps no other institution had ever done.

Today things are different. A woman has to assert herself if she is to have a meaningful life outside of the family.[2] The teaching outlet of a few years ago no longer exists. In this light, the feminine "spillover" into the masculine occupations was not an avant garde movement pioneering new opportunities but was founded out of desperation brought on by a loss of female positions.

Perhaps as a reaction to such changing circumstances, various reform movements and their youthful sponsors began to challenge the basic assumptions of society.[3] For example, in 1964, when a class of college women were asked about the desirability of being future housewives, 65 percent viewed the prospect in the affirmative; six years later only 31 percent held that remaining in the home was a suitable feminine role.[4]

Presently, women may not be rebelling against "occupation housewife" but only against the belief that regardless of their educatinal attainments they *must* be housewives.[5] They want the opportunity to choose. Yet there is no such thing as

225

partial freedom. Freedom is an absolute and in the marital state a woman's freedom is compromised. If it is thought that a woman, who happens to be married and has a profession, can easily retreat into the world of the housewife, she will be forever resented and suspected by her employers as having an unfair advantage. Alternatively, if she does not assert herself through a revision of the marriage contract, it will be impossible for her to pursue a career in a particular area without being fearful of her husband's quixotic geographical preferences. While many women may prefer the old role, the trend will probably be on the side of the educated and articulate activists. Moreover, as we saw, if a professional woman feels that she can retreat into the home, that feeling may be a comfortable trap which may keep her from fulfilling her true potential. Men have to succeed, and so they do. What we are therefore envisioning is not a revision of roles but an absence of roles, a new social order for all Americans. This seems to be happening. In a Daniel Yankelovich survey taken in the early 1970s it was found that "whatever the differences to emerge from the interviews with 3,522 young people, they were generally more pronounced among the 1,762 women included." Especially interesting is the gap in the attitudes between college and noncollege women. For instance, when the question of having children was posed, 50 percent of the noncollege women as against 35 percent of the college women believed offspring to be essential to a more fulfilling life.[6] These statistics are intriguing for a variety of reasons. For one thing, they seem to indicate that women's liberation is having some effect even on those who decide not to go to college. In addition, with more and more women going to college, the data portend a continuing radicalization of the female student population. Finally, what also emerges is that college women have a much more altered view of marriage than their less educated comrades.

> To the college woman, marriage means a chance to continue a career, to work out a marital relationship where the role of wife has changed. To the noncollege woman, marriage still means entrapment.[7]

Whatever way one looks at the statistics, no matter

what group is subjected to scrutiny and by whatever means, it is apparent that some form of dramatic upheaval of life-styles is taking place. Raising children, judging by the labor statistics, is no longer the major preoccupation of American women. The new methods for controlling the population gradually if begrudgingly, brought forth new, more open attitudes. The battles waged by Margaret Sanger may be unknown to a generation of young women but her legacy will be forever with them.[8] With fewer children and more labor-saving devices, women faced the prospect of becoming functionally obsolete if their roles were not radically reconsidered. Even such unexpected trends as the extension of the life expectancy must have had a devastating effect on women's thinking.[9] For with the new medical advances, women are increasingly outliving their mates for ever longer periods of time. If their entire lives were dedicated to procreation and to being wives, then these years alone could constitute a tremendous mental agony—either to the woman in question or to society as a whole.

There can be little doubt, therefore, that the contemporary family is undergoing an unprecedented reappraisal.[10] Women in college who desire to get married no longer assume that marriage and a career are mutually incompatible. President Bunting reiterated the changing tendencies but cautioned: "I think these young women are planning an experiment that is very important. . . . And I don't think our graduate schools are ready for them."[11]

Abundant data confirm these observations. An analysis of the attitudes of Stanford women in 1972 revealed that only one out of twenty-five women interviewed anticipated performing the role of a full-time housewife five years hence. This contrasts sharply with a 1965 survey of Stanford women when 70 percent concurred in the belief that they would not seek employment until their children were at least six years old.[12] The important thing about these attitudes is that the woman who stays away from disciplinary involvement completely for six years inevitably loses touch with her subject, gradually adopting a new routine and concurrently losing confidence in her overall professional ability. Initially it is perhaps easy for the young woman to think of the housewife assignment as temporary. However, after a while, women become desocialized from the effects of their college education and liberated from their earlier ambitions. Fortunately, this seems to be changing. More women than ever before are seeking full and uninterrupted professional employment. In 1964 women comprised 23 percent of the college teachers, 15 percent of those in public relations, 19 percent of the designers, 18 percent of the accountants, 10 percent of the pharmacists, and 7 percent of the chemists. Barely ten years later, in 1974, the respective figures were 31 percent for college teachers, 29 percent for public relations, 24 percent for designing, 24 percent in accounting, 17 percent as pharmacists, and 14 percent in the field of chemistry. These changing roles were confirmed in the new curricular choices of many college women.[13]

What effects has all this had on the male world? It remains an obvious truism that the sexes are so interdependent that the thinking of one must have a profoundly inhibiting or encouraging effect on the aspirations of the other. The transition period for men, forsaking the old notions before the adoption of the new, is perhaps the most difficult. Margaret Mead in her characteristically succinct manner sums up the problem:

> For men it will be essential to find responsible ways of protecting the sense of masculine identity during the period when men, reared to depend on a traditionally attributed superiority over women, will inevitably feel threatened by new forms of aspiration, competition, and achievement as women move out of the home into a wider world.[14]

In changing roles, women must unavoidably change their relationship with men.[15] Prenatal definitions of what constitutes maleness and femaleness will have to be modified. For if the woman desires to be her own protector, then the male is relieved of a function which has differentiated him from females. Accordingly, will there be a general revision in the thinking of American men or will only a begrudgingly piecemeal modification take place to accommodate women where necessary and to hold firm where possible? Some authorities suggest that a basic and irreversible reform is already subtly happening.[16] Mead presents one possibility.

> There would be a growing disregard for sex as a basic mode of differentiation. Boys and girls would be given a similar education and like demands would be made on them for citizenship, economic contribution, and creativity.... Boys and girls would be differentiated not by sex-typed personality characteristics, but by temperament.[17]

Whatever the ultimate solution, it is clear that humankind must modify its structure to fit its technology. Tremendous support for women as well as men is required if the transitional stage is to be successfully traversed. The docile character adopted by many women must be abandoned.[18] Once women realize that their careers will win them status that is separate from their husbands, a status not dissolved with divorce or death of a mate, they will not easily surrender this newly won security.[19] The trend has become apparent: more mothers than ever before are receiving college degrees and college educated mothers are more inclined than those with a lesser education to insist upon education for their daughters.[20] The new realities appear imminent. For if women are "security" oriented people, then they know that, unlike in the past, there is little security in marriage—only in their own accomplishments. The "Feminine Mystique" of yore was based in part on the security and happiness that supposedly could be found in marriage and the family. Now such marriages have the opposite consequences. Women, whether obsessed with the need for security, or whether liberated from the entanglements of their earlier socialization, must all seek a common solution in independent careers. A radically new society appears in the offing to which academe must respond. Hochschild sums up the intimate interconnection between university and society.

> We cannot change the role of women in universities without changing the career system based on competition, and we can't change that competitive structure without also altering the economy....[21]

The rate of change will probably accelerate as change occurs.[22] For women are talking about a change not only in the way they view themselves and other women but also in the way they are depicted by men as well.[23] In addition, as society gives them new status and finances they will crave more decision-making authority within the restructured family and will demand to work and to be paid on an equal basis with men.[24] The impact will be revolutionary. In a shrinking job market, where all too many men must now compete for a steadily decreasing piece of the professional employment pie, there now exists the spectre of the potential work force instantaneously doubling. New values other than work and money must substitute for old values which are no longer achievable.

If this new situation is indicative of the problems men must surmount, it is no small consolation that the obstacles confronting women are equally unenviable. Women must assume new responsibilities and obligations.[25] If, for example, they are to compete with men for the finite number of available jobs, they cannot choose between their traditional and liberated roles without also allowing men a comparable choice. For unless women abandon en masse their former sexual role they will not be taken seriously, either by men or by themselves, and their sentiments will be viewed as ephemeral. The man's role, while it offers freedom, is correspondingly unpleasant. Reiterating a point, for women to succeed, they must not be offered the alternative of retreat into the home. Unless sex roles are finally abandoned we will encounter the problem of men being compensated at a higher rate to provide for their family's sustenance. If the government intervenes in this equation to ensure absolute equity without recognizing the necessity to first abolish socially contrived sexual functions, considerable disorder may well result. The man's job has a societal function that cannot be ignored. Thus despite the fact that many women are heads of families and constitute the exclusive financial support, many more men are heads of families. If the job market is finite, and women merely take positions without adopting the ensuing function of those positions, that of family breadwinner,

widescale disruption could follow. If such adverse consequences were impending, people might revert to the posture of
least resistance—which in this case might mean women's
traditional role. Women are totally free if they want to be
totally free; they cannot elect to be free.

THE FREEDOM TO FAIL

Women face other burdens, of which they may as yet be
unaware. John Gardner, in talking about the differences of
attitudes between British and Americans makes an observation that could well be applied to American women.

> It must never be forgotten that a person born to low
> status in a rigidly stratified society has a far more ac-
> ceptable self-image than the person who loses out in our
> free competition of talent. In an older society, the hum-
> ble member of society can attribute his lowly status to
> God's will, to the ancient order of things or to a corrupt
> and tyrannous government. But if a society sorts people
> out efficiently and fairly according to their gifts, the
> loser knows that the true reason for his lowly status is
> that he is not capable of better. That is a bitter pill for
> any man [Woman].[26]

It is not necessary to point out that many women have indeed been sheltered from "personal" failure since their role
as "occupation housewife" was socially preordained. A man,
on the other hand, succeeds or fails on his own. Some may
reply that women will change the system dramatically into a
more humane order. Yet competition seems more likely to
remain; it prevails universally in capitalist, socialist, and
even in communist countries. In many socialist lands the
competition is just as fierce, albeit for nonmonetary incentives such as public recognition; and failure is just as bitter.
Women may, of course, change this seemingly fundamental
competitive scheme, but the probability is that they will radically alter the family structure instead, leaving competition
intact.

231

Implicit in much of the folklore concerning the women's movement is that they would be the chief beneficiaries of proposed reforms. What is usually overlooked is the idea that women's "freedom" is essential for the welfare of our society. For example, the technological revolution is opening up profound possibilities as well as ominous dangers. Cynthia Epstein cites one illustration.[27] In our society, since men have a greater social value, couples will generally prefer to have sons. Writing earlier, Simone de Beauvoir reported similar findings.[28] What will happen when couples can decide the sex of their offspring through the ingestion of prescribed medication? The consequences of this seemingly innocent medical advance, which appears imminent, could be more profound than the French Revolution. Imagine an entire society composed of the male sex! Attitudes regarding the equality of the sexes must be universally internalized if we are to thwart this hypothetical although very real impending calamity.

Also, as we all know, there is always the danger of being squeezed to death before we die of hunger. The new population control technology seems to have abated this trend, at least in the West. However, society cannot have it both ways: either it provides meaningful work outside of the home for its women or it must allow them to find a rationale for their existence through procreation. Population increases, judging from historical statistics, are generally permanent and it may well be advisable to anticipate the consequences of an excessive population rather than seek difficult solutions once the problem has arrived.

Finally, there is the problem of wasted talent.[29] By and large, the structures of society help to determine which groups will assume ascendancy and which will be socialized into mediocrity. Acknowledging today's complex society, and remembering that many other civilizations have fallen because they failed to make the necessary accommodations to changing conditions, one may well ponder how long America can continue as a great nation by tacitly keeping half of the population from making a meaningful contribution. America has on its horizon the opportunity to be the first civilization in the history of the world to harness the full talents of all of its people. To a revisited academe goes this monumental charge and on its success hinges the future well-being of us all.

FOOTNOTES FOR CHAPTER X

[1]Epstein, *Woman's Place: Options and Limits in Professional Careers,* p. 10.

[2]Bailyn, "Notes on the Role of Choice in the Psychology of Professional Women," p. 701.

[3]Cross, *Beyond the Open Door,* p. 148.

[4]Ibid., p. 147.

[5]Trow, "Higher Education for Women," p. 20.

[6]Nadine Brozan, "Widening Gap in Views Is Registered Between College and Noncollege Women," *New York Times* 22 May 1974, p. 45.

[7]Ibid.

[8]Lindsay Miller, *Newest Course on Campus. Women's Studies* (New York: ERIC Document Reproduction Service, ED 065 108, May 1972), pp. 1-24.

[9]Stimpson, *The Women's Center,* p. 10.

[10]Bobbi Granger, *Proposal for a Department of Women's Studies at the University of Pennsylvania* (Philadelphia: ERIC Document Reproduction Service, ED 070 414, April 1972), pp. 1-2.

[11]"Women Won't Let Marriage Interfere with Grad School, Mrs. Bunting Says," *Chronicle of Higher Education,* 13 January 1967, p. 4.

[12]The Carnegie Commission on Higher Education, *Opportunities for Women in Higher Education,* p. 31.

[13]"Special Section/Women—'A Close-Up of Women in US. . . And Ways Their Status Is Changing,'" *U.S. News and World Report,* 8 December 1975, p. 57.

[14]Margaret Mead, "The Life Cycle and Its Variations: The Division of Roles," *Daedalus* 96 (Summer 1967): 874.

[15]Sally Navin, "Future Planning of College Women: Counseling Implications," *Vocational Guidance Quarterly* 21 (September 1972): 14-15.

[16]Alper, "Achievement Motivation in College Women: A Now-You-See-It-Now-You-Don't Phenomenon," p. 196.

[17]Mead, "The Life Cycle and Its Variations: The Division of Roles," p. 872.

[18]Jaroslav Pelikan, "The Liberation Arts," *Liberal Education* 59 (October 1973): 296.

[19]Kinnard White, "Social Background Variables Related to Career Commitment of Women Teachers," p. 651.

[20]Cross, "The Woman Student," p. 31.

[21]Hochschild, "Inside the Clockwork of Male Careers," p. 75.

[22]Parrish, "Women, Careers and Counseling: The New Era," p. 14.

[23]Richter and Whipple, *A Revolution in the Education of Women—Ten Years of Continuing Education at Sarah Lawrence College*, p. 7.

[24]Goode, *The Contemporary American Family*, p. 45.

[25]Koontz, "Counseling Women for Responsibilities," p. 15.

[26]Gardner, *Excellence—Can We Be Equal and Excellent Too?* p. 83.

[27]Epstein, *Woman's Place: Options and Limits in Professional Careers*, pp. 40-41.

[28]de Beauvoir, *The Second Sex*, p. 286.

[29]*Graduate Education for Women: The Radcliffe Ph.D.*, pp. 80-81.

BIBLIOGRAPHY

Abramson, Joan. *The Invisible Woman: Discrimination in the Academic Profession.* San Francisco: Jossey-Bass, 1975.

An Affirmative Action Program to Redress Past Inequities and to Establish a Policy of Equal Treatment and Equal Opportunity at the University of Wisconsin for All Women. Madison, Wisc.: ERIC Document Reproduction Service, ED 067 982, 10 May 1972.

Almquist, Elizabeth M., and Angrist, Shirley S. "Role Model Influences on College Women's Career Aspirations." *Merrill-Palmer Quarterly* 17 (July 1971): 264-270.

Almquist, Elizabeth M. and Angrist, Shirley S. "Career Salience and Atypicality of Occupational Choice among College Women." *Journal of Marriage and the Family* 32 (May 1970): 242-247.

Alper, Thelma G. "Achievement Motivation in College Women: A Now-You-See-Now-You-Don't Phenomenon." *American Psychologist* 29 (March 1974): 195-202.

American Women, Report of the President's Commission on the Status of Women. Washington, D.C.: Government Printing Office, 1963.

"Amherst College to Admit Women in '75." *New York Times,* 3 November 1974, p. 58.

Angrist, Shirley S. "Counseling College Women About Careers." *Journal of College Student Personnel* 13 (November 1972): 494-498.

Astin, Helen S. "Career Development of Girls During the High Schools Years." *Journal of Counseling Psychology* 15, no. 6 (1968): 538-539.

Astin, Helen. S. *The Woman Doctorate in America.* New York: Russell Sage Foundation, 1969.

Attwood, Cynthia. *Women in Fellowship and Training Programs.* Washington, D.C.: ERIC Document Reproduction Service, ED 081 371, November 1972.

Bailyn, Lotte. "Notes on the Role of Choice in the Psychology of Professional Women." *Daedalus* 93 (Spring 1964): 701-707.

Barzun, Jacques. *Teacher in America*. Boston: Little, Brown and Company, 1945.

Bass, Ann Trabue. "The Development of Higher Education for Women in This Country." *Contemporary Education* 41 (May 1970): 285-288.

Baumrind, Diana. "From Each According to Her Ability." *School Review* 80 (February 1972): 166-175.

de Beauvoir, Simone. *The Second Sex*. New York: Alfred A. Knopf, 1953.

Bem, Darly J., and Bem, Sandra L. "On Liberating the Female Student." *School Psychology Digest* 2, no. 3 (1973): 10-14.

Benson, Ruth Crego. "Women's Studies: Theory and Practice." *AAUP Bulletin* 58 (September 1972): 283-286.

Bereaud, Susan; Daniels, Joan; and Stacey, Judith. *And Jill Came Tumbling Down—Sexism in American Education*. New York: Dell Publishing Company, 1974.

Bernard, Jessie. *Academic Women*. University Park, Pa.: Pennsylvania State University Press, 1964.

Bernard, Jessie. "You Can't Destroy This Movement." *U.S. News and World Report*, 8 December 1975, p. 72.

Bettelheim, Bruno. "The Commitment Required of a Woman Entering a Scientific Profession in Present-Day American Society." In *Women and the Scientific Professions*. Edited by Jacquelyn A. Mattfeld and Carol G. Van Aken. Cambridge, Mass.: The M.I.T. Press, 1965.

Bird, Caroline. *Born Female*. New York: Pocketbooks, 1975.

Bird, Caroline. "Women's Colleges and Women's Lib." *Change* 4 (April 1972): 60-65.

Brann, James W. "An Introduction to Life at the Top." *Chronicle of Higher Education*, 12 July 1967, p. 1.

Breasted, Mary. "Yale Shuts Gates to Curb Assaults." *New York Times*, 5 February 1976, p. 60.

Brozan, Nadine. "Widening Gap in Views Is Registered Between College and Noncollege Women." *New York Times*, 22 May 1974, p. 45.

Bunting, Mary. "A Huge Waste: Educated Womenpower." *New York Times*, 7 May 1961, sec. 6, p. 23.

Burn, North. *Cooperative and/or Coeducation*. Hartford, Conn.: ERIC Document Reproduction Service, ED 065

078, May 1970.

Burstyn, Joan N. "Striving for Equality: Higher Education for Women in the U.S. Since 1900." *University College Quarterly* 18 (January 1973): 22-32.

Bushnell, John H. "Student Culture at Vassar." In *The American College: A Psychological and Social Interpretation of the Higher Learning.* Edited by Nevitt Sanford. New York: John Wiley and Sons, 1962.

Cain, Louise G., Symposium Chairman, ed. *Women on Campus: 1970 A Symposium.* Ann Arbor, Mich.: The University of Michigan Center for the Continuing Education for Women, 14 October 1970.

Calderone, Mary S. "New Roles for Women." *School Review* 80 (February 1972): 275-279.

Campbell, Jean W. "The Nontraditional Student in Academe." In *Women in Higher Education.* Edited by Todd Furniss and Patricia Albjerg Graham. Washington, D.C.: American Council on Education, 1974.

Campbell, Jean W. "Women Drop Back In: Educational Innovation in the Sixties." In *Academic Women on the Move.* Edited by Alice Rossi and Ann Calderwood. New York: Russell Sage Foundation, 1973.

The Carnegie Commission on Higher Education. *Opportunities for Women in Higher Education: Their Current Participation, Prospects for the Future, and Recommendations for Action.* New York: McGraw-Hill Book Company, 1973.

Carroll, Mary Ann. "Women in Administration in Higher Education." *Contemporary Education* 63 (February 1972): 214-215.

"The Case for Women's Colleges." *Intellect* 102 (March 1974): 344-345.

Cheit, Earl F. "What Price Accountability?" *Change* 7 (November 1975): 30.

Clarenbach, Kathryn F. "Can Continuing Education Adapt." *AAUW Journal* 63 (January 1970): 63-64.

Clark, Burton R. "The 'Cooling-Out' Function in Higher Education." *American Journal of Sociology* 65 (May 1960): 571-575.

Clarke, Marnie A. "Transitional Women: Implications for Adult Educators." *Adult Leadership* 24 (December 1975): 125-126.

"Coed Status Pleases Vassar Despite Problems." *New York Times,* 19 November 1974, p. 45.

Cohen, Audrey C. "Women and Higher Education: Recommendations for Change." *Phi Delta Kappan* 53 (November 1971): 164-167.

Cole, Charles C., Jr. "A Case for the Women's College." *College Board Review,* no. 83 (Spring 1972), pp. 17-21.

"College Sports Sanction Plan Set for Women." *Chronicle of Higher Education, 12 January 1976, p. 6.*

Conway, Jill K. *"Coeducation and Women's Studies: Two Approaches to the Question of Woman's Place in the Contemporary University." Daedalus* 103 (Fall 1974): 239-249.

Cope, Robert G. "Sex-Related Factors and Attrition Among College Women." *Journal of the National Association of Women Deans, Administrators, and Counselors* 33 (Spring 1970): 121.

Crockford, Richard. "The Forgotten Sex in Education." *Junior College Journal* 42 (October 1971): 17-19.

Cross, Patricia K. *Beyond the Open Door.* San Francisco: Jossey-Bass, 1972.

Cross, Patricia K. *College Women: A Research Description.* Chicago: ERIC Document Reproduction Service, ED 027 814, 5 April 1968.

Cross, Patricia K. "The Woman Student." In *Women In Higher Education.* Edited by Todd Furniss and Patricia Albjerg Graham. Washington, D.C.: American Council on Education, 1974.

Cross, Patricia K. and Valley, John R. "Introduction." In *Planning Non-Traditional Programs.* Edited by Patricia K. Cross and John R. Valley. San Francisco: Jossey-Bass, 1974.

Cross, Patricia K. and Valley, John R. eds. *Planning Non-Traditional Programs.* San Francisco: Jossey-Bass, 1974.

Deinhardt, Barbara. "Mother of Men?" In *Women in Higher Education.* Edited by Todd Furniss and Patricia Albjerg

Graham. Washington, D.C.: American Council on Education, 1974.

Dement, Alice L. "What Brings and Holds Women Science Majors?" *College and University* 39 (Fall 1963): 44-50.

Dinerman, Beatrice. "Sex Discrimination in Academia." *Journal of Higher Education* 62 (April 1971): 253-264.

Douvan, Elizabeth. "Internal Barriers to Achievement in Woman—An Introduction." In *Women on Campus: 1970 a Symposium*. Edited by Louise G. Cain, Symposium Chairman. Ann Arbor, Mich.: The University of Michigan Center for the Continuing Education for Women, 14 October 1970.

Dressel, Paul L. *College and University Curriculum*. 2nd ed. Berkeley, Calif.: McCutchan Publishing Company, 1971.

Dunkle, Margaret, and Simmons, Adele. *Anti-Nepotism Policies and Practices*. Bethesda, Md.: ERIC Document Reproduction Service, ED 065 037, January 1972.

Eckert, Ruth. "Academic Woman Revisited." *Liberal Education* 57 (December 1971): 479-487.

Edmiston, Susan. "Portia Faces Life: The Trials of Law School." *Ms*. 2 (April 1974): 74, 76, 78, 93.

Engin, Ann W.; Fodor, Iris; and Leppaluoto, Jean. "Male and Female—The Mutually Disadvantaged: The School Psychologist's Role in Expanding Options for Both Sexes." *School Psychology Digest* 2, no. 3 (1973): 2-6.

Epstein, Cynthia Fuchs. *Woman's Place: Options and Limits in Professional Careers*. Berkeley: University of California Press, 1971.

Farley, Jennie. *Women's Studies: Where to Now?* Ithaca, N.Y.: ERIC Document Reproduction Service, ED 086 078, 1973.

Feldman, Saul D. *Escape from the Doll's House—Women in Graduate and Professional Education*. New York: McGraw-Hill, 1974.

Ferber, Marianne A., and Loeb, Jane W. "Performance, Rewards, and Perceptions of Sex Discrimination Among Male and Female Faculty." *American Journal of Sociology* 78 (January 1973: 999-1000.

Fields, Cheryl. "Women's Studies Gain; 2,000 Courses

Offered This Year." *Chronicle of Higher Education,* 17 December 1973, p. 6.

Flexner, Eleanor. *Century of Struggle: The Woman's Rights Movement in the United States.* New York: Atheneum, 1974.

Frankel, Phylis. "Sex-Role Attitudes and the Development of Achievement Need in Women." *Journal of College Student Personnel* 15 (March 1974): 114-119.

Freeman, Jo. "Women's Liberation and Its Impact on the Campus." *Liberal Education* 57 (December 1971): 468-478.

Friedan, Betty. *The Feminine Mystique.* New York: W. W. Norton and Company, 1963.

Friedan, Betty. "Up from the Kitchen." *The New York Times,* 4 March 1973, sec. 6, p. 9.

Friskey, Elizabeth A. "College Women and Careers." *AAUP Bulletin* 60 (September 1974): 317-319.

Furniss, Todd, and Graham, Patricia Albjerg, eds. *Women in Higher Education.* Washington, D.C.: American Council on Education, 1974.

Gardner, John W. *Excellence—Can We Be Equal and Excellent Too?* New York: Perennial Library, Harper and Row, Publishers, 1971.

Getman, Lisa. "From Conestoga to Career." In *Women in Higher Education.* Edited by Todd Furniss and Patricia Albjerg Graham. Washingtdon, D.C.: American Council on Education, 1974.

Ginsberg, Eli, et al. *Life Styles of Educated Women.* New York: Columbia University Press, 1967.

Goldberg, Philip. "Are Women Prejudiced Against Women?" *Transaction* 5 (April 1968): 29-30.

Goldberger, Paul. "Girls at Yale." *Today's Education* 59 (October 1970): 50-51.

Goode, William J., ed. *The Contemporary American Family.* Chicago: Quadrangle Books, 1971.

Gornick, Vivian. "Why Radcliffe Women Are Afraid of Success." *New York Times,* 14 January 1973, sec. 6, p. 56.

Gornick, Vivian, and Moran, Barbara K., eds. *Women in a Sexist Socity.* New York: Basic Books, 1971.

Gouldner, Abby, ed. *At Kirkland.* Clinton, N.Y.: ERIC Document Reproduction Service, ED 063 912, 1972.

Gove, Walter R., and Tudor, Jeanette F. "Adult Sex Roles and Mental Illness." *American Journal of Sociology* 78 (January 1975): 814-816.

Graduate Education for Women: The Radcliffe Ph.D. A Report by a Faculty-Trustee Committee. Cambridge: Harvard University Press, 1956.

"Graduate-Level Women Reduce Dropout Rate." *Chronicle of Higher Education,* 21 January 1974, p. 7.

Graham, Patricia Albjerg. "Women in Academe." In *The Professional Woman.* Edited by Athena Theodore. Cambridge, Mass.: Schenkman Publishing Company, 1971.

Granger, Bobbi. *Proposal for a Department of Women's Studies at the University of Pennsylvania.* Philadelphia: ERIC Document Reproduction Service, ED 070 414, April 1972.

Greenberg, H., et al. "Personality and Attitudinal Differences Between Employed and Unemployed Married Women." *Journal of Social Psychology* 53 (February 1961): 91-92.

Hammel, Lisa. "We Are the A's: Associate, Assistant, Adjunct, Acting." *New York Times,* 26 October 1973, p. 48.

Hansot, Elizabeth. "A 'Second-Chance' Program for Women." *Change* 5 (February 1973): 49-51.

Harbeson, Gladys E. "The New Feminism." *AAUW Journal* 63 (January 1970): 53-55.

Harmon, Lenore W. "Anatomy of Career Commitment in Women." *Journal of Counseling Psychology* 17 (January 1970): 77-80.

Harris, Ann Sutherland. "The Second Sex in Academe." *AAUP Bulletin* 56 (September 1970): 283-295.

Heist, Paul. "The Motivation of College Women Today: The Cultural Setting." *AAUW Journal* 56 (January 1972): 55-56.

Herman, Michele H., and Sedlacek, William E. *Career Orientation of University and High School Women.* College Park, Md.: ERIC Document Reproduction Serivce ED 074 950, 1972.

Hochschild, Arlie Russell. "Inside the Clockwork of Male Courses." In *Women and the Power to Change*. Edited by Florence Howe. New York: McGraw-Hill, 1975.

Hoffman, Lois Wladis. "Early Childhood Experiences and Women's Achievement Motives." *School Psychology Digest* 2, no. 3 (1973): 20-21.

Hole, Judith, and Levine, Ellen. *Rebirth of Feminism*. New York: Quadrangle/The New York Times Book Company, 1971.

Hook, Sydney. "Semantic Evasions." *College and University Journal* 2 (September 1972): 16-18.

Hopkins, Elaine B. "Unemployed! An Academic Woman's Saga." Change 5 (Winter 1973-1974): 49-53.

Horner, Matina S. "Fail: Bright Women." *Psychology Today* 3 (November 1969): 36-38, 62.

Hornig, Lilli S. *Affirmative Action Through Affirmative Attitudes*. Albany, N.Y.: ERIC Document Reproduction Service, ED 076 091, November 1972.

Houle, Cyril O. *The External Degree*. San Francisco: Jossey-Bass, 1973.

Howe, Florence. "Introduction." In *Women and the Power to Change*. Edited by Florence Howe. New York: McGraw-Hill, 1975.

Howe, Florence. "Women and the Power to Change." In *Women and the Power to Change*." Edited by Florence Howe. New York: McGraw-Hill, 1975.

Howe, Florence, ed. *Women and the Power to Change*. New York: McGraw-Hill, 1975.

Howe, Florence, and Ahlum, Carol. "Women Studies and Social Change." In *Academic Women on the Move*. Edited by Alice Rossi and Ann Calderwood. New York: Russell Sage Foundation, 1973.

Howell, Mary C. "Professional Women and the Feminist Movement." *Journal of the National Association for Women Deans, Administrators and Counselors* 37 (Winter 1974): 84-86.

Huber, Joan. "From Sugar and Spice to Professor." In *Academic Women on the Move*. Edited by Alice S. Rossi and Ann Calderwood. New York: Russell Sage Foundation, 1973.

Hunt, Beverly English. "Characteristics, Perceptions and Experiences of Married Women Students at Lansing Community College." Ed.D. dissertation, Michigan State University, 1966.

Husbands, Sandra Acker. "Women's Place in Higher Education?" *School Review* 80 (February 1972): 270.

Jacobson, Robert L. "Coeducation's Siren Song Lures Colleges." *Chronicle of Higher Education,* 31 May 1967, p. 6.

Jacoby, Susan. "What Do I Do for the Next 20 Years?" *New York Times,* 17 June 1973, sec. 6, pp. 42-43.

Jencks, Christopher, and Riesman, David. *The Academic Revolution.* Garden City, N.Y.: Anchor Books, Doubleday and Company, Inc., 1969.

Jensen, Beverly. "Single-Sex Education: The Cause for Women's Colleges." *College and University Business* 56 (February 1974): 16-17.

Keezer, Dexter M. "Watch Out Girls!" *The New Republic,* 6-13 September 1969, pp. 30-31.

Klemsrud, Judy. "After Wellesley, Women's Liberation." *New York Times,* 7 June 1971, p. 28.

Kelmsrud, Judy. "Barnard's New Alumnae Tell What They Now Want Out of Life." *New York Times,* 2 June 1971, p. 36.

Klemsrud, Judy. "The Spocks Bittersweet Recognition in a Revised Classic." *New York Times,* 19 March 1976, p. 28.

Knight, Michael. "Yale's First Full Class of Women, About to Graduate, Looks Back with Pride and Hope." *New York Times,* 3 June 1973, p. 39.

Komarovsky, Mirra. "Cultural Contradictions and Sex Roles." *American Journal of Sociology* 3 (November 1946): 184-189.

Komarovsky, Mirra. "Cultural Contradictions and Sex Roles: The Masculine Case." *American Journal of Sociology* 78 (January (1973): 873.

Komisar, Lucy. "The New Feminism." *Saturday Review,* 21 February 1970, pp. 28-29.

Koontz, Elizabeth Duncan. "Counseling Women for Responsibilities." *Journal of the National Association for*

Women Deans, Administrators and Counselors 34 (Fall 1970): 13-15.

Koontz, Elizabeth Duncan. *Plans for Widening Women's Educational Opportunities*. Racine, Wisc.: ERIC Document Reproduction Service, ED 067 990, 13 March 1972.

Kovach, Bill. "Wellesley Says It Won't Go Coed." *New York Times*, 9 March 1973, p. 43.

Kreps, Juanita. *Sex in the Marketplace: American Women at Work*. Baltimore: The Johns Hopkins University Press, 1973.

Landy, Marcia. "Women Power and the Word." *College and University Journal* 2 (September 1972): 19-22.

Langdon, George, and Griffen, Clyde. *Report on Men's Education*, Poughkeepsie, N.Y., 1968.

Lantz, Joanne B. *On the Position of Women in Society*. Report of the American Personnel and Guidance Association. Bethesda, Md.: ERIC Document Reproduction Service, ED 049 486, 1971.

Larson, Barbara. *Affirmative Action and Academic Women: A Crisis in Credibility*. Bethesda, Md.: ERIC Document Reproduction Serivce, ED 084 585, November 1973.

Lavine, Thelma Z. "The Motive to Achieve Limited Success: The New Woman Law School Applicant." In *Women in Higher Education*. Edited by Todd Furniss and Patricia Albjerg Graham. Washington, D.C.: American Council on Education, 1974.

LeFevere, Carole. "The Mature Woman as Graduate Student." *School Review* 80 (February 1972): 281-282.

Lefkowitz, Mary. *Final Report on the Education and Needs of Women*. Wellesley, Mass.: ERIC Document Reproduction Service, ED 081 329, September 1970.

Leifer, Aimee Dorr. *When Are Undergraduate Admissions Sexist? The Case of Stanford University*. Bethesda, Md.: ERIC Document Reproduction Service, ED 095 740, 18 April 1974.

Leppaluoto, Jean. *Attitude Change and Sex Discrimination: The Crunch Hypothesis*. Bethesda, Md.: ERIC Document Reproduction Service, ED 071 548, 1972.

Letchworth, George E. "Women Who Return to College: An Identity-Integrity Approach." *Journal of College Student Personnel* 2 (March 1970): 103-105.

Littleton, Betty. "The Special Validity of Women's Colleges." *Chronicle of Higher Education,* 24 November 1975, p. 24.

McLure, Gail T., et al. "Sex Discrimination in Schools." *Today's Education* 60 (November 1971): 33-35.

Margolis, Diane Rothbard. "A Fair Return? Back to College at Middle Age?" *Change* 6 (October 1974): 34-37.

Markus, Hazel. *Continuing Education for Women: Factors Influencing a Return to School and the School Experience.* Bethesda, Md.: ERIC Document Reproduction Service, ED 078 296, April 1973.

Martin, Donna. "The Wives of Academe." *Change* 4 (Winter 1972-1973): 67-69.

Mattfeld, Jacquelyn A. *Many Are Called, But Few Are Chosen.* Bethesda, Md.: ERIC Document Reproduction Service, ED 071 549, 6 October 1972.

Mattfeld, Jacquelyn, and Van Aken, Carol G., eds. *Women and the Scientific Professions.* Cambridge, Mass.: The M.I.T. Press, 1965.

Mayer, Evelyn A. "Women at the University of Virginia." *Journal of the National Association for Women Deans, Administrators and Counselors* 35 (Summer 1972): 158-164.

Mayhew, Lewis B. *Colleges Today and Tomorrow.* San Francisco: Jossey-Bass, 1971.

Mayhew, Lewis B., ed. *The Carnegie Commission on Higher Education.* San Francisco: Jossey-Bass, 1973.

Mead, Margaret. "The Life Cycle and Its Variations: The Division of Roles." *Daedalus* 96 (Summer 1967): 872-874.

Mead, Margaret. *Male and Female.* New York: William Morrow and Company, 1949.

Mead, Margaret, and Metraux, Rhoda. "Image of the Scientist Among High School Students." *Science,* 30 August 1957, pp. 385-389.

Merton, Robert K. *Social Theory and Social Structure.* New York: The Free Press, 1968.

245

Miller, Lindsay. *Newest Course on Campus. Women's Studies.* New York: ERIC Document Reproduction Service, ED 065 108, May 1972.

Mitchell, Susan B., and Alciatore, Robert T. "Women Doctoral Recipients Evaluate Their Training." *Educational Forum* 34 (May 1970): 534-535.

Montagu, Ashley. *The Natural Superiority of Women.* New York: Collier Books, 1974.

Moore, Kathryn M. *The Cooling Out of Two-Year College Women.* Bethesda, Md.: ERIC Document Reproduction Service, ED 091 021, April 1974.

Moos, Malcolm, and Rourke, Francis E. *The Campus and the State.* Baltimore: The Johns Hopkins University Press, 1959.

Mueller, Kate H. "Sex Differences in Campus Regulations." *Personnel and Guidance Journal* 32 (May 1954): 530-531.

Mulligan, Kathryn L. *A Question of Opportunity: Women and Continuing Education.* Washington, D.C.: ERIC Document Reproduction Service, ED 081 323, March 1973.

Nachmias, Vivianne. "Panelist." In *Women and the Scientific Professions.* Edited by Jacquelyn A. Mattfeld and Carol G. Van Aken. Cambridge, Mass.: The M.I.T. Press, 1965.

Nadelson, Carol, and Natman, Malkah T. "The Woman Physician." *Journal of Medical Education* 47 (March 1972): 176-182.

Navin, Sally. "Future Planning of College Women: Counseling Implications." *Vocational Guidance Quarterly* 21 (September 1972): 14-15.

"New College Trend: Women Studies." *New York Times,* 7 January 1971, pp. 37, 70.

Newcomer, Mabel. *A Century of Higher Education for American Women.* New York: Harper and Row Publishers, 1959.

Niles, Judith. *Women and Fellowships.* Washington, D.C.: ERIC Document Reproduction Service, ED 091 970, April 1974.

"1974 Divorces Were at Nearly 2% Rate." *New York Times,* 21 April 1976, p. 18.

"Number of Women's Colleges, 300 in 1960, Down to 146."
Chronicle of Higher Education, 3 May 1973, p. 3.

Oltman, Ruth M. *The Evolving Role of the Women's Libera-
tion Movement in Higher Education.* Washington, D.C.:
ERIC Document Reproduction Service, ED 049 489, 15
March 1971.

Ortega y Gasset, Jose. *The Revolt of the Masses.* New York:
W. W. Norton and Company, 1957.

Orwell, George. *Animal Farm.* New York: The New American Library, 1946.

Osborn, Ruth Helm. "Developing New Horizons for Women."
Adult Leadership 19 (April 1971): 326-328, 351.

Parrish, John B. "Women, Careers and Counseling: The New
Era." *Journal of the National Association for Women
Deans, Administrators and Counselors* 38 (Fall 1974):
12-14.

Patrick, Theodore Anne. "Personality and Family
Background Characteristics of Women Who Entered
Male-Dominated Professions." Ed.D. dissertation,
Teachers College, Columbia University, 1973.

Patterson, Michelle, and Sells, Lucy. "Women Dropouts from
Higher Education." In *Academic Women on the Move.*
Edited by Alice S. Rossi and Ann Calderwood. New
York: Russell Sage Foundation, 1973.

Pelikan, Jaroslav. "The Liberation Arts." *Liberal Education*
59 (October 1973): 292-297.

Peterson, Martha E. "Women, Autonomy, and Accountability
in Higher Education." In *Women in Higher Education.*
Edited by Todd Furniss and Patricia Albjerg Graham.
Washington, D.C.: American Council on Education,
1974.

Pfiffner, Virginia. "The Needs of Women Students?" *Community and Junior College Journal* 43 (August/September
1972): 12-14.

Pottinger, Stanley J. *Affirmative Action and Faculty Policy.*
New Orleans: ERIC Document Reproduction Service,
ED 062 929, 5 May 1972.

Pottinger, Stanley J. *Statement on Guidelines for Application
of Executive Order 11246 to Higher Education Institutions Receiving Federal Funds.* Washington, D.C.: ERIC

Document Reproduction Service, ED 069 225, 4 October 1972.

Radley, Virginia. *Involvement of Women in the Governance Process: Decision Making.* Bethesda, Md.: ERIC Document Reproduction Service, ED 086 061, 29 April 1974.

Radlow, Lillian. "Boys and Girls Together(?)" *The Independent School Bulletin* 29 (December 1969): 12.

Raffel, Norma. "The Women's Movement and Its Impact on Higher Education." *Liberal Education* 59 (May 1973): 248.

Rees, Nina. "Panelist." In *Women and the Scientific Professions.* Edited by Jacquelyn A. Mattfeld and Carol G. Van Aken. Cambridge, Mass.: The M.I.T. Press, 1965.

Reeves, Mary Elizabeth. "An Analysis of Job Satisfaction of Women Administrators in Higher Education." *Journal of the National Association for Women Deans, Administrators, and Counselors* 38 (Spring 1975): 135.

Reinfeld, Patricia M. *Woman: Yesterday, Today, Tomorrow.* Sewell, N.J.: ERIC Document Reproduction Serivce, ED 091 254, 1974.

Report of the Commission on the Future of Wellesley College. Wellesley, Mass.: ERIC Document Reproduction Service, March 1971.

Report of the Committee on the Status of Women in the Faculty of Arts and Sciences. Cambridge, Mass.: ERIC Reproduction Document Service, ED 057 714, April 1971.

Report of Conference on the Undergraduate Education of Women. Allentown, Pa.: ERIC Document Reproduction Service, ED 043 283, 8-10 July 1969.

Rich, Adrienne. "Toward a Woman-Centered University." In *Women and the Power to Change.* Edited by Florence Howe. New York: McGraw-Hill, 1975.

Richardson, Mary Sue. "Self Concepts and Role Concepts in the Career Orientation of College Women." Ph.D. dissertation, Teachers College, Columbia University, 1972.

Richter, Melissa Lewis, and Whipple, Jane Banks. *A Revolution in the Education of Women—Ten Years of Continuing Education at Sarah Lawrence College.* Bronxville, N.Y.: Sarah Lawrence College, Center for Continuing Education and Community Studies, 1972.

Riesman, David, and Stradtman, Verne. "Academic Transformation." In *The Carnegie Commission on Higher Education*. Edited by Lewis B. Mayhew. San Francisco: Jossey-Bass, 1973.

Roberts, Joan. "Problems and Solutions in Achieving Equality for Women." In *Women in Higher Education*. Edited by Todd Furniss and Patricia Albjerg Graham. Washington, D.C.: American Council on Education, 1974.

Roberts, Sylvia. *Equality of Opportunity in Higher Education—The Impact of Contract Compliance and the Equal Rights Amendment*. Washington, D.C.: ERIC Document Reproduction Service, ED 074 920, 15 January 1973.

Robinson, Lora. *Women's Studies: Courses and Programs for Higher Education*. Washington, D.C.: ERIC Document Reproduction Service, ED 074 997, 1973.

Roby, Pamela. "Institutional Barriers to Women Students in Higher Education." In *Academic Women on the Move*. Edited by Alice Rossi and Ann Calderwood. New York: Russell Sage Foundation, 1973.

Rosen, Norma. "Mount Holyoke Forever Will Be Mount Holyoke Forever Will Be for Women Only." *New York Times*, 9 April 1972, sec. 6, p. 65.

Rosen, R. A. Hudson. "Occupational Role Innovators and Sex Role Attitudes." *Journal of Medical Education* 49 (June 1974): 554-561.

Rossi, Alice S. "Barriers to the Career Choice of Engineering, Medicine, or Science Among American Women." In *Women and the Scientific Professions*. Edited by Jacquelyn A. Mattfeld and Carol G. Van Aken. Cambridge, Mass.: The M.l.T. Press, 1965.

Rossi, Alice S. "Equality Between the Sexes: An Immodest Proposal." *Daedalus* 93 (Spring 1964): 610-632.

Rossi, Alice S. "Women in Science: Why So Few?" *Science*, 28 May 1965, pp. 1198-1201.

Rossi, Alice S., and Calderwood, Ann, eds. *Academic Women on the Move*. New York: Russell Sage Foundation, 1973.

Rudolph, Frederick. *The American College and University—A History*. New York: Vintage Books, 1962.

"Ruth Adams, Head of Wellesley, Named an Officer of Dartmouth." *New York Times,* 21 January 1972, p. 24.

Sandler, Bernice. "Discrimination Is Immoral, Illegal and, Offenders Find, Costly." *College and University Business* 56 (February 1974): 27-30.

Sandler, Bernice. *A Feminist Approach to the Women's College.* Washington, D.C.: ERIC Document Reproduction Service, ED 071 561, November 1971.

Sandlund, Britt. "Adult Education of Women in Sweden." *Improving College and University Teaching* 20 (Winter 1972): 64-65.

Sanford, Nevitt, ed. *The American College: A Psychological and Social Interpretation of the Higher Learning.* New York: John Wiley and Sons, 1962.

Schlossberg, Nancy K. "The Right to Be Wrong Is Gone: Women in Academe." *Educational Record* 55 (Fall 1974): 257-262.

Schmalzried, Beverly. "Day Care Services for Children of Campus Employees." In *Women in Higher Education.* Edited by Todd Furniss and Patricia Albjerg Graham. Washington, D.C.: American Council on Education, 1974.

Schneider, Liz. "Our Failures Only Marry: Bryn Mawr and the Failure of Feminism." In *Women in a Sexist Society.* Edited by Vivian Gornick and Barbara K. Moran. New York: Basic Books, 1971.

Schwartz, Pepper, and Lever, Janet. "Women in the Male World of Higher Education." In *Academic Women on the Move.* Edited by Alice S. Rossi and Ann Calderwood. New York: Russell Sage Foundation, 1973.

Scott, Ann. *The Half-Eaten Apple: A Look at Sex Discrimination in the University.* Bethesda, Md.: ERIC Document Reproduction Service, ED 041 566, May 1970.

Scott, John Finley. "The American College Sorority: Its Role in Class and Ethnic Endogamy." *American Sociological Review* 30 (August 1965): 515-526.

Seabury, Paul. "The Idea of Merit." *Commentary* 54 (December 1972): 41-45.

Sells, Lucy. *Availability (sic) Pools as the Basis for Affirma-*

tive Action. Scottsdale, Ariz.: ERIC Document Reproduction Service, ED 077 461, 5 May 1973.

Selznick, Philip. *TVA and the Grass Roots: A Study in the Sociology of Formal Organization.* New York: Harper Torchbooks, 1966.

Sicherman, Barbara. "American History." *SIGNS,* no. 2 (Winter 1975), pp. 465-480.

Sicherman, Barbara. "The Invisible Woman: The Case for Women's Studies." In *Women In Higher Education.* Edited by Todd Furniss and Patricia Albjerg Graham. Washington, D.C.: American Council on Education, 1974.

Simon, Rita; Clark, Shirley Merritt; and Tifft, Larry L. "Of Nepotism, Marriage, and the Pursuit of an Academic Career." *Sociology of Education* 39 (Fall 1966): 344-358.

Simpson, Alan. "Coeducation." *College Board Review,* no. 82 (Winter 1971-1972), pp. 17-23.

"Smith College and the Question of Coeducation—A Report with Recommendations Submitted to the Faculty and the Board of Trustees by the Augmented College Planning Committee." Northampton, Mass., April 1971.

Smith, Constance. "The Radcliffe Institute." *Improving College and University Teaching* 20 (Winter 1972): 42-43.

Somerville, Rose M. "Women's Studies." *Today's Education* 60 (November 1971): 35.

"Special Section/Women—'A Close-up of Women in US . . . and Ways Their Status Is Changing.' " *U.S. News and World Report,* 8 December 1975, p. 57.

Stafford, Rita Lynne. "Do Women Believe the Inferiority Myth?" *AAUW Journal* 61 (January 1968): 58-59.

Staines, Graham; Tavris, Carol; and Jayaratne, Toby Epstein. "The Queen Bee Syndrome." *Psychology Today* 7 (January 1974): 55-60.

Steinmann, Anne; Levi, Joseph; and Fox, David. "Self-Concept of College Women Compared with Their Concept of Ideal Woman and Men's Ideal Woman." *Journal of Counseling Psychology* 2 (Winter 1974): 372-374.

Stent, Angela. "The Radcliffe Institute: Is There Life After Birth?" *Change* 7 (September 1975): 13.

Sternick, Joanna Henderson. "But I Love It Here'—Coeducation Comes to Dartmouth." *Journal of the National Association for Women Deans, Administrators, and Counselors* 37 (Spring 1974): 142-143.

Stimpson, Catharine. "The New Feminism and Women's Studies." *Change* 5 (September 1973): 43-48.

Stimpson, Catharine. *What Matter Mind: A Theory About the Practice of Women's Studies*. Bethesda, Md.: ERIC Document Reproduction Service, ED 068 078, August 1972.

Stimpson, Catharine, et al. *The Women's Center*. New York: ERIC Document Reproduction Service, ED 063 913, 1971.

Stone, Elizabeth. "Women's Programs Grow Up." *Change* 7 (November 1975): 17-19.

Taines, Beatrice. "Older Women, Newer Students." *Community and Junior College Journal* 44 (August/September 1973): 17.

Theodore, Athena, ed. *The Professional Woman*. Cambridge, Mass.: Schenkman Publishing Company, 1971.

Thom, Patricia; Ironside, Anne; and Hendry, Eileen. "The Women's Resources Center—An Educational Model for Counselling Women." *Adult Leadership* 24 (December 1975): 129-132.

Thomas, M. Cary. "Present Tendencies in Women's University Education." In *And Jill Came Tumbling Down*. Edited by Susan Bereaud, Joan Daniels, and Judith Stacey. New York: Dell Publishing Company, 1974.

Thomas, Ronald. "Coed Housing in One Fell Swoop." *College and University* 49 (Spring 1974): 276-277.

Tidball, Elizabeth. "Perspective on Academic Women and Affirmative Action." *Educational Record* 54 (Spring 1973): 130-135.

Tidball, Elizabeth. "Women on Campus—And You." *Liberal Education* 61 (May 1975): 288-291.

Tobias, Sheila. *New Feminism on a University Campus: From Job Equality to Female Studies*. Pittsburgh: ERIC Document Reproduction Service, ED 065 073, 1970.

Tobias, Sheila. "Teaching Female Studies: Looking Back Over Three Years." *Liberal Education* 58 (May 1972): 258-263.

Tobias, Sheila, and Kusnetz, Ella. "For College Students: A Study of Women, Their Role 'and Stereotypes." *Journal of Home Economics* 64 (April 1972): 17-20.

Tompkins, Pauline. "What Future for the Women's College?" *Liberal Education* 58 (May 1972): 298-302.

Trecker, Janice Law. "Woman's Place Is in the Curriculum." *Saturday Review,* 16 October 1971, pp. 83-92.

Trow, Jo Anne J. "Higher Education for Women." *Improving College and University Teaching* 20 (Winter 1972): 19-20.

Truman, David B. *The Single Sex College—In Transition?* South Hadley, Mass.: ERIC Document Reproduction Service, ED 065 031, 1971.

Veblen, Thorstein. *The Theory of the Leisure Class.* New York: The Viking Press, 1945.

Warren, Jonathan. "Awarding Credit." In *Planning Non-Traditional Programs.* Edited by Patricia K. Cross and John R. Valley. San Francisco: Jossey-Bass, 1974.

Wasserman, Elga R. "Coeducation Comes to Yale College." *Educational Record* 51 (Spring 1970): 143-147.

Watkins, Beverly T. "This Year's Freshmen Reflect New Views of Women's Role." *Chronicle of Higher Education,* 12 January 1976, p. 31.

Weisstein, Naomi. "Woman as Nigger." *Psychology Today* 3 (October 1969): 20, 22, 58.

"Wellesley President Says School Can Do Without Men." *New York Times,* 23 April 1973, p. 22.

Wells, Jean A., and Magruder, Harriet C. "Education Programs for Mature Women." *Education Digest* 37 (January 1972): 42-45.

White, Barbara Ehrlich, and White, Leon S. *Women's Caucus of the College Art Association Survey of the Status of Women in 164 Art Departments in Accredited Institutions of Higher Education.* New York: ERIC Document Reproduction Service, ED 074 901, January 1973.

White, Kinnard. "Social Background Variables Related to Career Commitment of Women's Teachers." *Personnel and Guidance Journal* 45 (March 1967): 650-651.

White, Lynn, Jr. *Educating Our Daughters.* New York: Harper & Row, Publishers, 1950.

Wilms, Barbara. "Getting at the Women's Market in Higher Ed." *College Management* 8 (August/September 1973): 32-33.

"Women Make Strides: On Bases and into Mory's." *New York Times,* 30 March 1974, pp. 1, 25.

"Women Won't Let Marriage Interfere with Grad School, Mrs. Bunting Says." *Chronicle of Higher Education,* 13 January 1967, p. 4.

Woodward, Kenneth L., with Elaine Sciolino. "Clio Tells Herstory." *Newsweek,* 8 December 1975, p. 51.

Woody, Thomas. *A History of Women's Education in the United States.* Vol. 2. New York: Octagon Books, 1974.